# 'THE FENIANS WERE DREADFUL MEN'

# 'THE FENIANS WERE DREADFUL MEN'

## The 1867 Rising

Pádraig Ó Concubhair

MERCIER PRESS

IRISH PUBLISHER – IRISH STORY

MERCIER PRESS

Cork

www.mercierpress.ie

© Pádraig Ó Concubhair, 2011

ISBN: 978 1 85635 717 3

10 9 8 7 6 5 4 3 2 1

A CIP record for this title is available from the British Library

Printed and bound in the EU.

# CONTENTS

In the presence of God, I swear I hold a true and lasting allegiance to the Irish Republic, now virtually established, I will maintain it in all its integrity and independence. I will faithfully obey any superior officer and be ready at a moment's notice to act as a soldier when called up. I take this oath in the spirit of a true soldier of Liberty. So help me God.

*Copy of the Fenian oath found on John Dolan, who was arrested in Sunderland on 1 June 1867*

Some of the Fenian convicts of the present day might be respectable citizens and farmers but for the agitation of Daniel O'Connell.

*Sir Robert Anderson in January 1867, condemning the Liberator (Historical Sketch on Fenianism in Larcom papers)*

The rebel can reckon on nothing in life; he is sure to be calumniated, he is likely to be robbed and he may even be murdered, but let him once go out of life, and he is sure of a fine funeral.

John Devoy, *Recollections of an Irish Rebel*

The decision to fight in 1867 was a counsel of despair.

John Devoy, *Recollections of an Irish Rebel*

# ACKNOWLEDGEMENTS

The greater part of the research for this book was carried out in the National Archives of Ireland in Bishop Street, Dublin, and the National Library of Ireland in Kildare Street, Dublin. Thanks to the staff of both institutions for their help over the last four years. Roinn Bhéaloideas Éireann in the National University of Ireland, Dublin, is a treasure trove for the researcher on this period and the Local Studies section of Kerry County Library is a tremendous asset to any historian.

Much material relevant to the period is to be found in the National Archives of the United Kingdom at Kew and the British Library in both St Pancras and Colindale, and the staff in the two institutions were most helpful. Material for the chapter on the Clerkenwell explosion was sourced in the archive sections of Holborn and Islington Public Libraries and this was made freely available to me. I am very grateful to the archivists in both centres.

# INTRODUCTION

Thanks to the men of Cahersiveen and Foilmore, who 'jumped the gun' and began their long, cold and weary march to Killarney on the night of 11–12 February 1867, Kerry appears on maps that show the places in Ireland where the Irish Republican Brotherhood took the field during the short-lived Fenian rising. The Brotherhood had been established in 1858, another Irish revolutionary movement that would vainly attempt to establish an Irish republic. But the Fenian rising was much more than a series of isolated and sporadic outbreaks and failed attacks on various constabulary barracks in different parts of the country. For the first time since 1798, a countrywide organisation had been established to seek Irish independence through force of arms, and defeat in the field did not mean the death of that movement. 'The Fools, the Fools, they have left us our Fenian dead,' Pádraig Pearse later declaimed at the grave of Jeremiah O'Donovan Rossa. It was men like O'Donovan Rossa and the many other members of the Irish Republican Brotherhood, the secret organisation which survived after the failed rising, who while they were alive nurtured and conserved the republican tradition and tended the 'Phoenix Flame' which blazed into light in the General Post Office in Dublin at Easter 1916. A deeper understanding of the strengths and weaknesses of the Fenian movement is needed, and by concentrating on the movement in Kerry and Limerick and the involvement of men from these two counties in the wider movement, not only in Ireland but also in the United Kingdom and in the United States, we can progress towards this understanding. The Fenian threat to the established order was ever present, not just in the 1860s but for many years afterwards, so to the Castle and to Westminster the Fenians indeed 'were dreadful men'.

# CHAPTER 1

# THE FENIAN STORY

Being at an Irish seaport in 1847 I spoke to a man about to emigrate
to America. I advised him to remain at home.

'No, Sir!' said he, 'I will go to the Land of Liberty.'

'But what of your sons?' was my reply.

'Oh! They will come back,' was his response, 'with rifles on their
shoulders.'

*'Young' Henry Grattan, House of Commons, July 1848*

The Fenian Brotherhood, founded in 1858, resembled neither its
precursor (the Young Ireland movement of 1848) nor the United
Irishmen (the instigators of the rebellions of 1798 and 1803). No
longer did the leaders of the struggle for freedom come from the
intelligentsia and the gentry of Ireland. They were now 'of the
people and from the people'. So, in his introduction to *Devoy's Post
Bag*, P. S. O'Hegarty wrote: 'The first two [i.e. the United Irishmen
and Young Ireland] had been in origin upper-class and middle-
class movements. They came to the people from above and they
began as constitutional and reforming movements, but Fenianism
was a popular movement from the beginning and a separatist
movement from the beginning.' Or, as Sir Robert Anderson,
the British 'spymaster', so elegantly put it in a police report: 'It is
worthy of observation with what regular gradations sedition and

treason have been declining in respectability, ever since 1798. Thus Fenianism is all the more dangerous as the members have little else to lose besides their lives.' The *Illustrated Police News* of 27 April 1867 commented on:

> the remarkable difference between those charged in 1848 of high treason and those now lying in gaol for the same crime. With exception of four medical students, four commercial clerks and fourteen drapers' assistants, the rest are mechanics [i.e. workmen] or agricultural labourers. There are no gentlemen, no poets, no orators, no public writers as there were in 1848.

Another difference was that the leaders no longer looked for aid to France, the country of the tricolour. They sought help from the First Republic, the United States of America. In the draft notes for his *Historical Sketch on Fenianism* (Larcom papers), Anderson wrote: 'Now, there commenced, on the other side of the Atlantic, a conspiracy differently organised and upon different methods from that [of the Young Ireland party], which preceded it.'

Emigration to America during and following the Great Famine, meant that America now had a significant Irish population. In 1851 alone, 221,100 Irish people had emigrated to the United States and in that same year Michael Doheny, one of the leaders of the 1848 rebellion, founded the 69th Regiment, 'The Fighting Irish', one of the many militia groups in New York where the use of arms could be learned. 'They were,' he said, in a speech recorded in the *New York Phoenix* and kept in police files, 'the unpaid bearers of the free flag of this enlightened and liberal state, the sons of sires who, on their deathbeds, bequeathed to them the treasured and exhaustless legacy of hatred of Saxon rule in their native land.' It was no wonder then that these emigrants felt the need to avenge the deaths from fever and hunger that happened during the Great Famine of 1845 and the evictions that followed it.

Their natural leader was John Mitchel, who had been transported before the beginning of the 1848 rebellion and escaped from Van Diemen's Land (present-day Tasmania) in July 1853. On his arrival in New York in January 1854 he founded the Irish nationalist newspaper, *The Citizen*. He saw the Crimean War (1854–5) between England, France and Turkey on the one side and Russia on the other as a clear example of the maxim of 'England's difficulty being Ireland's opportunity', but it seemed that very few of the leaders of the 1848 rising agreed with him.

Someone who did agree, albeit writing five years later, was Sub-Inspector (later Superintendent) Thomas Doyle, who had been sent to America by Dublin Castle to keep an eye on the new Irish revolutionary society there. In November 1860 he reported: 'It was when the British army stood before Delhi and Lucknow and the affairs of India required the presence there of a powerful British force that the Phoenix [i.e. Fenian] Society, as now organised, was initiated in New York.'

One of those who had not agreed with Mitchel was Charles Gavan Duffy, his comrade in the Young Ireland movement. Disheartened by the numbers of Irishmen joining the British army to fight in the Crimea, as well as the collapse of the Tenant Right Movement which had aimed to secure land reforms for all tenants regardless of religious affiliation, Duffy sold his interest in *The Nation* newspaper and emigrated to Australia. There he became prime minister of Victoria and was the first former Irish rebel for many hundreds of years to be knighted by a queen.

Despite the opportunity he felt was presented by the Crimean War, Mitchel saw no hope of organising a successful rebellion at this point and this fact, together with his support for slavery which made him very unpopular with the liberal leaders in New York, caused him, in 1855, to sell his paper and move to Knoxville, Tennessee. Following this, he remained on the periphery of the Fenian movement.

Nevertheless, in December 1857, Michael Doheny and John O'Mahony, another 1848 exile living in New York, contacted a third of their number, James Stephens, who had fled to Paris after the 1848 rebellion, but had returned to Ireland in 1856 and was teaching French in Dublin. They sent him a clear message: would he explore the opportunities for a new rebellion and instigate preparations for an Irish-American military invasion? This was something they felt they could not do themselves for fear of re-arrest if they came back to Ireland but Stephens could – since according to official record he had been dead and indeed buried since the 1848 rebellion! As Anderson recorded: 'What were represented to be his remains were actually interred with considerable ceremony in Kilkenny.' Stephens did as he was asked. He felt uniquely qualified for the position and made himself provisional dictator of the new Fenian movement, travelling all round Ireland meeting many like-minded, or, as in the case of William Smith O'Brien and John Blake Dillon, two more of the 1848 leaders, unlike-minded, people. Strange as it might seem, at one time Dublin Castle considered Smith O'Brien to be the *éminence grise* of the Fenian Brotherhood, a view encouraged no doubt by a letter written by him from his house at Cahermoyle, County Limerick, on 5 April 1861:

> I wish it to be understood that while I labour (I fear with little success) to persuade my countrymen to abstain from looking to a foreign nation for the establishment of our National Welfare, I ask no man to pledge himself against the adoption hereafter of whatever course of action may appear to him best suited for the eventualities which may arise.

*James Stephens,*
*Fenian head centre.*

JAMES STEPHENS.
THE FENIAN HEAD CENTRE FOR IRELAND.

Stephens had promised that he would have 10,000 men enrolled in four months, but he would need £80 a month to do this. The American leaders agreed and their envoy, Joseph Deniffe, reached Dublin on St Patrick's Day, 1858. On that day, Stephens founded a revolutionary society and called it the Irish Revolutionary Brotherhood, a name that later was transmogrified into the Irish Republican Brotherhood (IRB). It was to be a secret society; indeed Anderson wrote: 'Stephens has frequently attributed the failure of Smith O'Brien's attempt to the want of a secret oath binding the members of the conspiracy together and enjoining obedience to their superior officer.'

The society was organised in 'circles' of 810 men. The leader of each such circle was called a centre. Each centre was responsible for a group of nine captains, each captain for nine sergeants and each sergeant for nine men. It was a system based on that used in revolutionary societies on the continent, with which Stephens had become familiar during his sojourn in Paris. The organisation was thus centred on cells of ten members, which in theory cut down the opportunities for successful infiltration by spies, but it was unsuitable for the mass movement into which the IRB shortly developed. As Fenian historian Seán Ó Luing wrote, 'it was impossible to keep a large-scale organisation free of leakages', while John Devoy remarked, 'the Irish are a loquacious people'.

Stephens' journeys were not unknown to the Irish Constabulary, a police force that, according to their inspector-general, 'might be compared to a spider's web, which when touched caused the almost instant approach of the spider to that spot' and whose principal *raison d'être* was to keep a sharp eye on any revolutionary societies that might develop. This mysterious stranger, christened *An Seabhach* by Jeremiah O'Donovan Rossa, figured in police reports as Mr Shooks. Sub-Inspector Curling in Kenmare came nearer the mark when he reported that: 'The members of the society only wanted instructions [to rise] from America or from a Mr Stephenson who is supposed to be in France – who he is I cannot say.'

By 1865 the police were able to provide a more exact description of Stephens for their colleagues across the Irish Sea:

He is forty to forty-five years of age, five foot seven or eight inches tall, pretty stout build with an active appearance. He has the accent and demeanour of a Frenchman, and speaks French tolerably well as he has resided for a long time in France. He is an Irishman by birth and the French accent may be affected to suit his purpose. He dresses very respectably, chiefly in dark clothes and wears a silk hat or a cloth cap. When travelling he wears a brown Inverness cape, in damp or wet weather gaiters, and he carries a small cloth bag in his hand.

One of the few places Stephens discovered an existing revolutionary organisation was in the Skibbereen–Killarney–Kenmare area of south-west Cork and south-east Kerry, where O'Donovan Rossa had founded the Phoenix Society to keep alive the desire for an independent Ireland. In October 1858 Constable James Guider reported from Kilgarvan that the people of the district were forming themselves into a secret society, 'sworn to oppose the government and to aid a foreign foe'. He requested permission 'to dress in plain clothes on Sunday nights and be out after hours in the village, to enable him to watch the suspects' movements closely'. Later in the year Sub-Constable Connor identified Daniel Shine of Gortbrack as 'a dangerous ringleader – an expelled student [from Maynooth] of the Roman Catholic Church and talented accordingly, he being seven years in the college'. By the end of November the police were able to supply a list of forty-one members of the society in Kenmare, whose occupations ranged from that of national teacher – four of them – through various tradesmen, farmers and publicans, to one who was described as having 'no trade or calling but that of a drunkard'. On 13 December 1858, egged on by reports received from some of the Catholic clergy in the area, the Castle ordered the arrest of the leaders of the organisation. Archdeacon John O'Sullivan, the parish priest of Kenmare, wrote to the *Tralee Chronicle*:

> In the middle of December the lads were seized by the police in the dead of the night and on the following day they were, in the height of the rain, carried off to the county gaol on the Long Car, handcuffed, with their parents and friends rending the air with their shrieks, and the lads, who had escaped the informer, with their knees knocking with fright, only then they said, 'Father John was right!'

A Fair Trial Fund was established by *The Nation* to pay their defence lawyers and among the subscribers was William Smith O'Brien. Prosecutions followed, but as Anderson remarked: 'They were not at the time as successful as expected.' One that was, albeit at the second attempt, was the prosecution of Daniel O'Sullivan of Ardgroom, who was teaching at Shelburne School, Kenmare. On 7 March 1859, he was tried before Baron Green in Tralee and sentenced to ten years' imprisonment for 'conspiracy to levy rebellion on the queen', by someone described by the Castle as 'one of the most merciful judges on the bench, after he had given the matter a night's consideration'. The two other 'conspirators', Florence O'Sullivan and John D. O'Sullivan (despite the surnames, all three were unrelated), were freed having pleaded guilty to the charge against them, as it was felt that Daniel's sentence would serve as an example to the young men of the area. Daniel himself was released a year later and emigrated to the United States. In June 1860 in answer to a parliamentary question by Mr White, the member for Trinity College, the home secretary said: 'He [O'Sullivan] was released on licence and as a convict on licence he was bound to report from time to time to the constabulary and not permitted to leave the country.' Despite this a police report of June 1861 stated that: 'When John O'Mahony, that truculent intriguing man and the proprietor of the *Phoenix* newspaper, returned to America in that month [of May], he was accompanied by Sullivan [*sic*], the *Phoenix* convict.' This is confirmed by a cutting in police files from the *New York Phoenix*, which mentioned that when they landed in New York from the SS *Edinburgh* on 21 May, Daniel O'Sullivan, responding to an address of welcome presented to him by the Fenians of New York, said:

It was not in pursuit of personal fame or glory that I have come to the United States. No, it was the threatened vengeance of a tyrant landlord who had the power to ruin my family and who might do so had I remained at home; it was this that compelled me to fly my own mountain home. Besides being constantly watched for by the bloodhounds of the law, I could not serve the cause of Ireland with the same efficiency as before.

In the United States, some time before April 1859, John O'Mahony founded a support movement, the Fenian Brotherhood, the name by which the whole Fenian body soon came to be known. By November 1859, according to the *New York Phoenix*, military training was widespread in North America and forty different regiments (i.e. companies) were regularly drilling in New York. These men later became the nucleus of the Irish Brigade of the Union army in the American Civil War. Thomas D'Arcy McGee, the former Young Ireland leader and by 1859 a member of parliament in Canada, stated at the time: 'The Fenians were regarded as a recruiting agency by the Federal administration.'

The movement also spread to Britain where Thomas Clarke Luby, yet another of the 1848 men, was one of the chief organisers and where it made many contacts with various British radical associations. Those were the years of the Great Rebellion, as the Indian Mutiny (1856–8) is called in that subcontinent, and the Franco-Austrian War (1859), which was fought in Italy and led towards the unification of that country. These events strengthened radical ideas in Britain and encouraged those who were working towards a rebellion in Ireland. As Anderson commented: 'The Crimean war and the absence of the English army in India were [each] a fresh stimulus to the [Fenian] movement.'

Stephens' first great *coup* was the organisation in Ireland in October 1861 of the funeral of Terence Bellew McManus, an 1848 man who had died in San Francisco in January 1861 at the age of fifty, ten years after his escape from the convict settlements of Tasmania. At San Francisco 22,000 people took part in the funeral procession to the docks. From there the body was sent by SS *Uncle Sam* to Panama, across the isthmus via the Panama Canal Railway and on to New York on the SS *Champion*. News of the funeral (partly carried by the Pony Express) had reached New York by 7 September and when the coffin reached the city on 13 September it was escorted to the cathedral by the New York Police Department, followed by 'O'Connell's Band' and ten men from each company of the 69th Regiment of Militia. Archbishop Hughes of New York presided at a solemn requiem mass for the dead patriot in St Patrick's Cathedral. When the remains arrived in Ireland, the bishop of Cloyne allowed the rosewood coffin (described in *The Nation* of 2 November 1861 as 'complete with elegantly chased silver handles and an engraved representation of the goddess of Freedom, holding a cap of liberty and pointing to a sun rising upon a broken column') into his parish church in Queenstown (Cobh), County Cork. But the bishop of Cork refused to allow the body into any of the city churches and it was taken to the hospital chapel of the Sisters of Mercy. An account of the funeral in the *Tralee Chronicle* of 9 November 1861 gave an idea of the extent of successful recruitment of soldiers by the Fenians:

> As the cortege crossed Benson's Bridge into Bridge Street, on its way to the railway station, a group of military men, mostly non-commissioned officers in full dress uniform, joined it in a body. One private soldier stated that, in the course of his duty, he had fallen in with McManus in Australia and such was his regard for him, he would have come from any part of the world to attend his funeral.

In Dublin, the Archbishop, Cardinal Cullen, would neither allow the body into any church in the diocese nor permit any of his priests to take the funeral service. McManus lay in state for a week in the Mechanics' Institute in Abbey Street and Anderson reported that on most days upwards of 9,000 people passed by the bier. It was left to Father Peter Lavelle, from Partry in County Mayo, to bury the patriot, an act that earned him the undying enmity of Cardinal Cullen. He was afterwards 'the subject of inveterate persecution, arraigned before the highest ecclesiastical tribunal on earth', as he himself wrote in a pamphlet now in the Castle files, and it was only due to the support he received from John McHale, the archbishop of Tuam, that he was able to defend himself from severe ecclesiastical punishment. Whatever may have been McHale's views on the Fenians, Father Lavelle could do no wrong in his eyes because of his leadership in the struggle against the New Reformation (when strenuous efforts were made to convert Catholics to the Established Church) in Partry, County Mayo. Lavelle later told an audience that it was written in Colmcille's prophecies that 'a red-headed bishop in Leinster would bring about Ireland's ruin'. Cardinal Cullen had red hair.

Meanwhile, the American delegates to the funeral had stayed in the Shelbourne Hotel, Dublin, causing Thomas Clarke Luby to remark that their presence was anything but welcome to many of the usual guests: 'Our transatlantic braves would hardly prove *personae gratae* to old Martin Burke's [the then owner] ordinary patrons' (Fenian briefs).

Daniel O'Donoghue (commonly known as The O'Donoghue), MP for Tralee, who at the time was the leading figure of the Irish Parliamentary (Home Rule) Party, subscribed £20 towards the funeral expenses. He would have been very surprised that his letter to the secretary of the funeral committee ended up in the police files of Dublin Castle accompanied by a pencilled note: 'Although not sworn (as far as is known), he has always been suspected as a member of the Fenian Brotherhood.'

Meanwhile, back in America, civil war had broken out between the northern and southern states. Ostensibly fought on the question of freeing the slaves, the real reason was to decide who should have supreme power, the individual states or the central government. Sub-Inspector Doyle neatly summed this up in his report of January 1861 to Dublin Castle: 'The only alternative to civil war and dissolution of the Union is concession to the Slave States implying political humiliation of the free Northern States.' There is a pencilled note on the report: 'This will give the Phoenix [i.e. Fenian] Society some employment – Mahony [*sic*], Doheny &c. – if they have the pluck!'

Many of the Irish leaders encouraged American Irishmen to join either the Northern (Federal) or Southern (Confederate) armies to prepare themselves for the day when they could resume the struggle in Ireland. Among these was Richard O'Gorman, a prominent lawyer in New York, who had led the 1848 rising in north Kerry and west Limerick. Stephens thought that he had turned his back on the cause of Ireland, but when Michael Doheny died suddenly in October 1862, O'Gorman took charge of setting up a fund to help his family. This drew a fierce attack on him from Stephens. In a letter to John O'Mahony, Stephens wrote: 'Would that this work had fallen to the duty of an Irishman instead of that miserable hybrid, Richard O'Gorman. It cuts against the grain to find that you are inclined to forgive him half his backslidings for the feeling he has shown on this occasion.'

Not all Fenians felt the same way. Two years later at the time of the Fenian Fair in Chicago in 1864, Charles Ring, one of the

*Fenians in New York encouraged to join the Union army.*

leading Fenians in that city wrote to O'Mahony: 'Send a speaker such as Meagher or Richard O'Gorman, who would readily fill the largest hall in the city and bring in a large amount of money.'

Nor was O'Gorman forgotten in Ireland. When John O'Connor, a stonemason and leader of a Fenian circle in Tipperary town, fled the country 'nine days before the warrant was issued for his arrest', among the treasonable documents found at his father's house by Head Constable Ellis were 'a few copies of Richard O'Gorman's speech on the Freedom of Poland'. On 15 August 1863, Charles Joseph Kickham, another of the 1848 men, addressed a meeting on the mountain of Sliabh na mBan, County Tipperary, 'under a flag of red, white and green, with an Irish harp without the crown'. The *Tralee Chronicle* of 21 August 1863 reported that he said that no progress could be made towards Irish independence through parliamentary methods and referred to Michael Doheny, Thomas Francis Meagher and John O'Mahony, 'the descendant of the ancient Fenian chiefs', all of whom had fought in 1848. He hoped that: 'Ere long the modern Fenians would assemble in their might, with the tried and trusted O'Mahony at their head.'

Many American Irishmen followed the advice of the Irish leaders. On 28 November 1864, *The Irish People* quoted from the *New York Irish American*: 'The untrained peasant who fled from a policeman's baton in Ballingarry [scene of the 1848 rising] and looked with awe on a red coat and lead buttons on Sliabh na mBan [where the United Irishmen gathered at the time of the Rebellion of 1798], today stands erect in the Federal Uniform, a distinguished warrior inured to hunger and fatigue and the shocks of war.' John Mitchel lost two sons fighting on the Confederate side. They were among the seven regiments of Irishmen recruited for that army. Thomas Francis Meagher, another Young Ireland leader who fought at Ballingarry, County Tipperary, in 1848, lived up to his nickname 'Meagher of the Sword' and was to prove Daniel O'Connell wrong by the courage he displayed, when he bravely led a division of the Union army at the Battle of Fredericksburg. (O'Connell had said about the men of Young Ireland: 'They speak about swords but they would be afraid of a poker!')

More than 150,000 men of Irish descent served in the Union army, one-sixth of the whole force, and according to United States government statistics 50,537 of these were born in Ireland. Among those who died in the war was Frank Brennan of Kenmare, serving with the 97th Regiment of New York. He was killed at the Battle of the Wilderness on Sunday 6 May 1864. He was twenty-four years old and a prominent Fenian. Colonel John O'Mahony attended his funeral at Calvary Cemetery. The deaths of two soldiers from Ballylongford are also recorded. Timothy King was killed at the Battle of Fair Oaks and his brother Richard died on 21 May from wounds received at Spotsylvania. Timothy was thirty-four years old and 'had come to America in his early youth'. The brothers were both members of the Fighting 69th Regiment of New York. Captain John Foley, another Kerryman, was with Richard when he died. Anderson wrote: 'Colonel [Michael] Doheny estimated that 2,500 drilled men and 50,000 who sympathised with the Brotherhood joined the Union army, but the long and wasting war left it [the Fenian Brotherhood] nearly ruined, although in another aspect it made the few survivors more dangerous and resolute.' Thomas Clarke Luby, who was in America from March to September 1863, wrote from Suffolk, Virginia on 13 April: 'I visited the camp of the 69th and slept in a tent with John O'Mahony, while shells went over our heads (very high, though), whizzing and whirring through the air.' However, it transpired that the shells were from a Federal gunboat 'sent to try the range'. Luby soon found out that real war did not resemble the gentlemanly version that had been pursued by the Irish Confederates in 1848: 'Yesterday morning General Corcoran shot a colonel [Lieutenant-Colonel Kimball] dead; he [Kimball] tried to stop him on the road in an insubordinate manner.'

The Civil War caused the supply of money from America to the Irish Fenians and to Stephens himself, which was never very great, to dry up completely, so in 1864, at 12 Parliament Street in Dublin, Stephens founded a newspaper, *The Irish People*, both as a propaganda vehicle and a means of raising money. It was highly successful in the former aim, but it lost money rather than made it, even though Stephens, in a not untypical bout of optimism, had written to John O'Mahony in October 1863: 'It will give us from £1,500 to £5,000 a year.' Stephens wrote the leading article, 'Isle, Race and Dream', for the first edition. Luby later remarked: 'A few more of the Captain's [Stephens'] articles requiring fearful expenditure on all-night coffee, brandy and tobacco, together with various guide books and Mrs Hall's *Pictorial Work on Ireland* and our newspaper, if not the very "Irish Republic, now virtually established", will be hopelessly bankrupt'. Stephens wrote only two more leaders, and then Luby himself tried his hand. J. F. X. O'Donnell, who had stood to arms in Waterford at the time of the Cappoquin rising in 1849 and would do so again in Cork in 1867, described Luby as the 'Prose Homer of the Shirtless'.

Reports in the newspaper show that there was strong opposition to *The Irish People* from various members of the clergy: 'Father X heard that Miss Y gets *The Irish People*. He told her it was a mortal sin every time she read the paper. She said she believed not and would continue to read it. He said: "You are a Protestant so will be refused the sacraments."'

A Kerry teacher wrote:

> From my being a subscriber to *The Irish People* for upwards of twelve months, I was dismissed from the charge of a National School held westwards of Kenmare at the request of Reverend Michael Walsh PP Sneem, by Archdeacon O'Sullivan, Kenmare. The manipulations that were effected in victimising me I care not for, as I always held an utter abomination to their capacity and feel quite happy to lose some of my chains.

The *Tralee Chronicle*'s view of *The Irish People*, on 1 March 1864, was: 'This journal is written with great ability and, while we cannot approve of the policy which guides it, we may say we admire the style in which the articles are presented.'

When the American Civil War ended in 1865, the first ex-army officers returned to Ireland to begin active preparations for a rising there. They were described by Anderson as 'having spent so long in the army in the field, they were on their return unfit for civil employment. They join eagerly in the scheming and plotting of the Fenian Brotherhood and long for the opportunity of fighting again (this time) on Irish soil.' The *Dublin University Magazine* said: 'It was plain from their bearing that they were trained soldiers, accustomed to campaigning, with all the shifts incident [*sic*] to the sort of warfare carried on during their own civil war.'

The government was soon alarmed by the sound of their American accents and even more so by the information it was getting from the spies who had been placed in the top tiers of the Fenian movement in both Ireland and America, which was a highly effective way of discovering the Fenians' plans. On 28 December 1865, the Lord Lieutenant of Ireland, Lord Wodehouse wrote to the British Prime Minister, Lord John Russell, in London:

> I am very glad that the second regiment is coming immediately. We have a number of American-Irish prowling about Dublin, and the disaffected remembrance of the massacres which disgraced Ireland in 1798 and previous rebellions have sunk deep in Irish imagination. The views and the designs of the Fenians are so distinctly revolutionary that it is not surprising that the loyal landowners fear a Jacquerie [i.e. a massacre]. If any serious outbreak occurred I have no doubt that it would quickly assume that form, and that disgraceful atrocities would be perpetuated. At the same time it is my firm belief that no such outbreak will occur if reasonable precautions are taken. Meanwhile the general distrust which prevails is doing incalculable harm to the country.

Sometimes the Fenians made it easy for the government spies. In June 1865, Colonel Thomas Kelly (who was to succeed James Stephens as leader of the Fenians) wrote: 'Any man with square-toed [army] boots will be dogged everywhere.' When John Cromien was arrested in Dublin on 17 February 1866, Superintendent Daniel Ryan of the 'G' Division of the Dublin Metropolitan Police reported that he had divested himself of his ordinary dress and assumed broad-toed boots and the broad-brimmed hat of the Fenians to attract attention on the streets. As Cromien owned a public house at 51 South Great George's Street, this may have been a form of advertisement, and police evidence stated that 150 Fenians were seen going into the house in one evening, that drilling was carried on there and that a crucible and a smelting pot, together with coke and lead for making bullets were found on the premises. Cromien was released on substantial bail on 2 November 1866. By that time Superintendent Ryan was so experienced in the detection of conspirators that in the following month he was able to write: 'I have seen John O'Grady whose appearance is so extremely Fenian that I would be induced to arrest him if I but met him by accident in the street.'

Already, by 2 October 1865, fourteen men had been arrested in Killarney on the word of an informer, John Sullivan, a baker from Milltown, and five were brought to Tralee gaol a fortnight later. The *Freeman's Journal* reported:

Tralee; Monday. This day five young men, Jeremiah Shaw, John Galivan, Peter Breen, Robert Fleming and William Looney, all arrested in Killarney, arrived here by the five o'clock train. The men were very tightly handcuffed. On arrival at the station they were met by a large body of police who proceeded to form an open square. In the middle, the five young men were placed under a heavy escort of some thirty police and marched at a steady pace down the New Line, up Castle Street and in the direction of the county gaol.

Most of the fourteen were released on bail, on their own surety of £40 and two independent sureties of £20, but Peter Breen (a post office worker), Jeremiah Shaw (the manager of a tobacco shop) and Robert Fleming (a law clerk) – who, rather ironically, worked in the crown solicitor's office – were kept in gaol until the following May when they were released on the condition that they went to America. The informer, Sullivan, who was known as Sullivan Goulah, had sworn that these three men were looked up to as having the command in Killarney and that at meetings Fleming would sing 'The Green Flag' and 'O'Donnell Aboo'. Breen left for America on 7 May 1866 and Fleming on 15 May. Fleming's employer had been well aware of his connection with Fenianism as Sub-Inspector Columb had told him about this in September 1865, 'begging him to avoid showing any indication of his knowing it, for the present' – presumably so Fleming could be watched.

In September 1865 John McCafferty was arrested as he attempted to land at Queenstown from the tender of the SS *City of Limerick*. The police reported that:

> … papers of a most treasonable character, including the books *Infantry Tactics* by General Silas Casey and Cooke's *Military Movements* illustrated by Colonel Patton were found on McCafferty, together with two of Colt's revolvers, a belt and ammunition and £50 in gold. A number of the other passengers were armed with rifles which were seized.

The local magistrates were so certain that an attempt would be

*The arrest of Captain Charles O'Connell (formerly of the Union army) as he arrives at Queenstown.*

made to rescue McCafferty from Cork gaol that fifty marines were landed from the *Frederick William* and the *Prince Consort*, but 'the town was quiet and the night passed without anything taking place'. After he had been arrested and charged, McCafferty was released and sent back to the United States, a decision that greatly annoyed the Home Office in London when he became one of the many American officers who returned two years later to take part in the rising.

The Fenians were not solely relying on the American armies to supply them with trained soldiers. Many of the Irish soldiers in the British army also supported the Fenians in their aims and were prepared to fight for them. The Irish regiments in the British army and other regiments with a large proportion of Irish soldiers suddenly found themselves transferred to duty in Malta or in the West or East Indies. As early as 1865, when the 53rd and 61st Foot Regiments were to be stationed in Canada, Lord Derby, the former prime minister, wrote: 'They are tainted with Fenianism and should be passed on to the West Indies as soon as possible.' For example, one of the returned American officers, Captain Guiry, a former soldier in the Confederate army, had been very effective in recruiting soldiers into the Fenian Brotherhood in his native Limerick. In September 1865 the Castle had targeted him:

Arrest J. J. Geary [*sic*] escaped Fenian agent aged thirty, five feet eight or nine, fair hair, small fair whiskers, hair cut short, medium make, rather small towards eyes. He is a native of Newcastle West. He may wear a grey suit of tweed and a Jenny hat or tweed trousers and vest [waistcoat] and black frock coat and silk hat.

Lord Strathnairn commented:

Guiry, the head of the Fenian Conspiracy in the south of Ireland, now a fugitive from arrest with a price on his head, and two other Fenian leaders, both lately sent to penal servitude, were introduced to the Sergeants' Mess of the 2nd Regiment by the drum major without the adjutant or the CO knowing anything about it.

Among those in the mess were Sergeant Ormsby (master of musketry), Sergeant Mahon (master cook) and Sergeant Burns (master tailor), 'all more or less implicated in the Fenian movement'. Lord Strathnairn recommended that 'the propriety of sending them to the colonies be considered'.

Other Fenian recruiting agents displayed a skill at billiards, which endeared them to soldiers and drew the following reproof from the War Office:

> The practice of many officers playing at Public Billiard Tables is reprehensible and leads to very bad consequences, one of which is that they may play with the most disreputable characters. This result actually took place (in Cork). Lieutenant Edgecombe and Ensign Carmac of the 73rd played with a treasonable agent whose chief mission was to seduce soldiers from their allegiance.

When, in September 1865, Lord Strathnairn had issued a circular, warning of the dangers of Fenianism, he felt the replies 'showed the same futility of a false *esprit de corps* which produced such deplorable results in an immeasurably worse case [the Indian army mutiny], when officers, declaring their conviction that their men were free from all disloyalty, were almost shot by them'. According to *The Times* (London) in the summer of 1859 soldiers at Meerut had refused to obey transfer orders saying: 'I'm an Englishman, not a slave, and won't be transferred like an 'oss.' It went on to record: 'They abstained from violence but were cheeky to a degree. In the same way almost all the answers [to the circular] denied the existence of Fenianism in their regiments and it has since come out that Fenianism of a very bad description was in those very regiments.'

In October 1866, at the royal barracks in Dublin, ten men of the 92nd Highlanders, the 83rd Regiment and the 5th Dragoon Guards received sentences ranging from life down to five years' imprisonment for offences in connection with membership of the Fenians. Samuel Lee Anderson, the solicitor-general, listed twenty-four soldiers convicted in Ireland that year. General Sir Hugh Rose, Lord Strathnairn, the commander-in-chief of the British forces in

*Lord Strathnairn (Sir Hugh Rose), commander-in-chief of the British forces in Ireland.*

Ireland, said: 'The soldiers were very bad and far too many cases of individual but not collective treason have occurred. Those who were sworn into the movement display a dark fanaticism.' He went on to say that, in his opinion, military Fenianism was engendered by 'discontent arising from a Nationality aggrieved by the Conquest and a Religion, it is averred, injured by the Reformation' (papers of Sir Hugh Rose).

The unionist *Dublin University Magazine* blamed the national schools for this growth of nationalist sentiment in the army:

Twenty years ago the young men from the farmer's humble steading and the peasant's cabin who entered the army were unable to read. Nowadays they have had the advantage of the teaching of the

National Schools. They have mastered the rudiments of knowledge, but only to become enabled to drink more greedily the poisonous instruction supplied by astute agents.

In contrast John O'Mahony praised the national schools. In a cutting from the *New York Phoenix*, found in police files, he wrote: 'The youth of Ireland has run far ahead of us in education and knowledge during the past decade and if the Irish National Schools – the only boon England ever gave us – have produced many more such as these two young men, I feel assured that Ireland cannot remain long enthralled.'

O'Donovan Rossa, who was the business manager of *The Irish People*, was one of the men who tried to recruit soldiers of the British army into the movement, sometimes with surprising results, as Luby recounted:

One day as I was going to the printers' room, I heard an unusual noise issuing from another room. I looked into the chamber and saw squatting on the floor ten or a dozen legionaries of Perfidious Albion playing cards, some smoking pipes and making merry. I observed in a gentle tone of voice, 'Boys, I don't in the least grudge your being here. In one sense I'm only too glad to see you. But I put it to your own common sense – is it prudent or safe?' The jolly Sons of Mars grinned good-humouredly, but unanimously agreed with me that it wasn't and promised that it shouldn't occur again.

Another odd visitor to 12 Parliament Street to buy *The Irish People* was the Marquis of Clanrickard. Luby, writing in the 1890s in *An Gael*, a nationalist newspaper published in New York, remarked that if the marquis had ever read *The Irish People* aloud for the edification of his son – a notorious landlord evictor – it didn't seem to have done him (the son) any great good. Others were more successful at recruiting followers for the organisation. Luby went on:

> After Pat O'Leary's arrest in Athlone, where in July 1865 he was sentenced to seven years' penal servitude for 'seducing soldiers' [from their oath of allegiance], Bill Roantree was appointed to take up his unfinished work. Bill proved a worthy follower in his footsteps. I was his paymaster, commissioned by Stephens to pay him a weekly stipend for expenses for treats to the gallant Sons of Mars. After the general arrests, John Devoy succeeded to the role of propagandist among the soldiers. Later he was assisted by Edward St Clair Pilsworth.

Pilsworth had been a volunteer with Garibaldi's army in Italy in 1850, and since his father had been a sergeant major in the British army he had been brought up among soldiers and spoke with an English accent. This made him a very effective recruiter.

Pat 'Pagan' O'Leary was a curious character. He traced all the weaknesses of the Irish psyche back to the conversion of Ireland by St Patrick and he could see no hope for the country until the worship of the ancient pagan gods would take the place of Christianity. Heaven was to be replaced by Tír na nÓg, which was much easier to enter. The only people barred from this Elysium were inveterate foes of the Fenians such as police informers, Cardinal Cullen of Dublin, Bishop Moriarty of Kerry and Father Mawe, who was the parish priest of Tralee and dean of Kerry. Father Mawe held consistently to his anti-Fenian views. On September 1869, when the first 'Amnesty Meetings' to seek the release of Fenian prisoners were organised, he wrote to the *Tralee Chronicle*:

> There should be no paltering with the Fenian faction, no attempt at palliating the gravity of their crimes – crimes aimed at the overthrow

of society and the destruction of religion. It is comforting to the priests and people of Tralee to see the Fenian faction here – the objects of pity and contempt – brought so low as to be obliged to go about begging of the respectable people of the town to come to their assistance, even though they lately boasted that they would have their Amnesty Meeting *in spite of the dean or the devil!*

Both Bishop Moriarty and Father Mawe also featured in a contemporary ballad, describing the supposed fate of those who had given information against the Fenians who attacked the barracks in Kilmallock, County Limerick, in March 1867:

> I've travelled all hell but I never have been
> In a dungeon more certain to please.
> A friend of mine living near Cahersiveen
> Showed me in and the like of it never was seen,
> So I stole from his Lordship the keys
> While the young devils drink
> To old Mawe and the Kerry PPs.

When O'Leary was arrested, the governor of Mountjoy said that he must be registered in the prison records as a 'Roman Catholic, a member of the Established Church or a Dissenter [i.e. Presbyterian)]'. This inspired O'Leary to compose:

> It seems to me, Governor, rather bad
> Though men may be Fenians to drive them mad.
> If men keep out of gaol they can choose their divinity
> But if they're in it they're bound to believe in the Trinity
> Or if such a belief can only be shammed
> At least to attend and hear themselves damned.

*Amnesty meeting in Hyde Park to demand the release of Fenian prisoners.*

In Killarney in October 1866, Richard Barry, 'a well-known ballad singer', was arrested at the Market Cross and charged before the magistrate, Mr Gallwey, with singing that 'decidedly Fenian ballad, the Stars and Stripes'. Remarking that 'the people of Killarney, who lived in the freest country in the world, were not so foolish as to have any connection with the Fenians' – an opinion that he changed before long – Mr Gallwey sentenced Barry to six months' imprisonment.

Canon Sheehan, whose novel *The Graves of Kilmorna* gives a stirring picture of those times, described such a ballad singer in graphic terms:

I see now, as clearly as I saw then, the short well-knit figure of the ballad singer in the Main Street; I see the gas light from the shop flickering on his coat; I see the coat shining and glistening because the rain was pouring down in cataracts and torrents; I see his face pale but stern looking, his black hair falling on his shoulders; I hear his fine voice singing up along the deserted street that fine ballad 'Out and Make Way for The Bold Fenian Men'.

Encouraged by the growing numbers in the movement, Stephens fixed the day of the intended rising for 21 September 1865, the anniversary of the date of Robert Emmet's rebellion, but the government acted first. On 14 September the police raided the offices of *The Irish People* to arrest the staff and Fenian leaders. At 11 p.m. that night, Superintendent Ryan reported to the Castle:

No one was found in the house. But no less than ten of the principals and employees of the establishment were arrested in Parliament Street, Dame Street and Crane Lane between 9.30 p.m. and 9.45 p.m. These were O'Donovan Rossa, Shawn Clancy, James Murphy, James Thomas Ashe or Roantree, Cornelius O'Mahony, James O'Connor, Mortimer Moynihan, Michael O'Neill Fogarty, William F. Roantree and Pierce Nagle. [The last name is doubly underlined in Ryan's report, not surprisingly, since he was one of the Castle's principal agents.] They had made their exit by clambering over the roofs of the adjoining houses and thus reaching the street. They were marched to the police stations at College St and Chancery Lane.

Among the papers of Sir Thomas Larcom, there was a letter from Tamworth in Sir Robert Peel's almost indecipherable handwriting, dated 17 September 1866. Peel had been Chief Secretary for Ireland until December 1865 and was clearly still interested in

*Seizure of* The Irish People *newspaper.*

what was happening in the country. The letter thanked Larcom for sending a copy of Superintendent Ryan's report on the seizing of *The Irish People*:

> They do not appear to have been very largely supplied with ammunition at Dublin and it will be delightful if the arrest of half a dozen editors and subeditors will tend to eviscerate this great Fenian movement, as Burke [the private secretary who manned the Irish Office in London and was to be assassinated by the 'Invincibles' in 1882] seems to think will be the case.

A pamphlet published in Paris described the scene as follows:

Le Vendredi soir, 15 Septembre, Dublin prenait un aspect lugubre et mélancolique de Varsovie. Les troupes de la Reine avaient ont consigneés dans les casernes, les posts militaries avaient eté doublés, la ville livreé à la police. Ces measures donneret aux rumours le plus extraodinaires – que les américains Fenians etaient déjà arrives et que le drapeau vert a sa harpe d'or flottait sur le rivage irlandais.

[Mistakes from the original have been retained]

(Dublin took on the mournful and melancholy aspects of Warsaw. The queen's soldiers had occupied the barracks, the military posts had been increased and the city abandoned to the police. The measures gave rise to the most extraordinary rumours – that the American Fenians had already arrived and that the green flag with its golden harp waved over the Irish shores.)

But Stephens remained at large. As the *Daily Express* – a newspaper not fond of the Fenians – commented: 'He lived in Sandymount, quietly digging in his little garden, indulging his refined taste in the cultivation of flowers or bestowing a gardener's care on the substantial vegetables which were destined to appear upon his dinner table.' He was, however, captured on 11 November 1866. On the same day, Lord Wodehouse wrote to Lord John Russell: 'I regard it as a greater blow to the conspirators than all we have done hitherto. We have now in prison all the leading men except Geary, who was Head Centre in Cork.' On 23 November he wrote again:

Stephens is, I am told, a Kilkenny man, educated as a civil engineer. He was at the cabbage garden conflict during the Young Ireland rising in 1848 and was in the Phoenix organisation in 1858. He made his livelihood at one time as a teacher and oddly enough gave lessons to the children of Judge FitzGerald, who is to try him.

But that trial never opened as Stephens escaped from Richmond prison on 26 November 1866. On hearing the news, 300 Fenian miners celebrated by taking part in a torchlight procession in Gold Hill, California. Wodehouse wrote: 'This is a most mortifying occurrence – no doubt he escaped with the connivance of the warders, but *Quis custodiet ipsos custodes?* [Who will guard the guardians themselves?]' In the official enquiry which followed, it emerged that the precautions taken to prevent escape were so strict that even the prisoner's food was minutely searched. Mangan, the hall porter, had detected a bottle of whiskey inside a fowl.

A contemporary ballad ran:

Perhaps you'd like to know,
Says the Sean Bhean Bhocht
What way did Stephens go?
Says the Sean Bhean Bhocht
When from Richmond snug and tight
He marched out at dead of night
And never said good night,
Says the Sean Bhean Bhocht.

They thought it very hard
Says the Sean Bhean Bhocht
He should only leave his card,
Says the Sean Bhean Bhocht
At Mr Lawson's gate,
If he early came or late
He would rather let him wait
Says the Sean Bhean Bhocht.

The Queen had kindly fixed
Says the Sean Bhean Bhocht
For a party nicely mixed
Says the Sean Bhean Bhocht
To give him honour due
Through her judges staunch and true
And policemen all in blue
Says the Sean Bhean Bhocht.

When Marquis found him out
Says the Sean Bhean Bhocht
His warders tall and stout
Says the Sean Bhean Bhocht
He roused them on their quest
And says he, 'May I be blest
For the bird's not in his nest'
Says the Sean Bhean Bhocht.

Marquis was the governor of the prison and lost his post because of Stephens' escape.

Raids followed all over Ireland. In Tralee Sub-Inspector McGuire and Head Constable Burchell confiscated nineteen copies of *The Irish People* from O'Flaherty's shop and others were seized from the 'flying news vendors' in the street and from the newsagents in Listowel, Killarney and other towns in Kerry. However, Stephens remained at large.

On 17 February 1866 the Act to Suspend the Right of Habeas Corpus had been passed by the British parliament and effectively allowed imprisonment without trial. It was said to have had the quickest ever passage of any bill through parliament, and arrests began even before the House of Lords had approved it. Lord

Strathnairn did not agree with the suspension of the right of Habeas Corpus and described it as 'an inefficient remedy for the present and none whatsoever for the future'. He would rather have seen: 'Such or something like the Act of George III – the Whiteboy Act 1765 – which would do far more to put down Fenianism than the cumbrous and inefficient remedy of the suspension of this great Constitutional Privilege.'

In Tralee two days after the act came into force, warrants were issued for the arrests of Cornelius Healy, Charles McMahon, John and Thomas Sullivan and William Flynn. Not all the warrants were executed, but the local police were warned to keep their eye on such suspicious characters. Many were former soldiers in the American Union army. Thomas O'Neill was arrested at Killelan near Cahersiveen; Cornelius Healy was arrested in Tralee on the Monday following the passing of the act and described himself as being a captain in a United States cavalry regiment. He was held in Tralee gaol for three weeks before discharge, on condition of his leaving the country. Governor Smyth of New Hampshire made representations on his behalf, stating that he had served in the 5th New Hampshire Regiment during the Civil War. On the same day in Dublin, Henry O'Connor, printer, of 2 Cuffe Lane, a native of Tralee and Eugene O'Shea of Tralee, leader of a Fenian circle, whose *nom de guerre* was Frank Leslie, were also arrested, having been identified by Head Constable Walker of Tralee. They were detained until the 17 September when they were released on condition that they too returned to America. On 1 March Florence McCarthy, the son of a licensed vintner from Killarney, was arrested. He also was a former soldier in the Union army and he was detained for six weeks before being freed on the same condition.

Two days later, Eugene O'Shea's brother, John, a shipwright who lived in The Mall, Tralee, and Patrick Leane of Castleisland were also arrested. Both O'Shea brothers as well as Patrick and Thomas Regan had been named as centres for Tralee in the informer Pierce Nagle's list of some 120 provincial centres, as was John S. O'Connor, newsagent, of Kenmare. William Leonard (a soldier and a native of Listowel), who gave his name as John Hearn, was arrested in Dublin after his arrival from England on 16 March. He was released after five months. On Thursday 16 April 1866, Patrick Leane, who had been arrested in the roundup following the suppression of *The Irish People*, was discharged by Magistrate Cruice on his own bond of £100 and a surety of £50, as was John O'Shea on 8 June.

Thus, in the weeks after the suspension of the Habeas Corpus Act the average number in custody was 550, and this rose to 669 by the second week in April. According to Sir Thomas Larcom, Permanent Under-Secretary at Dublin Castle: 'Telegrams flowed to the Castle and arrests were made in such numbers that I sent a circular to resident magistrates telling them not to arrest on suspicion.' The Castle itself was very fond of dispatching telegrams, all sent in code and later in cipher, as many of the postmasters – such as Mr FitzGerald in Cahersiveen – and the telegraph operators were suspected of disloyal tendencies. A police spy, Thomas Talbot, had written in March 1865: 'Fenians are now every place in Railways, Telegraph Offices, Banks, Post Offices &c.' An example of a police telegram of this period read: 'Impossible arsenal O'Driscoll headmast cephalic thara deadly', which meant 'Important arrest O'Driscoll, head centre, this day'.

On 10 December 1866, Thomas Lynch of Glenflesk was arrested in Bantry, County Cork. The local resident magistrate (RM) wrote to the Castle: 'The Fenian prisoners in Cork gaol were well fed by Lynch. Sworn in by James Creedon, not alone is he Head Centre for Bantry but for Macroom and Skibbereen.' In spite of an encomium from the great drapery firm of Ferrier Pollock of

William Street in Dublin – 'frequent intercourse and large dealings justify our strong impression that Thomas Lynch is not a guilty man' – and a memorial for his release which contained the signature of Bishop Moriarty of Kerry, Lynch remained in Mountjoy until the end of July 1867.

William Leonard of Listowel was re-arrested in Dublin on 27 April 1867. Described as 'a private in the Military Train' he was charged with concealing mutiny and sentenced at the Dublin City court martial to five years' penal servitude because 'he had deserted and came to Dublin to take part in the rising'. With seventeen other prisoners he was dispatched to Millbank Convict Prison on the gunboat *Earnest*, which sailed for Holyhead at 9.15 a.m. on the morning of 3 July 1867, 'accompanied by Principal Warder Lawless, eighteen Prison Officers and an Escort of Mounted Police'.

After these arrests of the Fenians, the *Daily Express* reported that in Boyle, County Roscommon:

> The females of the middle- and lower-classes have espoused the Fenian cause and expressed their feelings by a most profuse patronage of green ribbon. It was to be seen on the persons of all from the babies in arms to the oldest matrons, to such an extent that the parish priest has denounced it from the altar but with very little (if any) effect.

This demonstration was repeated in towns all over Ireland. In New York in 1862/3 the Fenian Sisterhood had been founded, its object being 'the attainment of Irish Government for Ireland'. It was open to all women who were Irish by birth or descent. Branches were formed all over the United States. By November 1864 Indianapolis had been organised, according to the *New York Phoenix*: 'The ladies are very patriotic and the sisterhood will make the movement here more attractive and will initiate emulation.' In New York, a crowd of 500, the vast majority of whom were ladies, attended at the Demilt Dispensary at the corner of 2nd Avenue and 23rd Street. There Miss O'Shea, the directress, administered the pledge of the society to each member: 'I, A. B. pledge my word of honour that I become a member of this society actuated by patriotic and honest motives. I will labour to foster and extend feelings of harmony and intense and intelligent love of country among Irish men and women.'

The movement quickly spread its influence to Ireland. Mr Archibald, the British consul in New York, wrote in September 1865 that: 'Women passengers (Fenian Sisters) are said to carry arms and ammunition to Ireland in their luggage.' He described Ellen Mahony, principal of a school in Chicago, as the 'Female head centre'. (She may have been John O'Mahony's sister.) When Jeremiah O'Leary, a national teacher in Croom, County Limerick, was arrested in March 1866, a police report said that: 'His sister is a member of the "Fenian Sisters" and has got all the young men in Croom to join the Fenians.' James Stephens was asked at a meeting in the Cooper Institute in New York in June 1866, 'Are the girls at home trumps in the cause of Ireland?', to which he replied: 'The girls at home are not only trumps in the cause of Ireland but are the ace of hearts itself.' In December 1866, Superintendent Doyle stated that: 'Very few (young men) are arriving (from America) who are not sent here under the auspices of the Fenian Conspiracy and many are accompanied by females who are made the purse bearers and as a general rule carry revolvers for distribution among the conspirators.' In January 1867, Doyle reported:

There were a considerable number of women attending the Fenian ladies committee rooms on Wednesday and Friday nights with seventy present on the preceding Wednesday. All had collected from

15/- to 25/- a week. £200 had been sent to Australia (for the benefit of the Fenian prisoners), besides remittances to England.

After the Limerick rising in March 1867, the police complained:

> Kate Carroll, sister to one of the prisoners, made fifty flannel vests for the insurgents and presented them to them on the morning of the rising together with a quantity of whiskey. Mary Ryan of Cromhill, first cousin to the Carroll's, made a number of green leather pouches, which some of the insurgents wore at Kilteely.

Mr Franks, the resident magistrate in Bruff, was certain that the wife of William O'Sullivan, the hotel-keeper in Kilmallock, who himself had been detained for complicity in the rising, 'had long since openly declared her Fenian tendencies in a most undisguised manner and has within the last week taken into employment a person named O'Donnell, engaged in most active operations, swearing in men, purchasing arms and collecting money for Fenian purposes'.

By September 1867 there were still 135 Fenians detained under the provisions of the Suspension of Habeas Corpus Act, of whom ninety-six were in the various Dublin prisons, ten in Limerick, and two – J. D. Sheehan and Timothy O'Connell – in Tralee.

With the benefit of hindsight, it is easy to agree with Devoy when he wrote in *Recollections of an Irish Rebel* some twenty years after the event that 1865 might have been the best year for a rebellion. Lord Strathnairn wrote in 1866: 'Had there been a rising in 1865 before military Fenianism had been properly dealt with, something disagreeable might – and probably would – have occurred' (papers of Sir Hugh Rose). True, guns and ammunition would have been at a premium – on 16 January 1865 Commissioner Mayne of Scotland Yard reported that: 'Fifteen Volunteer soldiers have left London for Dublin and they are sure to have taken their rifles and bayonets with them.' However, the number of trained soldiers available would have been very great and many experienced American officers were ready to lead them. As Lord Strathnairn commented in April 1867: 'Lord Cornwallis said seventy years ago – at the time of the 1798 rising – "they embark with a spade and will return with a musket" – it was a prediction liberally fulfilled.'

The Castle was not only aware of the Fenian threat but also taking it very seriously. This is clear from a thirty-seven-page document, *Plan of Operations of the Garrison of Dublin in the Case of Disturbances or an Insurrection on the Part of the Disaffected*, to be found among the State Papers in the National Archives in Dublin and dated 20 December 1865:

> Dublin possesses peculiar advantages for the suppression of popular commotions, for it is divided into two parts by the Liffey which, crossed by bridges, enable the troops to communicate and cooperate and at the same time prevent rioters from doing so. As well cannon can sweep the quays on both banks of the Liffey ...
>
> The objects of attack would probably be the Castle, the Bank [of Ireland], the College [Trinity], the [General] Post Office, the Railway Stations, Mountjoy and possibly the Vice-regal Lodge. The Four Courts would be a vital strong point and would be defended by three companies of the 8th Regiment of Foot, with each soldier bringing a day's ration of bread and cooked meat, two days' ration of coffee and sugar and, if required, a blanket for the night.

When the 1916 rebellion broke out, it could be seen that this document was prophetic.

In February 1866, Superintendent Ryan wrote:

> When it is borne in mind how long the society is in existence, the secret system adopted for its propagation which for years baffled every legal effort to restrain it, and the amount of subscriptions raised during a series of years, there will be no difficulty in accounting for the great hold it has taken in the community and the extent of its ramifications.

Evidence given at the trial of Thomas Clarke Luby, who had been arrested on 16 September 1865, revealed:

> We have discovered a great variety of papers ruled in squares. The squares are filled up – sometimes by a single line drawn across, sometimes by an O, sometimes by a V and sometimes by an inverted V. The O represents an unarmed man, the single line a man armed with a pike, the V a man with a rifle and the ∧ with some other firearm. The paper I hold in my hand is considerably well filled, but the circles representing unarmed men vastly predominate.

Luby's work in organising the IRB in Britain had not gone unnoticed and, when he was sentenced, Inspector Mayne of the Metropolitan Police wrote to Larcom, 'I rejoice to hear of his conviction.'

Larcom described how in 1866 revolvers were being sold at fifteen shillings and rifles at thirteen shillings each:

> This and much more valuable information is acquired from George Reilly, a respectable tradesman, who became very intimate with J. J. Kelly, tobacconist of Sackville St., a leading Fenian. Rifles were being imported into the country on an extensive scale, and the police have

seized a number in Cork. On one day £1,400 was withdrawn from the Savings Bank in Drogheda and the same was happening in other parts of the country.

Writing in the *Evening Telegraph* of 10 September 1892, Devoy said:

Had Stephens been ready to give the word then [at the time of his escape from Richmond], he could have had ten followers for every one that would have answered the call at a previous time. But there were not above 1,000 rifles in the whole organisation. A really bold conspirator having the splendid material that Stephens absolutely controlled, with 8,000 out of the 25,000 troops then in Ireland sworn members of his organisation, 150 Irish-American commissioned officers who had gone through the Civil War and the Irish masses in America at his back might not have been able to separate Ireland from England but he would have struck a blow at English power that would have forced England to concede a parliament in Dublin. The opportunity came and went without being seized.

Instead, Stephens was on the run and most of the main Fenian leaders in Ireland were incarcerated.

By the end of 1865 the Fenian headquarters in the United States had been established, according to the Castle, in an expensive house in a most fashionable district in New York (Union Square), over which the Fenian flag was hoisted. The house had been newly upholstered in green and gold and furnished in mahogany. The *Clonmel Commercial* – not a nationalist paper – wrote in March 1866:

True to the luxurious policy of the Fenian Leaders, their agents invariably travelled first-class, dined at first-class hotels and fared

*The Fenian headquarters in New York.*

sumptuously every day. The poor clod-hopper with his 8*d*. or 10*d*. a day supplied the funds that payed [*sic*] the landlord's bill. O'Mahony in Union Square, Stephens in Fairfield House, Colonel Byron astonishing the military and commercial circles of the towns he visited with his profuse extravagance and skill at Billiards.

However, in December 1865 John O'Mahony had been deposed as president of the Brotherhood. The 'Senate Wing' as O'Mahony's opponents were called, were led by William Roberts, a successful businessman from Brooklyn and a native of County Cork, and General Thomas (Fighting Tom) Sweeny from Dunmanway in the same county, who had spent twenty years in the Union army, losing an arm during the Mexican war. They could see no prospect of giving meaningful help to a rising in Ireland, so they decided to organise a second front by invading the British Colonies of Upper Canada, a plan that had been first proposed at the Fenian Congress in October 1865:

We are the Fenian Brotherhood, skilled in the arts of war,
And we're going to fight for Ireland the land that we adore,
Many battles we have won, along with the boys in blue,
And we'll go and capture Canada for we've nothing else to do!

The apparent reason for deposing O'Mahony was his personal decision to issue Fenian Bonds as a way of raising money for the proposed insurrection in Ireland, something that was not to be done until the American Fenians were on the point of sailing. But he had been slow to name the date for this invasion, which was no surprise, as it seems he had not thought through any strategy to promote such an attack.

On Thursday 10 May 1866 Stephens, having escaped from

Ireland, reached America on the *Napoleon III*, and on the following Tuesday he made an effort to reunite the two factions, something that was doomed to failure after the publication of his letter to O'Mahony condemning the Senate Group. 'Lash them from you like dogs!' He addressed a number of meetings at Jones' Wood, a large park outside New York. One meeting at the end of May led to a most interesting letter from L. Taylor, a native of Scotland, published in the *Toronto Globe* on 14 June 1866:

> While attending a meeting of one of the greatest peace associations of the world, The Bible Association, I have been brought into contact with the personified genius of war, James Stephens. On returning from the Grand Jubilee meeting of the American Bible Society, I could not understand the crowd of loafers I met on the street in front of the hotel. Nevertheless I could easily proclaim their nationality, for the wonderful Milesian cast of countenance was stamped on every mother's son of them. A few wore American army uniform, a few were tolerably well dressed, but the majority looked as if it were only yesterday they had left the bogs of Connaught or dear old dirty Kerry. The mystery was soon solved, when the head clerk directed my attention to one of the latest entries in the register, viz. James Stephens, Ireland. In a moment the old spirit of 'Duthach nam beann nan glean, nan gaisgeach' [a Gaelic Motto, which could also be seen on the notes of the Caledonian Bank] rose in me and I said, quietly but firmly: 'Give Mr Stephens my compliments and tell him we are ready for him.'
>
> I trust the Great Chief fully endorses O'Mahony's programme, viz. 'to let us weak and unoffending colonists alone, our only crime being that we owe allegiance to the hated Sasanach'. If Roberts and Sweeny come we must give them the Quaker's response: 'Friend, thou hast no business here.' But if the Fenian army were to take the field in

Ireland, does the Chief Organiser really suppose that King William's Boys would stand by with folded arms and see their country over run by the Fenian host. Let the Boyne and Derry give their proper reply to that!

As for Mr Stephens himself, he holds no connection with the school that produced Grattan, Burke, Curran, Sheridan, still less the famous Dan [O'Connell] or own [sic] McGee. He speaks more like a cautious, deliberate, canny Scot than an enthusiastic, impulsive, outspoken Irishman.

I have headed this letter Under the Green [which is] literally true, for we are treated [at the Fenian meetings] not alone to music and addresses, balcony and moonlight speeches but the charming green with the harp of old Ireland waves over us and underneath is a streaming pennant studded with stars, the banner and ensign of the New Republic. But this is not the Star of Destiny, nor the Star of Hope, nor yet the Morning Star, but the star of which the Apostle Jude speaks, 'worldly stars for which are reserved the darkness forever'.

In October 1866, Stephens spoke at a further meeting in Jones' Wood: 'We shall be fighting in Ireland before the first of January next.' According to the *New York Times* – no friend to the Fenians – 'This was more rational than proposals to secure the amelioration of Ireland by bombarding the island Campo Bello from the coast of Maine.' But before January 1867 came, the officers who were veterans of the Civil War had come to the conclusion that the battles would continue to be fought in Stephens' imagination and he too was deposed from the leadership and replaced by Colonel Thomas Kelly. A year previously Kelly had written to O'Mahony: 'There is no reason why success could not be achieved [in Ireland] if men were properly equipped and led.' He intended to live up to this statement.

Stephens' life was threatened and he was described as a coward and a traitor. It was said that at a meeting of the New York Directory Captain John McCafferty drew a revolver and threatened to shoot him. Sir Robert Anderson, in his *Précis of Reports on Fenianism in the USA* (Foreign Office papers), mentioned the information he received from the informer Geoffrey Massey about this meeting, which was held in New York on 29 December, and that 'Stephens' credit was impaired with a large class of the Irish'. Stephens fled to France at the end of January 1867.

John Martin, the former Young Ireland leader, wrote to *The Nation*: 'It is generally expected that a popular insurrection will break out in Ireland this winter and that a long-prostrate people, very carefully disarmed and debarred from all military activity, will throw themselves in frenzy against the trained hosts of one of the greatest empires of the world.' Martin proved himself a true prophet – unlike the *Dublin Evening Mail* of 17 December 1866: 'We believe that no sane person now believes in any danger of a rising, or in the existence of a domestic Fenian conspiracy.'

# Chapter 2

# Preparations in Kerry and by Kerrymen

The rising, so long prepared and planned, perished without the occurrence of anything that could be dignified with the name of battle against the forces of the crown. This was not owing to any want of courage or determination on the part of those who took the field. They would have delighted and gloried in the chance of making a fight for Ireland.

*T. D. Sullivan, 1885*

The Fenian rising in Kerry began on the night of 11 February 1867. It could be argued that Fenianism itself began in Kerry, because it was to that county that James Stephens, the founder of the Irish Republican Brotherhood, accompanied Michael Doheny in his epic flight to freedom following the rebellion of 1848. The country around Killarney made a deep impression on them, as Doheny wrote in *The Felon's Track*:

We were assured that the most inventive and hazardous scrutiny would never track our footsteps to the dizzy height of Carn Tuathail. But we had another and, it must be confessed, a more powerful motive. In either alternative which our fate presented [i.e. exile or death] there was no hope of ever beholding these scenes again and we could not omit this last opportunity of minutely examining what was grandest and loveliest in our native land.

He and Stephens also formed a high opinion of the people of Kerry. Doheny continued: 'It was easy to perceive that the people had cherished in their hearts the same imperishable purpose and hope [that Young Ireland had] of overturning the dominion of the stranger.' He spent his last night in Kerry in a cabin on the hills above Kenmare sleeping on a settle bed with a mattress of new-mown hay. In the morning the owner took him to the summit of a nearby mountain. 'Here we are, Mr Doheny,' said the man, 'higher than the proudest of your enemies!' Doheny was astonished that his name was known and that, in spite of this, none of the many people he and Stephens had met, the majority living in direst poverty, had claimed the substantial reward they might have gained by denouncing them to the police.

The revolutionary group, the Phoenix Society, founded by Jeremiah O'Donovan Rossa in Skibbereen, spread its gospel in the area, and Stephens in his journeys around Ireland returned to Kenmare and Killarney in 1858. In Kenmare he taught French at Miss Norris' school, as well as to the children of Mr Horsley, the Poor Law Union inspector in Killarney. When he reached Killarney, Stephens found the town decorated for the consecration as Bishop of Kerry of Dr Moriarty, who was then the president of All Hallows Missionary College in Dublin. In former days, Dr Moriarty had been a supporter of Young Ireland, but his politics had changed: 'I am loyal to England, heart and soul, but there is not a priest in the diocese that agrees with me.' His brother, Oliver, was a resident magistrate in Limerick and was a most reliable channel of information on the Fenians to Dublin Castle.

Almost thirty years later, Father C. McMahon from Kerry attended a lecture by Michael Davitt, the founder of the Land League, in aid of the James Stephens' testimonial fund in the Rotunda in Dublin on Tuesday 28 July 1885. Father McMahon recalled in the *Tralee Chronicle* of 1 August 1885 how Davitt described Stephens in those far off days:

A silent and mysterious figure was gliding through the land, visiting the remotest hamlets and infusing wherever he went a glow of enthusiasm into the manhood of each district. He was enkindling a spirit of robust revolutionary feeling which was to laugh, to scorn the difficulties, the dangers and the disasters from which the national cause in a few years after was destined to rise from defeat. The youth of the country was taught the tremendous power and advantage of combination. The principles of Thomas Davis and the songs of *The Nation* began to be cultivated in the popular mind. Faction fighting disappeared, provincialism vanished, religious animosity began to soften and subside and England's government soon discovered that the seeming 'Last Conquest of Ireland', which it hoped the Famine of 1848 had accomplished, was no conquest at all and that the rule of Dublin Castle was again confronted with the deathless spirit of Irish liberty.

It was also at that time Stephens developed the idea that in the event of the establishment of an Irish Republic the example of America should be followed and a new capital city be created in the fashion of Washington DC – and that this would be situated in Killarney, where he wrote: 'Our holiest love of Ireland was quickened by the shores of Loch Lein.'

In the winter of 1860–61 John O'Mahony visited Ireland and came to Kenmare. The ever-alert local constabulary reported on those who met him: 'O'Donovan and Sullivan (Bonane), Moynihan and Stack were always together and with them are the National Teachers William O'Brien, Mary O'Brien, John O'Driscoll and Lucy Davis.' This was not surprising. A government return of 1866 gave the names of thirty-four teachers involved in Fenianism and twenty-nine of these had been arrested by 12 July 1867. Dublin Castle drafted a letter in September 1866 to the Commissioners of Education requiring a declaration from teachers that they would not belong to any secret society – except the Freemasons – but the commissioners do not seem to have implemented this. A nationalist commentator remarked: 'In any case teachers dismissed have no redress. An appeal to the commissioners gets the reply "serves you right".'

Perhaps it was one of these teachers who was responsible for the 'Fenian Geography Lesson', later quoted by T. F. O'Sullivan, the noted Kerry historian and a native of Listowel:

What is Bermuda famed for?

As the prison of John Mitchel.

Who sent him there?

The Saxon Government.

For what crime?

For the love of Ireland, and for his noble and brave attempt to save
    her from starvation, degradation, misery and slavery.

Will he ever come back again to Ireland?

He will, please God and that right soon.

What will he do when he returns?

Make Ireland a nation once more.

The Sullivan (Bonane) who met O'Mahony was probably Florence O'Sullivan, an apothecary's assistant, who had been arrested in

1858, and lodged in Tralee gaol as a member of the Phoenix Society. A petition in his favour sent to Lord Naas, the chief secretary at the Castle, on 3 January 1859 entreated that his age (he was only nineteen years old) and previous good conduct might extenuate his offence. Seven local magistrates and six local clergy including Archdeacon O'Sullivan of Kenmare and Bishop Moriarty signed the petition.

James Stephens and Thomas Clark Luby visited Tralee and Listowel in 1861. Indeed, Luby's family was said to be originally from Kerry, though John O'Leary, who was editor of *The Irish People*, stated that they were from Tipperary. A police report of this visit recorded:

> The active manager of the Fenian Clubs – a kind of a travelling secretary – is named Stevens [*sic*] or Captain Stevens. S ... saw him in Cork. He was implicated in the 'rebellion' of 1848 and usually travels under the name of Murphy. His secretary is a man named Mooney or Looney.

Luby, when recalling this visit, said:

> On leaving Killarney we walked across country by tarns and over mountains. Hopoch Lake I well remember having been there before [in 1848] with Stephens and Deniffe – we made our way to a small station near Killarney on the Tralee line and so came to Tralee. Here at one of the hotels Mrs Sullivan, the proprietor's wife, evidently mistook the Captain [Stephens] for 'The Great Hogani' [probably Hogan], the chieftain of a renowned equestrian troop whose marvellous feats were at that moment flaming red letters on the walls of the metropolis of the Kingdom of Kerry. Probably the lady set *me* down as a boneless acrobat or a trapeze artist.

From this we posted by car to Listowel. Just as we had all but reached the town, the two 'clever ones', as Mrs Luby used facetiously to describe us, narrowly escaped a possible abrupt winding up of their distinguished two careers. The left wheel of the inside car suddenly dropped off and the two of us were knocked – if not into a cocked hat, at least into a heap in the corner. Pulling ourselves together we found that no bones were broken. I don't think I had any hurt worth speaking of and the 'Captain' might have received a few trifling bruises.

We dismissed the car and entered Listowel on foot. There we saw and regulated [Dennis] McNamara, a good man whom I had made centre in Listowel while Jim [Stephens] was off in America [December 1858 to March 1859]. I stayed in McElligott's Hotel [now The Listowel Arms] on that first visit, having left Father Kenyon's in Tipperary [a priest who had been a leading light in the Young Ireland movement] to come to Listowel. At the hotel I saw a very nice old gentleman, a brother of Father Matthew. I remember I got a rare ducking the next day going to catch the boat crossing the Shannon to Clare.

On this visit we went on to Limerick and Clare with McNamara and he returned with us to Kilrush and on by car to Ennis as the night was very wet. We came back by way of Tarbert. There we stayed one night, not in a hotel, but in a humble house of entertainment where we slept in beds with amazingly clean sheets. We went on to Abbeyfeale where McNamara left us. He was a Clareman and very proud of his native county.

In 1862 Stephens and Luby made another visit to Kerry. They brought with them a trunk of pamphlets containing Michael Doheny's account of the funeral of Terence Bellew McManus – which Devoy noted went to six editions, each of 1,000 copies –

combined with fierce and venomous attacks on A. M. Sullivan and his newspaper *The Nation*. (The Fenians blamed Sullivan for the arrest of O'Donovan Rossa and the other leaders of the Phoenix Society.) Stephens and Luby stayed for one night at Benners Hotel in Tralee and then Stephens went on to Limerick by the post-car early next morning. Luby stayed on to meet Patrick Foley, leader of a Fenian circle, in the Square. Foley had fled to America to avoid arrest after the 1848 rising but had returned to Tralee where he had a successful business as a tin and copper smith. Foley was also able to fix smoky chimneys and in the local paper published testimonials to that effect from, among others, Wilson Gunn of Ratoo House, Thomas Blennerhasset of Shanavalla and Reverend W. Disney, the rector of Ballymacelligott, none of whom apparently recognised the cuckoo that had entered their nests. Foley had sent word that he was unable to join Stephens and Luby the previous night, remarking that his wife was wide awake. Nor was she the only one. Luby wrote: 'The captain had hardly left me at six in the morning when I had two unlooked for and unwelcome visitors, a sergeant and constable of the police.' Luby was questioned by the local head constable about the contents of the trunk, but he was finally allowed to leave and later returned to Dublin by train.

Fenian sympathies were widespread among the young working men of Tralee and the local branch of the Catholic Young Men's Society was dissolved in March 1863 when the president, Father Kearney, refused to accept the toasts of 'The Memory of the Dead' and 'Irish Exiles' at the St Patrick's Day banquet of the society. Dublin Castle was under no illusions about many branches of the society and Sir Thomas Larcom wrote: 'However peaceful and loyal the rules are, there can be no doubt they have been converted to bad purposes in several places and used for foreign [i.e. for the papal brigade] rather than loyal enlistment.'

Dr Greg, the Church of Ireland bishop of Cork, had a different view on the Kerry Fenians. At a meeting of the Irish Society, which had been founded many years before to teach the natives to read the Bible in their own language, he said: 'If I wanted to see an Irishman of the old nobility, one of the ancient aristocracy I would find him in the valleys of Kerry. These are the real descendants of the Fenians – the loyal Fenians!'

In March 1864, an Irish National Fair was held in Chicago to raise funds for the Fenian movement. T. F. O'Sullivan listed the Kerry people who provided items for the occasion, and details of others are to be found in the columns of *The Irish People* of 28 March 1864. They included:

John S. O'Connor, Killarney, soil from the grave of Wolf Tone [*sic*] and some ornaments made from Killarney Wood (Arbutus).

John D. Flynn, Tralee, a pike from the 1848 rising.

Thomas O'Regan, Tralee, a lady's brooch in the shape of an uncrowned harp.

John W. O'Neill, a book with an account of the trials of Wolf Tone, the Brothers Shears and Robert Emmet.

James Lambe, Tralee, a cluricaune carved in bonework.

A young lady, Tralee, an antique shawl pin.

James Wren, a bog oak brooch, some Kerry Crystals and some real Irish Shamrock.

Mrs Hyland of Dublin, a native of Kerry, an old bog oak harp breast pin and a very old Irish coin of the reign of King Florence [*sic*], representing St Patrick driving the serpents out of Ireland and worth a very high price.

John O'Shea of Tralee and New York must have stocked a stall all by himself. He sent:

... a copy of *Smith's History of Kerry*, an old coin of the time of St Patrick, two dozen stone arrows found in Gleann an Air, seven miles from Dingle, by Mr O'Shea himself and supposed to belong to Fionn Mac Cumhaill, a George Washington cent, a Charles II coin of 1683, a coin of 1753 with the Maid of Erin, a medal with a likeness of Daniel O'Connell and his pedigree, a Father Mathew medal from 1835, a 1798 pike and a dagger found in the Desmond Castle, Tralee, three arbutus scarf pins shaped like an Irish pike, some mineral specimens from Tralee, a flinging stone from Ventry harbour and a lady's tape measure in a handsome tortoise shell, mounted in silver.

He also forwarded 'a pair of old dragoon spurs, a toothpick belonging to O'Connell, a sod of turf cut with the sleán in Abbeydorney, a bog oak crucifix and a leather purse'. But O'Shea was to pay for his support of the Chicago Fair when he visited Tralee in October 1866. He was arrested as he returned from a Freemasons' dinner in Killarney and spent ten days in the local gaol before being released.

He was not the only one to suffer for this reason. A letter to the *Freeman's Journal* stated:

Young ladies from the Model Schools, promoted to the Central Institution in Dublin, organised at headquarters a large patriotic scheme of contributions to the Chicago Fair. But a letter from the patriotic young lady who was organising the whole scheme fell through treachery into the hands of an unsympathising inspector and led to the young lady losing her situation and her instant expulsion from the Normal School.

On 14 April 1864 the *Tralee Chronicle* published a letter from John D. Nagle of Dingle outlining the extent of support for the Fenians in America:

About the first of last month a young man living on the Blasket received a letter from his father, now resident in Indiana, USA … 'All the Kerry papers are received in this city. We know about the new lighthouse on the Tiaracht Rock and the burning in effigy of Father Collins in Skibbereen. He and Father Mawe in Tralee and Bishop Moriarty and Cardinal Cullen are all on the Black List. There are 500,000 Fenians here ready and willing to liberate Ireland at the earliest opportunity.'

The newspaper outlined its solution to the problem of American Fenianism on 7 April 1865:

Military authorities and cabinet ministers in America have been found encouraging Fenianism and sending it ahead across the Atlantic. Let the people of Ireland have something to thank England for instead of Famine and oppression, give them a field where they may earn a fair day's pay for a fair day's work and they will not visit America to be inoculated with freedom!

The *Tralee Chronicle* quoted from another letter received in Killarney in 27 June 1865:

I suppose you have heard of our society called the Fenian Brothers. It is organised to free Ireland. We are only 800,000 strong. Almost all are old veterans who carried the Green Flag wherever they went and have proved themselves good soldiers.

The *Cork Constitution*, a Unionist paper, gave a succinct summing-up of Fenianism in Munster:

It has an inestimable charm for the artisan and peasant class. The

Fenians have a settled air of quiet determination and a desire of knowledge in military exercise which shows their belief that an opportunity for their display will not be found wanting. They look confidently forward to aid from America and believe it only a question of time till the green wave proudly above the red.

In Dublin, William Moore Stack, a native of Carrueragh in Knockanure, County Kerry, had long been under suspicion as a Fenian organiser. Superintendent Ryan of the 'G' Division of the Dublin Metropolitan Police reported on 5 December 1865:

Stack, a law clerk, whose Christian name, place of residence or place of business I am unable to learn is, at the present time, actively engaged in tampering with soldiers and I have reason to know has done an immense deal of mischief in that line. He is intelligent and has a surprising knowledge of legal technicalities that might enable him to escape justice if he came into our hands in the ordinary way. It is in the evening he is generally with soldiers in singing saloons, and flagrantly answers the description accurately of a man who has been frequently observed in the company of soldiers under suspicious circumstances. He recently made a boast about how he could work upon soldiers and said that he has even succeeded to a very considerable extent with the Royal Artillery.

When the 28th Regiment came here a few days ago he said he hoped to make good work among them, as there were many Dublin-reared boys in the Regiment. He deplored the departure of the 1st Battalion of the Buffs (The Lancashire Regiment) and said they were all right.

In February 1866 Stack was said to be 'actively engaged in distributing arms'. Warrants were sworn for his arrest and for that of Dr Edward Power of 3 Upper Temple Street and 6 Gardner's Row, Dublin. According to his police description sheet, Dr Power was 'twenty-six years of age, five feet nine inches in height with brown hair, hazel eyes and a large mouth and nose and is out on Fenian business from five o'clock in the evening till five o'clock in the morning'. O'Donovan Rossa reported that Edward's father was John Power (agent in Tralee for Charles Bianconi, who is credited with founding public transport in Ireland) and that when Edward was arrested on 4 December 1866 a letter from Redmond Roche of the Medical Hall, Listowel, dated 30 June 1865, 'using suspicious language', was found in his desk: 'You can have the goods at your own valuation and an order to send them will be attended to with *neatness and dispatch*. Wishing your project all the success possible.' The police also seized a photograph of Dennis Downey, merchant tailor of Trinity Street, wearing a Fenian uniform.

Dr Power had been a member of the council of the National League, a precursor of the Home Rule Party, headed by John Martin, an 1848 man and the brother-in-law of John Mitchel, but had resigned, stating: 'The minds of the people are set upon a more practical mode of gaining their independence.' He was lodged in Mountjoy gaol but was removed to Kilmainham gaol on 6 February 1867. Superintendent Doyle reported: 'There was not twenty shillings' worth of furniture in the house, it was manifestly a Fenian meeting place.' A letter in the police files, which presumably came from Dr Power's house, read: 'Dear Doctor, I enclose fifteen shillings – for a couple of *bottles* the same as you prescribed for Mrs Kelly. She is doing well, thank God. The messenger is rather giddy – send your own.' These 'bottles' were liable to explode with a bang when the triggers were pulled.

Stack was taken in his own house, 17 North Portland Street, Dublin, 'with seven [actually eight] others at a Fenian meeting' on

11 December and on the same night as John J. Kelly (tobacconist) of 27 Upper Sackville Street (long identified by Larcom as a leading Fenian) and his brother George, who also had a tobacconist shop in 23 Grafton Street. Larcom considered that these arrests would be a 'fatal blow to the expected outbreak in Dublin', as would 'the arrival of additional regiments and the consequent power of the government'.

Among the others arrested at Stack's house were James Bowes, John Bennett Walsh and John Clune. Bowes was a native of Newbridge and was described by the police as a delegate from Manchester. He was sentenced to ten months' imprisonment and on release was to be sent back to England. Walsh and Clune were from Clare. On 19 February 1867, Walsh, aged twenty and a law clerk, living at 17 Portland Street, Dublin, was sentenced to seven years' penal servitude and transportation to Australia; he was released there on 9 June 1868. According to John Devoy, Clune was released because he became dangerously ill in Mountjoy: he had eaten prison soap, which contained arsenic, because he did not want to be deported to America. (Walsh and Clune were still involved in the movement in 1880. They were mentioned in a police report in February of that year, as attending a Fenian meeting on 13 January in J. J. Clancy's, Little Green Street, Dublin.)

Also arrested at Stack's house on 11 December 1866 were John Healy, a former soldier who had served four years as a sapper and miner, and James Dowling, whose real name was Daniel Byrne and whom the police suspected of spreading Fenian money among coastguards and the military. With them were Michael Cloney who, according to his own account, had just arrived from England to see his brother in the 85th Regiment, Eugene (Owen) O'Sullivan and David Peeble Stitt. O'Sullivan claimed to be a chimney sweep and to have merely called to Stack's house to receive payment for the chimney pots he had erected there the previous week. Superintendent Doyle remarked that not only was he a sweep, but that he had been cleaning chimneys at the Curragh camp and Newbridge military barracks, where he had, no doubt, acquired much useful information for the Fenians and was a dangerous man. He was discharged on bail on 6 February 1867, the prison doctor in Mountjoy stating that he was not likely to live if kept in prison. David Peeble Stitt, of 120 Aughrim Street, Dublin, who was a manager of house property for his mother, claimed to be a Protestant and a loyalist, who would be vouched for by the clergy of St Paul's. He said he had only three weeks' acquaintance with Stack, who had invited him to the house for a spree, but he still spent two months in Mountjoy, being released on bail on 13 February 1867.

Meanwhile in Kerry, in May 1866, the Chief Baron (judge of the assizes), Baron Deasy, had remarked on the absence of Fenian offences in the county:

> I am not surprised that the farmers of Kerry have kept aloof from the conspiracy. They are shrewd and quick-witted and they would be the first to suffer in a revolution. Their cattle, sheep, pigs, butter and corn would be seized or paid for in Fenian bonds, not worth the paper on which they are engraved.

Captain Asplin of HMS *Gladiator* reported: 'The majority of the disaffected were those in the different towns of Kerry, comprised of clerks, shopmen and low characters.'

On 15 December 1866 Stack petitioned from Mountjoy gaol for his release:

> About a week previous to my arrest a man named Mr Bowes came to the house (there being a lodging bill in the window) and asked if

71

he could get a room for a friend of his, a Mr Cloney [*sic*], who was to arrive from England. My wife set him the back parlour where I and those who were with me were subsequently arrested. On Sunday during the absence of myself, and my wife, at prayers, Mr Cloney and Mr Bowes arrived at the house where I found them on my return. I then accompanied them on a walk through Glasnevin cemetery and partly through the city, my rule having been always to oblige those occupying apartments in my house.

On Monday morning as I was leaving the house for business they asked me as a favour to allow them to have a few friends together in the evening to enjoy a glass together and asked me to join them and bring any of my friends I chose. In accordance with their desire I brought my friend Mr Stitt to my house and we had just joined them from my own tea-table when the police came in. There were several persons present who to my knowledge I had never before seen. I am not of course aware, nor I respectfully submit does it affect me, if anything illegal was found with any of the other parties and so I leave the matter in your hands, trusting to favourable consideration being given to my case.

The reply from the Castle on 21 December to the governor of Mountjoy was terse in the extreme: 'Detain'.

On 19 January 1867, Dr Daly, of 16 Talbot Street, Dublin, wrote that Stack's health was very delicate and that further confinement would be very injurious to him. But he was committed for trial on 1 February, pleaded guilty to treason felony and on 19 February he was sentenced to ten years' penal servitude in Millbank Prison. After the horrifying treatment the prisoners received in Millbank, Stack subsequently offered to give information regarding the Fenian conspiracy, echoing the words of another Kerryman: 'I should be amply repaid for my trouble if my efforts should result in my preventing a useless effusion of blood and save the country the horrors of an insurrection.' Superintendent Ryan's opinion was:

> Stack's knowledge of the conspiracy was local and could only affect Dr Power and those members of his circle already convicted. He was never a centre but he was foolhardy and a hard-working brother in seducing soldiers, which was the work assigned to him. If he had made a proposal of this kind prior to his conviction he might have materially aided the Crown in getting up cases prosecuted at the commission but now his information is out of date.

A note for the Castle stated: 'He is a dangerous person and government cannot consent to any arrangement with him. Put by for the present.' On 30 June 1867, Samuel Lee Anderson said: 'Stack is a dangerous person and government cannot consent to any arrangement with him.'

Neither was Superintendant Ryan in any doubt about Dr Power's involvement in the Fenian movement. He reported:

> Power's house which could contain [hundreds of] men is solely occupied by himself, his partner, his mother and his assistant. It was to be a rallying point for the Fenians and I am reliably informed that it was where James Stephens was to be put up immediately on his arrival in Dublin. There is little or no furniture in this house – it is one of three that were evidently used for drilling and is one of three situated as if at the three corners of a square, in the centre of the city. There are many surmises about how the government got the information that led to the arrest of Dr Power. Some are of the opinion that it was a soldier he tampered with a few weeks back and others imagine that it was a member of his own circle named Stack who informed on him for the purpose of gaining favour with some

official personage – he [Stack] being a law clerk. However, these surmises happen not to be correct.

*The Fenian prisoners before the grand jury.*

Power had also pleaded guilty to the charge of treason felony and on 19 February 1867 he was sentenced to fifteen years' penal servitude – the same sentence as John Devoy. On the next day, *The Irish Times* remarked: 'The prisoners seemed to be struck with astonishment at the length of their terms of imprisonment, and Power's face assumed a deadly hue.' This was not surprising as there is no doubt that by pleading guilty they expected to be released on licence, as were the Phoenix prisoners in 1859. Indeed Anderson had a note to this effect on their convict files. On 23 March Power was removed to Millbank Convict Prison. It was proposed that George Kelly should go to America, but he protested on the grounds that it would be the ruin of his widowed mother's business, and he was reluctantly released on bail at the end of April 1868 on two sureties of £100, 'the police to watch his movements'. He had been almost a year and a half in prison at that time. Superintendent Ryan had written in February of that year:

> If he [Kelly] is set at liberty when the government considers it unnecessary to detain any of his class he would have reason to congratulate himself on having escaped being brought to trial, because if he had been I have hardly any doubt he would now be undergoing penal servitude like Dr Power, Stack, &c. All were arrested about the same period and from the same circle.

Stack was one of the Fenian prisoners discharged in March 1869, largely as a result of amnesty meetings held all over Britain and Ireland. He went on to become a leading member of the Land League – for which he spent another year in Limerick and Mountjoy prisons. He was a founder member of the Gaelic Athletic Association (GAA) in Kerry and for the rest of his life he refused to hear mass in St John's church in Tralee in protest at the parish priest's denunciations of the Fenians.

In January 1871 Power was among the fourteen Fenians released from prison under amnesty by the British Prime Minister William Gladstone, on condition that they remained abroad until the expiration of their sentences. Six of the prisoners travelled on the *Cuba* to New York and eight others, including Power and William F. Roantree, sailed to the same destination on the Cunard Line SS *Russia*.

# CHAPTER 3

# DUBLIN CASTLE
# AND ITS AGENTS

It is in Ireland that the American [Fenian] organisation can be completely destroyed, not in America. They desire not that a wise and equal policy designed to bring about peace, industry and contentment should prevail in Ireland – not that they wish her ill, but because it would destroy the spirit of insurrection and discontent at home.

*Sub-Inspector Thomas Doyle, November 1860*

As early as July 1855, Sir Thomas Larcom, while permanent under-secretary at the Castle, reported:

Preparations are being made for a filibustering expedition, to Ireland, organised by Thomas Francis Meagher, Michael Doheny and [Thomas Addis] Emmet – descendant of [Robert] Emmet who was hanged in 1805 [*sic*]. They have collected arms – they boast of secret societies in Ireland in connection with them; they count on the militia to cooperate with them. Money was gathered and men enrolled but the sudden termination of the Russian war and the return of the [British] army [from the Crimea] afforded sufficient reason for letting matters rest for that time.

*The Fenian Alarm – night guard in Plymouth harbour.*

The information from the United States came to Larcom from George Boate, a former clerk of the petty sessions in Ardmore, County Waterford. On 20 September 1855 Boate wrote: 'The ship *Chatsworth* has left Boston for Liverpool with 200 steerage passengers. They may be volunteers to raise rebellion in Ireland. A blacksmith named Patrick O'Rorke [a native of Fossa, County Kerry] is with them.' When the *Chatsworth* arrived at Liverpool on 27 October the local police reported that the greater number of the passengers at once took ship for Ireland – clearly they were concerned that many of them were Fenians.

Castle hearts fluttered again in April 1860 when the American barque *C. B. Truit* of New York, laden with rifles, anchored for four months in Queenstown harbour. It later transpired that the rifles were destined for Garibaldi's army in Italy.

When Sub-Inspector Thomas Doyle of the Irish Constabulary was in America in 1857–8 he alleged that there were 75,000 Fenians in the United States and 15,000 in Massachusetts alone and that: 'Meagher and O'Mahony had a meeting with President Pierce and discussed the intended invasion but they got no encouragement in that quarter … [John O'Mahony] would, I am convinced, be willing enough to encounter risk, to hazard his own life in an attempt to become the "Garibaldi" of Ireland.' John Martin, another of the 1848 men but no supporter of the Fenians, remarked in a letter to *The Nation* in October 1865: 'John O'Mahony was an Irish Garibaldi, without hatred of the pope, without love of England.'

Garibaldi was a military leader who united Italy and rather ironically many sworn Fenians were among the thousand Irishmen who joined a papal brigade to prevent his annexation of the part of Italy ruled by the pope. Not only Fenians such as James Blaney Rice of 'Tehallen' (Tyholland), later to lead the movement in County Monaghan, joined the brigade, but also members of the Irish Constabulary – more than a hundred of these by August 1860. However, in May 1860, a proclamation under the Foreign Enlistment Act had made such recruiting illegal. Despite this, men were still being openly enlisted in England to fight with Garibaldi's army. As Constabulary Inspector Robert Curtis commented: 'Many young men are leaving the country with a view to joining the papal army; we cannot prove it nor prevent it.' The chief secretary, Edward Cardwell, remarked that one advantage had been attained because of the recruitment: 'the exodus of unquiet spirits'. Larcom, too, commented on 9 June 1860 in a similar vein:

The furore of constabulary enlistment begins to calm. As in epidemics, the loss to the epidemic is not to be measured by the whole number of deaths, because a considerable number would have died if there had been no epidemic and the epidemic seizes first on those who would have died from other causes. So in this case the papal epidemic has carried off, first, the unsettled restless youngsters from the constabulary, who probably would have resigned if there had been no such cause in action. None of the steady long-service men have gone, they have too much to lose.

This was true, as the police were already getting six times the amount in pay that they were promised as recruits in the papal army.

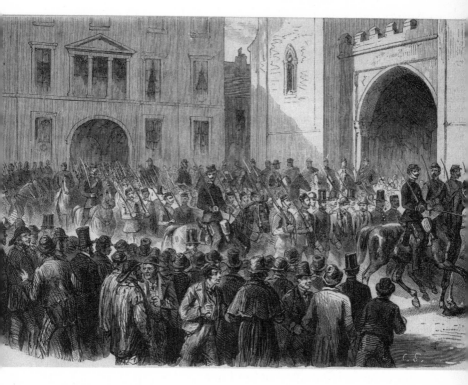

*Fenian prisoners at Dublin Castle.*

When Thomas Baines, an inspector in the Dublin Corporation, was arrested in August 1866, suspected of being a Fenian organiser, among the items found on his person was a pontifical cross of the Order of St Gregory, which had been presented to the members of St Patrick's battalion in the papal army and also another medal with the likeness of Pius IX and, within a wreath of laurels, the inscription *'Bene merenti'*. Baines had been putting his military experience to good use among the British garrison in Dublin, and on 19 February 1867 he was sentenced to ten years' penal servitude and transported to Australia for seducing soldiers from their allegiance.

Cardinal Cullen, the archbishop of Dublin, had no high opinion of either Garibaldi or the Fenians. He, of course, had first-hand experience of revolutions, as he had been in Rome in 1848 when the pope was driven from the city. He also had an uncle who had fought with the United Irishmen in 1798 and whose funeral had been attended by John Devoy's father (who had had to walk twenty miles each way in order to do so). In a letter published in September 1866 Cullen wrote:

> They [the Fenians] are followers of Mazzini and Garibaldi, Carbonari, Freemasons and international socialists. They are said to have proposed nothing less than to destroy the faith of our people by circulating works like that of the impious Voltaire and to seize the property of those who have any. Fortunately they had neither the wit nor the talents of Voltaire, but did not yield to him in anxiety to do mischief and in malice.

It is interesting to note that two sons of a leading 'Freemason', J. F. X. O'Brien, became priests, and the son of Garrett Stritch, who had to flee Ballyheigue in the 1870s because of his Fenian involvement, became cardinal archbishop of Chicago.

The Fenians gave back as good as they got. *The Irish People* reported:

> The bishops and priests who do the work of the enemy may be bad politicians and worse Irishmen. However, it *is* true that after the revolution men, women and children will take the place of flocks and herds on the extensive grass farms with which he [Dr Cullen] is acquainted.

A. M. Sullivan, no friend to the Fenians, in his *Story of Ireland* commented:

> At the very time the agents of the secret society were preaching to *The Irish People* the doctrines of revolution, *The Times* (London) wrote: 'Let all oppressed peoples know that liberty is a thing to be fought out with knives and swords and hatchets.' To be sure these propositions were formulated for the express use of the Italians at that time, but so utterly had England's anxiety to overthrow the papacy blinded her that she never reckoned that these propositions were being harkened to by the hot-blooded and impetuous Irish.

On St Stephen's Day 1866, County Inspector Smith reported to the Castle from Tralee:

> I regret to say that the opinion I formed twelve months ago regarding the unsatisfactory condition of the county remains unchanged. Disaffection has increased during the year and a bad spirit prevails in nearly all the towns. This is confined, however, to the lower orders, such as clerks, assistants in shops, tradesmen and the labouring classes. The workings of the evil disposed, though so secret as to baffle the exertions of the police in detecting them,

have not abated and I am certain that parts of the country which appeared to be uncontaminated have become imbued with the spirit of disaffection. However, the feeling of alarm and insecurity which prevailed amongst the well disposed has lately in some measure subsided, which I think may be attributed to the steps taken by the government.

In the meantime, Pierce Nagle, the 'prime informer' made his first communication to the police. Nagle was a part-time paper folder in the office of *The Irish People*, receiving by his own account, 'seven shillings and sixpence for working from Thursday to Saturday and wrote the address labels besides in his own house'. He was sacristan of St Laurence O'Toole church in Dublin and he worked at the building of the Augustinian church in John's Lane. His pay there was twelve shillings a week as attendant on the masons, a job secured for him by Denis Cromien, the clerk of works, a prominent Dublin Fenian and as ignorant as the rest of the organisation of Nagle's real purpose. Nagle was not inclined to be grateful for his post as he included 'Crommene' among the Dublin centres in a list he supplied to the Castle. Pat 'Pagan' O'Leary was also employed in building the church at the time.

Pierce Nagle was a native of Ballyboghan, near Clonmel. From 1853 to 1862 he had been a national teacher at Powerstown, County Tipperary. He had been reprimanded by his manager for 'mixing with the Fenians' so he resigned and went to America. He supplied a copy of the Fenian oath to the Castle and stated:

The members of the Brotherhood were encouraged to join the militia to acquire knowledge of drill. A man named David Bell, formerly a [Presbyterian] clergyman from Ballybay, County Monaghan, delivered lectures throughout the country in aid of Fenian funds. A rising was generally expected to take place after the harvest of 1865. The farmers in the south were drawing their money from the banks in gold.

In a note to Superintendent Ryan in June 1864 written at 2 Chapel Lane, off Lower Sheriff Street, Dublin, Nagle advised: 'Have a careful lookout from that week forward and to be cautious and wary in your movements for every one of the society are doubly wary and so clever as to know the slightest move of any kind.' He later said in court that, in August 1865, Stephens told him to give up his post in St Laurence O'Toole's and return to Clonmel. His wife would receive £1 a week and he would get his expenses. Nagle later vanished to Canada or South Africa, having been presented with a lump sum of £250 in November 1866 – an early example of the witness protection programme. As well as this, his father and brother had to be removed from their native Fethard for their own safety.

Two other effective police agents were Thomas Talbot and J. J. Corydon. Talbot had been a member of the Irish Constabulary for fifteen years. He joined the Fenian Brotherhood and became a centre for Tipperary and although a member of the Established Church – the Church of Ireland – he pretended to be a Catholic and received communion as such. While playing the part of John Kelly, a water bailiff, Talbot was searched three or four times by the police and attended the Friary chapel in Carrick-on-Suir in preference to the Catholic parish church. 'The service,' he said, 'was shorter and the sermon good.' All this made his crime much worse in Fenian eyes, and it was no surprise when he was later assassinated in Dublin. Earlier, Talbot had written to the Castle on 24 March 1865: 'On Patrick's night last, I was in the company of some Fenians in a public house and they boasted of having some of the brotherhood holding situations in Dublin Castle. Should any such be there and they see my reports, I would not be alive twenty-four hours.'

The agent who had most impact in Kerry was J. J. Corydon. Corydon's real name was John Joseph Corridan, and he was a native of Ballyheigue. His family had emigrated to America when he was twelve years old. He joined the 63rd New York Regiment of the Union army on 19 October 1861. In the summer of 1862 Corydon became a sworn Fenian, and he returned to Ireland at the close of the Civil War. He began giving information to the authorities in September 1866. In March 1867 Corydon was ordered by Colonel Massey to go to Millstreet and put himself under the orders of Colonel John James O'Connor in Kerry. Despite being instructed by O'Connor, 'to take command in north Kerry with Captain O'Brien, blow up bridges, tear up railway tracks and cut wires in that area and as far east as Rathkeale, if possible', instead Corydon returned to Dublin and began to provide information on the plans for the rising. As a result Colonel Massey was arrested. Corydon did his work voluntarily to break up the Fenian movement. He, too, echoed Daniel O'Connell's sentiments, saying that freedom was not worth the shedding of one drop of blood. On 10 July 1867 Corydon visited Naas gaol, which had received seven new iron gates, wrought iron bars in the cell windows and thirteen large padlocks, at a total cost of £149 8s. 8d. to render the prison more secure against the rescue or escape of the Fenian prisoners. There he identified Mortimer Moriarty, J. D. Sheehan and James O'Reilly, three of the Kerry prisoners. Together with Talbot, who had been promoted to the rank of head constable, Corydon gave evidence at their trial in Tralee.

One of his former comrades complained:

That scoundrel Corydon drew a captain's pay – that being supposed to be his rank in the Union army, while he was only a surgeon's assistant in a military hospital. A few nights before the arrests this rascal was playing cards with some of our fellows in Carey's Hotel. He was demure and plausible; you'd think butter wouldn't melt in his mouth.

The London magazine, *The Spectator*, did not think much of the informers: 'We suppose it necessary in the national interest to employ scoundrels of this kind, but if they could be used and then hung the world would be a cleaner and none the less safer place.' In the same vein the *Tralee Chronicle* remarked sarcastically: 'Everyone engaged with John Joseph Corydon in saving the state has found the undertaking delightfully graceful and remunerative.'

# CHAPTER 4

# THE FENIAN RISING
# IN KERRY

The vast majority of the lower orders in the south and west are as strong in their aversion to British rule as they ever have been and are ready, whenever any reasonable prospect of success presents itself, to risk their lives in what they term the struggle for freedom.

*Sir Robert Anderson, Historical Sketch on Fenianism in Larcom papers*

Cahersiveen – a meaner and muddier place I have seldom come across.

*The Times (London), 25 February 1867*

Why did Kerry rise on the night of 12 February 1867, while Fenians in other parts of Ireland did not rise? This was one of the many unresolved questions in the history of Fenianism. Recent biographical and other studies would suggest taking a fresh look at the question.

The background to the rising in Cahersiveen is simple: James Stephens, the organiser of Fenianism, had been deposed as he did not wish to be the leader of a rebellion, which he considered would have little, if any, chance of success. He claimed that the Fenians in Ireland had not been given the arms and supplies promised by the Fenian Brotherhood in America. However, many of the Fenian officers, particularly those who had fought in the American Civil War and had been responsible for brilliant feats of improvisation in battle, did not agree with him. They were confident they could overcome any difficulty that would arise. Moreover, a plan had been put in place to steal weapons from Chester Castle in England to be distributed in Ireland on 11 February. The plan was betrayed and the attempt was cancelled, but the Irish Fenians had been alerted to await delivery of the arms from 12 February and the men of Cahersiveen, unaware of the failure, assembled on that night as planned.

The great and the good were worried, but not unduly so, about the possibility of a rising. The *Tralee Chronicle* reported on 9 January 1867:

On 3 January 1867, the Knight of Kerry had organised an anti-Fenian demonstration in Valentia. It was attended by Reverend McGinn PP, Reverend Mr Sandford, rector, Mr John Driscoll, Lloyd's agent and Captain Needham JP. 'It is the greatest folly,' said the Knight, 'to talk of rebellion when butter is at £4 a firkin. It is utter madness with three ships to take on to destroy the greatest navy in the world. [At the time there were rumours in Kerry that three Fenian ships had sailed from New York.] I am perfectly satisfied that not one of the species "Fenian" is to be found within the precincts of the Island.'

He was wrong. In Cahersiveen, on the morning of 11 February Colonel John James O'Connor, the head centre for south Kerry and a native of Valentia (where the GAA field is named in his honour), shook hands with Captain Mortimer Moriarty as he boarded the mail car for Killarney. Captain Moriarty had been the first Fenian organiser in Canada and he had been on his way to join the Fenian attack on the island of Campobello off the coast of

Canada when he was arrested in 1866. He later escaped and now he planned to lead the rising in Killarney. Colonel O'Connor was to bring the Cahersiveen men to join him, but an informer had been at work. Mr Gallwey, JP, received an anonymous letter from 'A friend from Killarney' on 12 February 1867, 'the letter being left at my house a short time since by a girl':

Sir, I wish to inform you that there is a general rising of Fenians throughout Ireland tonight so any preparation you intend to make for your own safety do it at once. It is in compliment of Mr Coltsmann I give you this information, as he is a gentleman that has served me and my family. Please send him the enclosed note without the least delay. If it was known that I would give you so much information I would get a few bullets through my heart. I am no Fenian or neither would I act the part of a traitor or an informer – I can only give this information for your safety and more particularly Mr Coltsmann and his family.

P.S. Stephens is in the country and a lot of American officers. I have all this from one of themselves – the officer that will try to pass here tonight will come on the Cahersiveen car. I cannot write this note with ink for fear of being suspected.

The 'friend' may well have been John Glissane, because after the trials that followed the rising and the conviction of the Fenians, Glissane, his wife and two sons were sent to the Cape of Good Hope in South Africa. Dublin Castle spent £22 13s. 5d. on new outfits for them and a further £20 was to be given to Glissane on his arrival at the Cape.

Gallwey passed the letter on to Resident Magistrate Cruice and Sub-Inspector Colomb, and as a result a sergeant and two constables were sent to meet the mail car at Gortroe, Fossa, with directions to arrest any suspicious-looking stranger. Cruice later reported:

The anonymous letters to Messrs Gallwey and Coltsmann [two local magistrates] and our having acted on them by having the American agent [Moriarty] arrested on the Cahersiveen car before it reached the town and finding on him the letter [to the Killarney Fenians] no doubt prevented the rising taking place here that night.

A letter from Colonel O'Connor to J. D. Sheehan, the head centre for Killarney, was found in Moriarty's pocket giving details of the rising: 'Dear Sheehan, I wish to introduce to you Captain Mortimer Moriarty, who will do everything that is needful until I reach you myself. The private spys [*sic*] are very active but unless they smell a rat all should go off well without any trouble.' A copy was forwarded to the Castle.

According to the records of the Irish Folklore Commission:

D'eirigh na Finíní amach ar dtús i gCathair Uibh Ráthaigh agus chuireadar an captaen i 'jinjil' [caráiste] go Cill Airne mar ní raibh aon traen ann an uair sin ach do théighidís o áit go háit sa 'jinjil'. Do dhein duine éigin spiadóireacht air. Ach nuair a leandáil sé i gCill Airne do bhailigh piléirí timcheall ar an 'jinjil'. D'aithin sé ansan go raibh sé díolta. Do scread sé ach d'ith sé an méid paipéirí a bhí aige agus d'féad sé ach do tháinig siad ar litir a bhi aige don captaen i gCill Airne.

(When the Fenians rose in Cahersiveen, they sent on their captain in a horse-drawn carriage to Killarney, for there was no train there that time. But someone informed on him and when the police surrounded the carriage he knew he had been betrayed. He screeched and he ate as much as he could of the papers he had with him, but they found one letter destined for the Fenian captain in Killarney.)

*The Railway Hotel (later the Great Southern Hotel), Killarney – used as a
barracks at the time of the Fenian rising.*

Panic gripped the loyalists in Killarney when the news spread.
Cruice immediately telegraphed to Cork for reinforcements. Seven
officers and 165 men of the 2nd Battalion, the King's Royal Rifle
Corps, turned out in Cork at 10 p.m. and reached Killarney by train
at 3.30 a.m. on 13 February 1867. Since the military barracks was
in ruins they took over the Railway Hotel, which County Inspector
Smith regarded as the only house in the neighbourhood that could
afford them protection in an emergency. On the following day 100
men of the 14th Regiment and a troop of the 13th Lancers joined
them.

Many of the local landlords fled in fear from their mansions and
brought with them to the hotel their gold and silver plate with their
beds and baggage. *The Times* reported on 15 February 1867: 'The

children of Lord Castlerosse have been removed to England on their way to Europe to join their parents. Mr Herbert MP has gone to Killarney [presumably from Muckross House]. Respectable families are flying from their homes to places of safety.' But some were built of sterner stuff. The loyalist paper, the *Kerry Evening Post*, reported on 9 March 1867 that: 'During the dreaded Fenian outbreak, Mr Beale Brown, like a true Briton, took up his position and hung out his colours at Crotto [near Tralee] and Ballygoughlin [County Limerick]. Both himself and his son, Mr J. Beale Browne exhibited no more fear than if they had a flying column at their disposal.'

Cruice's next move was to alert the constabulary in Cahersiveen as quickly as possible, but the telegraph wires had been cut by the Fenians. A mounted constable was sent to Killorglin with orders to proceed from there to Glenbeigh and on to Cahersiveen. Colonel O'Connor had organised a dancing class for the night of the rising in Cahersiveen and Eileen Ahern, a young girl who was present on that night, recalled:

> Thomas Griffin, the dancing master, came into the room and told us to break up for the night. On my return home I heard footsteps after me and on looking around me I saw a party of about twenty men armed with pikes and marching two deep coming after me on the road leading from the Old Quay to the bridge. In a little time after I saw Michael Conway with a shot-belt across his breast and a coat thrown on one of his shoulders. He went in the same direction. [CSOR papers]

As Ahern said, after the dancing master ended the class much earlier than usual, the young men formed ranks in the main street and marched towards the barracks. This was the first stage in

Colonel O'Connor's plan but the planned attack on the barracks had to be abandoned when it became clear that the police were on guard as the lights remained on all night.

It was Joseph Noonan (one of the Fenian leaders, who was building a house for the officer of the coastguards in Cahersiveen), who had visited the barracks at 8.30 p.m. that evening and warned the police that an attack was imminent, but Noonan was not an informer. His actions were the result of the fact that on that night Head Constable O'Connell was in charge of the barracks. O'Connell's four sons had been sworn into the movement and one (William), at least, was marching with the Fenians that night. Noonan could not bear to think that any harm should come to O'Connell and so he told him of the Fenian plans. Devoy described how, while the police kept watch, O'Connell's daughter is said to have obtained the key of the armoury and smuggled out the police rifles under her cloak to give to the Fenians.

As recorded by the Folklore Commission, Micheál Ó Curráin from Na hOchtaibh in Waterville told a different story – one that agreed with the account found in the British Admiralty records:

Bhiodh na Finini a ndruilleáil timpeall na Caithreach go dti gur tháinig a lá orthu. Bhi mac sergeant romhtha [rompu] agus bhi a athair sa bhearraic ach an oiche bhiodar chun éiri amach is dócha go nduirt an mac leis an athair gan bheith sa bhearraic. Mas sea, do tugadh long – gunboat – anios ar a'gcuan [is d]á mbainfeadh aoinni den bhearraic go séidfheadh si Cathair Saibhin san aer, so nior bacadar dul go dti an bhearraic. Chuadar anonn thar Ghóilin go tigh muar [sic] Bharry agus thugadar gunnai as.

(The Fenians were drilling around Cahersiveen until the time came. The sergeant's son was with them and I suppose he told the father not to be in the barracks that night. So this gunboat came into the harbour and they knew that if they went near the barracks, Cahersiveen would be blown to pieces. So they crossed over to Barry's – the Big House – and they got guns there.)

The Fenians began their march from Cahersiveen to Killarney and were joined by the men from Foilmore. They attacked the coastguard station at Kells (Na Cealla) and captured five rifles, with accoutrement belts and sword-bayonets, cartouche-boxes and cartridges, ten rounds of rifle ball cartridges, thirteen caps in each, with three spare caps to allow for waste. Thomas Pierce, a coastguard officer, reported how when he saw twenty to thirty men with guns and pistols approaching the buildings:

> I made my way to the public road with the intention of proceeding to Cahersiveen and reporting to Captain White. I met another party of from twenty to thirty men armed, who challenged me to know who I was. I cried out 'Coastguard!' when the whole party presented at me and called on me to surrender. I stood still with my pistol in my hand and asked who was I to surrender to? They said: 'To the Irish Republic.'

A coastguard's wife, Elizabeth O'Bryan, whose house was searched by the Fenians, later testified: 'I knew Goulding, son to Paddy Goulding of Mount Foley. He had a rifle with a dirk on it and around his waist a coastguard's belt.' The local people remembered this because she was a local girl (her maiden name being Eilis Ni Guagáin) who had married a coastguard:

> Cuirfimid Goggin sa Sceilg,
> Cuirfeam ar bórd an Ri i,

Cuirfeam anonn that farra' i,
Féachaint an ndéanfai dion di.

(We'll bury Goggin on Sceilg,
We'll send her over to Court,
We'll send her far over the ocean,
To see who likes her most.)

Máire Ní Mhurchadha from Gort a' Phóisire near Kells also told the story:

Bhí cuid acu di-chéilli a ndóthain chun dul isteach go dti bean na Waterguards agus d'aithin si é (iad) is dócha (rud) nár locht uirthi. D'innis si cérbh e féinigh, buachaill de mhuintir Ghúilin, (Golden) in aice laimh liom. Sea, d'innis an bhean aimn an fhir agus do theic sé sin go Queenstown [Cóbh Chorcai], nuair a láimhsiodh é fein agus fear eile agus do chuireadh go Botany Bay é. I gceann tamaill, scaoileadh amach é, agus chuaigh sé go hAustralia. Tá a chlann ansan go fóill agus a mhuintir go han – mhaith as agus go an – saibhir timpeall na háite sin.

(Some of them were foolish enough to go to the house of the wife of one of the waterguards and she identified them – sure, you couldn't blame her. Yes, she identified my neighbour the boy of the Goldens. He fled to Queenstown but himself and another man were arrested there and sent out to Botany Bay. After a while he was released and he went on to Australia [sic]. His family is there still and well off.)

Mrs O'Bryan also recognised 'Mac snasta Sáirsint na bPilear', William O'Connell. 'Sergeant Connell's [sic] son spoke to me,' she said, 'and told me not to be frightened.' After the trials of those involved in the Kerry rising, the O'Bryans were transferred to Warrenpoint, County Down, for their own safety.

At Eisc a'Catha, the Fenians met Constable Duggan, the mounted policeman who had been sent from Killarney to warn the authorities in Cahersiveen of the rising. Having been shot down from his horse, Colonel O'Connor had Duggan taken to a nearby house and given water and brandy. 'I was wounded worse myself [in the American army],' O'Connor commented.

According to local tradition O'Connor asked Duggan, 'Why did you not stop when called upon?'

'I'm an Irishman too,' replied the constable, 'I had my duty to perform.'

The records of the Folklore Commission have an account by Micheál Ó Concubhair (Michil an Gabha) from Fatha of this incident:

'Twas thought they were going to rob the bank in Killarney and the bankers they carried away every shilling of money that was in it up to the Railway Hotel and put sandbags outside the windows to save it. But they [the Fenians] were sold partly behind Killorglin, by a servant girl. She gave an account of them that they were left and where they were going and there was a dispatch rider sent after them. They ordered him to give up his dispatches and he refused and in the legs, I think, they shot him. He asked them not to kill him, that he was the father of a family and they didn't but his horse was going round there.

In another record kept by the commission, according to Ó Curráin:

Bhuail capall iallaiste leo agus dheineadar halting air. Más sea, nior rinne se aon halting doibh. Chaitheadar leis agus leag Conway é agus fuaireadar liosta (d'aimneacha na bhFinin) ina chois agus a bhróg. Duggan ab ainm do.

(They met a man riding a horse and called on him to halt, but he wouldn't hear of it. So Conway shot him and they found an account of the Fenians in his boot! Duggan was his name.)

The Fenians continued to Glenbeigh and took over the Glenbeigh Inn. They took thirty-two penny loaves, thirty-three ha'penny loaves and some milk, costing five shillings and ten pence, and left a receipt for them in the name of the Irish Republic. When Colonel O'Connor saw that the innkeeper, Daniel O'Shea, was none too pleased with this he paid for the loaves out of his own money as well as an extra seven pence for a half stone of oats for his horse. O'Shea believed in the maxim that one good turn deserves another and when the Fenian trials came round Resident Magistrate Cruice complained: 'It was manifestly O'Shea's intention to go as far as he possibly could, with safety to himself, to render his information valueless, and Patrick Griffin would have been convicted if he were an honest witness.' Afterwards every effort was made by the authorities in Dublin Castle to deprive Daniel O'Shea of his position as postmaster in Glenbeigh.

Colonel O'Connor read Constable Duggan's dispatches and later he met the mail-car driver who told him of Moriarty's arrest. It was clear that the Fenian plans had been betrayed. No one joined him in Killorglin and the local centres told him that the rising had been postponed for a month. Like Richard O'Gorman who had led the 1848 rising in north Kerry, he ordered his men to scatter and to take to the mountains of the Cruacha Dubha (McGillycuddy's Reeks) to avoid capture. 'There will be another day,' he said, 'when I will return to lead you.' But many years were to pass before the day came and by 1916 O'Connor was long dead.

On hearing the news from Killarney, Edmund Day Stokes, Richard Chute and Robert Leslie, 'the principal magistrates in the county', demanded that the whole of County Kerry should be placed under martial law. A reward of £500 was offered for the arrest of those who shot Duggan, £250 for the arrest of O'Connor and £250 for the arrest of those concerned in the attack on Kells station. Despite these enormous rewards, witnesses were slow to come forward and no one betrayed O'Connor, who escaped to America, became sheriff of Shreveport in Louisiana and married Kate Kenny, a sister of General Kenny of the Confederate army. A few years later, as Colonel O'Connor lay on his deathbed, he told the priest about the bravery of the Cahersiveen men he had led to battle on that cold February morning. He died in December 1870. According to the *New York Phoenix*: 'Both Confederates and those who differed from him in politics – one and all came to his funeral – and paid kindness and respect to the remains of a gallant fellow-countryman.'

On 15 February 1867, the Sunday following the rising in Kerry, Bishop Moriarty preached in Killarney cathedral a sermon that was to make him famous (or infamous) in Irish history. It was printed in the *Freeman's Journal* of 18 February 1867:

The fact that they [Fenians] did harm to no one's property shows that the outbreak was not intended as one of rapine and plunder or a war on the gentry of the country. Kerry people are capable of acts of madness but they are utterly incapable of acts of robbery or such like outrage.

One word about the prime movers of this enterprise. Thank God, they are not of our people or if they ever were, they have lost the Irish character in the cities of America. But beyond them are criminals of far deeper guilt. The men who, while they send their dupes into danger, are fattening on the spoil in New York and Paris. The execrable swindlers who care not to endanger the necks of the men who trust them, how many are murdered by the rebels or hanged by the strong arm of the law provided they [the leaders] can get a supply of dollars for either their pleasure or their wants.

O God's heaviest curse! – His withering, blasting, curse on them! When we look down on the fathomless depth of this infamy of the heads of the Fenian conspiracy, we must acknowledge that eternity is not long enough nor hell hot enough to punish such miscreants.

A. M. Sullivan, the proprietor of *The Nation*, described the sermon as a 'rhapsody of undignified vituperation'. Bishop Moriarty was probably unaware of the damage done by the Fenians to Robert Ahern's potato garden in Cahersiveen, damage that Head Constable Howard estimated was worth three to four pounds. However, by September 1867 the Castle was in a generous mood and two five-pound notes were handed over to Ahern 'in as secret a manner as possible' by Sub-Inspector Ross in reparation.

Cardinal Tomás Ó Fiaich, writing in 1999 in *Seanchas Ardmhacha*, said that every student is familiar with the general statement repeated in all the manuals that the bishops and priests were vigorously opposed to the Fenians and condemned their activities. 'However,' he said, 'it is not to be expected that twenty-seven bishops and 3,000 priests would be of the same mind over such an issue.'

Since October 1866, the British garrison in Kerry had consisted of an officer and thirty-three men in the Lower Shannon forts, seven men based in Tarbert, five in Kilkerrin, five on Carrig island, nine on Scattery, four in Doonaha and three in Kilcredaun. Two companies of the 2nd Battalion of the 6th Foot Regiment were stationed in Tralee with five officers and 109 men. The Fenians were to be responsible for the subsequent considerable multiplication of these numbers.

On the same day as Bishop Moriarty's sermon, 15 February, Rear-Admiral Frederick wrote to the Castle from the *Black Prince*, his flagship at Queenstown:

> I went to Cork today to confer with Major-General Bates, commanding the district. Everything is quiet in that vicinity [i.e. Kerry]. Reinforcements have been sent to Sir A. Horsford at Killarney, and Colonel Palmer has proceeded thence with 250 men in pursuit of the insurgents in the direction of Kenmare. I reported this morning the sailing of the *Helicon* for that place and I hope she will arrive there early tomorrow morning. I have directed Captain Kennedy to send the *Blazer* to Tralee, if possible. I enclose a letter from Captain Asplin of the *Gladiator*. I received this morning this telegram from Lord Naas [Under-Secretary at the Castle], 'I hope the *Gladiator* may be allowed to remain at Valentia. Her captain and crew have done most excellent service.'

The *Blazer* did reach Tralee, and on 18 February Lieutenant Warren reported: 'All quiet in the neighbourhood of Tralee, but much excitement exists among the lower classes.'

There is an Admiralty account of the ships under Rear-Admiral Charles Frederick's command, which were on duty off Kerry on 15 March 1867:

> *Liverpool* cruising off coast between Shannon and Bantry
> *Gladiator* at Kenmare
> *Pigeon* at Kenmare – gunboat

*Sepoy* at Sneem – gunboat

*Racoon* at Valentia – Captain Parris

*Redwing* at Tralee – gunboat

*Hind* left Queenstown for Dingle and Ventry and will proceed to
Tarbert in accordance with request of magistrates forwarded by
the Lord-Lieutenant on 12th inst.

*Frederick William*, coastguard ship, and *Blazer*, tender, both on the
Shannon

A letter from Captain Asplin of HMS *Gladiator*, written the day
after the Cahersiveen rising, is interesting as it gives the British
point of view on the events:

Last night Mr White, inspecting officer of the coastguard, informed
me that a rising of the Fenians might be expected immediately at
Cahersiveen and requested my assistance, his force consisting of only

*The towns of Cahersiveen (opposite) and Killorglin (above).*

four men. I at once dispatched [the cutter] under Lieutenant Basil McArthur, manned and armed, with orders to anchor off the town and afford assistance if requested. In the event of any attack this was to be signalled by rocket to the *Gladiator.*

The linesmen who were repairing the telegraph line reported that they met a party of about 120 armed men, half way between here and Killorglin, who told them that 'it was no use repairing the lines as we shall destroy them as often as they are repaired'. The linesmen said, 'We won't repair them', and were then at the insistence of a Roman Catholic priest allowed to proceed. The armed party had shot one of the constabulary they met on the road, and the priest hearing of it had gone to the assistance of the wounded man; the bullet has since been extracted.

A fresh outbreak at Cahersiveen being considered probable last night I went up there at 8.30 p.m. with two boats manned and armed but returned before midnight the town being perfectly quiet.

In the same vein, Maurice James O'Connell, a Killarney magistrate, had written to the Castle on 15 February:

> Having accompanied a detachment sent to Killorglin last evening, I beg to state that I have no doubt that a second party of armed men came as far as Glencar. They retired to Cahersiveen and dispersed. If troops had not been sent here promptly, there would have been a general rising.

When he was recorded by the Folklore Commission in the 1940s, Pádraig Liath Ó Sullaibheáin from Muiring Ui Dhubha in the parish of Prior concurred with O'Connell's account:

> Bhí Muiris 'ac Shéamuis Ui Chonaill agus duirt se leis na saighdiúiri dearga agus na peelers dul go Coill Mhissus Shea no Coill Wynne i nGleann Beithe. Nior dhein siad rud air is dá dteighdis sa choill bhi an choill lán acu (na Finini). Tháinig se seo i gcoinne Mhuintir Chonaill in aimsir election ina dhiadh sin. Do bhios lá sa Cathair, mé i mo gheafar, agus Muiris 'ac Shéamuis roimh na saighdiúiri amach agus do chonac bean ag isliú sios sa tseanáil agus á breith ar francach marbh agus é caitheamh in airde ara bhurlach – ar Mhuiris 'ac Sheamuis.

> (Maurice James O'Connell advised the Redcoats and the police to go to Wynne's Wood in Glenbeigh but they would not be said by him, and weren't the Fenians all hiding there and would have been caught. The people didn't forget this when the elections came round. When I was a young fellow I was in Cahérsiveen one day and there was Maurice James in front of the soldiers. This woman – didn't she stoop down and catch up a dead rat from the channel and she threw it straight at Maurice James O'Connell.)

The British army was taking no chances. On 17 February 1867 Lord Strathnairn wrote to General Horsford:

> Would it not be good to patrol the suspected points on the line at uncertain times with cavalry and infantry combined, the detachments from different points meeting each other. I am glad you are detaching bodies of troops to scour the country. They should be – and I suppose they are – on the footing of moveable columns, moving with proper precautions, i.e. advanced and rear guard.

On 18 February Father John Healy, parish priest of Cahersiveen, wrote to the *Tralee Chronicle*:

> The cause of the mock-heroic enterprise was instructors who are importing the political theories of Republican countries and who are superseding the peaceful and constitutional teaching of O'Connell. While marching under the ruin where he was born, had those armed aggressors reflected on his famous dictum that any political change was too dearly bought by shedding one drop of blood, they would not have fired on a lone policeman.
>
> I wish the government to hear from a local source that there is no cause on any large scale of making examples *in corpore vili* in a remarkably quiet district (hitherto) for the terror of Fenians all over the nation.

Then on 19 February Lord Strathnairn reported to the British government:

> General Horsford's last effort does not throw much light on the Fenian disturbances in Kerry. *He* estimates a party of Fenians who are roaming through the county at only sixteen. He has made repeated

efforts to come up with them but hitherto he has not been able to do so. The very hilly and difficult nature of the country in Kerry conceals the movement of so small a body, difficult to discover, more especially as the people, even if not disaffected themselves, will not give information. Bishop Moriarty says that the band of insurgents consisted of sixty. I have also required the general to send detachments to several localities to support the police in their search for arms in the disaffected districts. Two parties of men supposed to be Fenians were seen at night near the barracks in Tralee by the sentinels but had disappeared when the patrols went after them.

Micheál Ó Concubhair's account shows that despite the threat posed by the Fenians, the fact that these men were known in the vicinity could have an impact on people's actions towards them:

I knew several of the Fenians. The doctor in Milltown, Dr Sheehan, his father was transported (for seven years) on account of his connection with the Fenians. He was in gaol for a long time. The Connells (of Lakeview) had great influence then and the Sheehans were bounding them and Sheehan's brother came down to Sir [Maurice] James O'Connell and asked him to sign a petition to lave [*sic*] Jerry come home.

'Well, Mick,' says he, 'I'll sign it for you though he *was* a Fenian!'

'Ah! He wasn't,' says Mick.

'He was,' says he, 'and every child born to his mother was another.'

Meanwhile in Killarney Magistrate Cruice had resolved to capture every single one of the Cahersiveen Fenians:

We marched the soldiers a distance of about five miles in the direction of Cahersiveen, but not having seen or heard anything the troops returned. I then proceeded with a hundred men in the direction of Kenmare in order to intercept the insurgents who had gone through the Gap of Dunloe. When we had marched twelve miles we found they had altered their course so we returned to Killarney. On the night of 8 March I proceeded with a party of police and thirty-two of the 60th Rifles to the Gap. We marched the three miles from the town to the Gap as the noise of the cars would apprise them of our coming. We went through the Black Valley (Cam ui Dhuibh), a distance of about thirty miles, but we did not succeed in coming up with them.

It was whispered in the locality that indeed there were Fenians hidden in the Tomies Wood on the south-west side of the lower lake but that some had met soldiers who were sworn Fenians and these allowed them through. Others, it was said, had been captured by Highland soldiers from Scotland and were allowed to escape when they spoke in Irish to their captors. The police arrested 'a son of James Connor', who was thatching Glena cottage at the bottom of the wood and who had taken Joseph Noonan and two others across the lake to Muckross in a fishing boat. Cruice reported:

> From fifty to sixty of the insurgents concealed themselves in Tomies Wood south-west of the lower lake about six miles from the town. Detachments were posted at each end of the wood and I remained there until three o'clock today. From what I can learn there is not any ground to think the insurgents were in the wood last night. They escaped through a pass, which as I am informed could not be protected and were seen escaping by some of the soldiers, leaving some arms and ammunition after them and also a saddle belonging to the policeman they had shot on the previous day.

A force of 116 infantry and twelve cavalry was sent to Cahersiveen.

The cavalry made a deep impression on the local people as recorded by the Folklore Commission:

Conac iad – na Finini – an t-am a thainig corr san saol. Bhios – sa, o, tá garsúin ansin, an ceann is lugha acu, bhios–sa timpeall na toirt sin agus b'fhéidir nios seana – chrionna. Bhuel, chualamar ag teacht iad, bhí eagla ar na daoine roimhis na bhFinini, go mb'é gur samhail a mharóidis na daoine. Nior dheineadar aon diobháil ach chuadar isteach i dtig Neidi O'Rale agus bhi braon bainne aige, mar bhi cupla bó aige ann agus d'itheadh an t-im agus an bainne, gach aon ghrota de – le hocras, is dócha. Ach dhiolodar as, chaitheadar an t-airgead isteach faoin doras chuige.

Ta páirc árd suas ansin – An Meanus – agus bhios–sa ansin ag ghlanadh prátai, ag tarrach na lutharnach as, nuair a chuala na daoine ag rith suas an bóthar soir agus an bóthar siar. Aoinne a bhi ar na bóithre ag rith, agus fear a' chapaill á scair a chapall agus á cheangail sa chlaidhe agus á fhágáil an trucail sa diog.

Bhuel, is gairid dom go bhfeaca chugham anios ná tri capall á léideáil agus ba iad na capaill is mo a bhfeaca riamh. Cheapas go rabhadar chomh hárd le binn a' tighe. Capaill móra agus ceannan bhán ionntua 'gus clúite. Ní clúite leis ab ea iad ach beagainti mar seo amach as a mburlach a bhiodar ceangailte. Bhi saighdiúiri dearga in áirde ar na haon ceann acu, na dtri chapall i gcónai i dteannta a chéile. Má bhí aon chapall amhain ansan bhi leath mhile de shaighdiúiri fen mbothar, pé in Eireannn é.

Dia linn, nior fhan duine acu, bhiodar amach ag lorg na bhFinineach. Ni haon Ri a bhi againn an uair sin ach Queen Victoria. Bhuel, bhaineadar amach Cathair Saibhin agus nior dheineadar aon diobháil ar a shon sin ach i ndiaidh na bhFinini, ach dá ndéanfaidis an rud ar an gcaptain a bhí orthu.

Cad é an tainm sin a bheith air? – Fan socair – *Connor* a bhi orthu mar captaen!!

Bhí na Finini i Ghabháil a' Phocáin, do leibheálfaidis iad go léir, ach ghlanadar soir agus stadar ag Coill na dTóime soir, chuadar i bhfolach ann. Dherú, mharbhóidis suid iad ar tháinig ann acu – na saighdiúri dearga.

(I saw them – the Fenians – at the time of the troubles. I was – I suppose – the same size as that young fellow there and a bit smarter. Well the people were afraid of the Fenians in case they might kill them. But they didn't do any harm, only that they went into Neidi O'Rale's house and they ate all the butter and drank all the milk in the house – with hunger I suppose. But they paid for it – they threw the money in under the door.

There's a field up on the hillside – An Meanus – and I was clearing it to plant potatoes – clearing the rushes, when I heard the people running up and down the road and a man with a horse and cart, he removed the tack from the horse and tied it to the fence and left his cart there in the gully.

The next thing was I saw the three biggest horses I ever saw in my life galloping towards me – they were as tall as the gable of a house. There was what you might take to be plumes on the horses – but they were only bayonets and there were three Redcoats riding them and they advanced in a line together and behind them were surely five hundred soldiers.

They made neither stop nor stay for all they wanted was to catch the Fenians and they continued on down into Cahersiveen. We had no king of course at the time only Queen Victoria. Well, they did no harm in Cahersiveen but if they could have laid hands on the Fenian captain!! –

What's this his name was? – I have it, he was Connor.

The Fenians were hiding in Gábhail a' Phocáin and later on in Tomies Wood and I tell you they would have dealt with the Redcoats if they caught up with them.)

On 1 March 1867 'CBB' from Killarney wrote to the *Tralee Chronicle,* enclosing a letter from a British officer explaining why the Fenians had not been caught: 'We see the helpless British infantry soldier, laden down with pack, tunic and shako, struggling like a staggering haystack over the slippery slate formation of the Kerry mountains, a thousand times more difficult from bog and bush than the slopes of the Himalayas.'

However, determination was Cruice's watchword, and on Saturday 10 March 1867 at 2 a.m. he led 130 soldiers and twenty-six policemen on a sweep towards the lower lake. All were back in the town by 9.35 a.m., 'tired, hungry and exhausted', but without any prisoners. On 18 March word reached Cruice that Colonel O'Connor had been seen in Millstreet, about twenty miles from Killarney. He ordered out the military and led them there on a terrible night of rain and snow, but again without success. The police by now had had enough of Cruice and refused to accompany the soldiers. Cruice complained to the lord lieutenant but he could not follow up his complaint as he nearly died from pneumonia after the exertions of his march.

In 1940, at the age of sixty-three, Pádraig Ó Donnchú from Clúthar Nois, in the Black Valley, told the collector from the Folklore Commission about the Fenians:

Is cuimhin liom go maith iad (na Finini) agus na saighdiúiri agus na peelers a bheith ag rith ina ndiaidh, Ghabh na Finini mar seo inniu agus ghabh an dream eile amárach ann. Ghlaodar – na Finini – istigh i dtig m'athair, beannacht Dé lena ainm. Bhí prátai fuair beirithe o réir ann agus feol a bhi beirithe is gubáiste [cabáiste] is dócha, agus d'itheadar na prátai fuar – á, na créatúiri – agus an feol aguis an gubáiste agus bhailiodar leo ansin. Bhí timpeall deich fhicid fearaibh acu ann, gunna ages 'na haoinne acu. Nuair a tháinig na saighdiúiri dearga ni bhfuair siad riamh aon tuairisc orthu. Bhí giústisi is daoine móra lena gcois, dar leat, chun órdú thabhairt dóibh chun lámhachadh dá bhfeicidis na Finini.

Bhiodar, na Finini bochta sin, ar thaobh na gcnoc is do mharóidis milte acu da mba mhaith leo é – na saighdiúiri sin agus iad ag titim thall is abhus is bfhéidir ocras orthu go léir. Tá sin tamall maith ó shoin anois.

(I remember the Fenians well and the police and soldiers chasing after them – one day they'd be here and another day there. They came into my father's house – God be good to him – and there were cold potatoes there and boiled bacon and cabbage and they ate it – the misfortunes – and off with them again. There were about thirty men and each had his gun. When the Redcoats came they couldn't find them – they had magistrates and gentry with them to give them the order to shoot the Fenians.

Yes, the poor Fenians were on the hills, but they could have killed the soldiers if they wanted – the soldiers were falling over here and there and they weak with the hunger. That happened a long time ago now.)

By the end of March 1867 there were two troops of the 12th Lancers distributed between Killarney, Killorglin and Cahersiveen. There were two officers and thirty-one men in Killarney, an officer and fourteen men in Killorglin and an officer and thirteen men in Cahersiveen. There were now three troops of the 6th Foot in Tralee with five officers and 160 men, one troop in Cahersiveen with two officers and sixty-six men, and one in Kenmare with two officers and seventy men. In addition, six troops of the 1st Battalion of the 14th Foot made up of twenty-four officers and 352 men commanded by Colonel Budd were divided between Killarney under Captain Le Mesurier, Kenmare under Major Grogan, and Killorglin, Cahersiveen and Sneem.

It had been proposed earlier in March to withdraw the Kerry detachments of soldiers. In a letter to Lord Strathnairn, who had described the Fenians as 'the class above the masses', Larcom wrote:

> As far as the state of that county is concerned I do not think it is necessary to retain troops at Kenmare, Sneem and Cahersiveen, but news has reached me this morning that the American wire has again been cut. Now in the face of threatened events, we *must* keep this line open. It would be presumptuous in me to suggest to you *how* this had best be done. I therefore ask you to communicate at once with His Excellency on the subject and you may be sure that I will approve of any course that you and he agree on. Patrolling so long a line would be difficult. If the company would strengthen the working party – protection might easily be given to the men sent to repair from Cahersiveen, Killorglin and Killarney. I see fully the difficulty of the duty but the object is of such importance that we must effect it if possible.

On 6 March 1867 the Knight of Kerry, the main landowner on Valentia Island, had written to Sir Thomas Larcom at the Castle:

> We are far safer here than we would have been had we not had our own premature and unsuccessful outbreak, however it appears to me to be a mistake to withdraw the military from Cahersiveen as that district is as disaffected as it can well be. The soldiers had been brought there by a long toilsome march and their presence was most salutary – just consider what I say *quatissium releat*. It is thought that O'Connor is still in the neighbourhood but if the soldiers and

part of the police were withdrawn it would not be easy to capture him.

Colonel Cruzon, the British officer in charge in Cahersiveen, protested: 'The strongest detachment of troops should be kept in Cahersiveen and it should be relieved as often as possible. I never saw so vile a spot – the appearance and manner of the people stamp it as a den of mischief.'

Máire Ní Mhurchadha from Gort a' Phóisire, near Kells, reported that her grandfather saw the troops come ashore:

Tháinig loingeas isteach sa chuan agus do dubhluiodh 'na haon tigh le waterguards agus as san amach ni bhiodh ach peelers agus waterguards sios suas agus eagla agus scanradh ar 'na haoinne (rompu).

(A warship came into the harbour, and from that hour the town was black with peelers and waterguards marching up and down and terrifying the people out of their wits.)

Sub-Constable Sullivan, who was serving in County Down, was dispatched in plain clothes to his native Cahersiveen, the Castle note stating: 'It was deemed expedient to send him there as a disposable man with a view to discovering some of the insurgents.' It is not clear how successful Sullivan was but it was soon discovered that he had not returned to Iveragh for the good of his health. As he came near the village of Waterville at 10.30 p.m. on the night of 16 April shots were fired at him, but he escaped injury.

Despite this, the police were not idle. By the beginning of March many of the Fenians had returned from the mountains. Thirteen were arrested, although one was later released, but Edward Murphy, the crown solicitor, reported:

Four respectable persons who had the opportunity of seeing those who marched from Cahersiveen on the 13th were confronted with the twelve men but did not identify anyone – indeed their unwillingness to give evidence was not concealed. There was no case for committing them to the county gaol, and it was for many reasons undesirable to keep them in the Bridewell [prison] where they had access to each other.

Finally, six were charged and brought to trial in Tralee where, as Murphy remarked on 7 June 1867: 'There is a good class of jury which will not be deterred from doing their duty by local influences.' One was sentenced to ten years, one to seven years, two to five years and two were acquitted.

On 20 April 1867 word reached Dublin Castle from Head Constable Addis in Hammersmith that Joseph Noonan was in London, and on 25 April Constable Garrett Gunning set off from Killarney on the 7 a.m. train to identify him. He was arrested in London on 30 April but made a daring escape from the train bringing him to Holyhead for the journey to Ireland where he would be tried. Constable Gunning stated:

With Sergeant Savage of the London police we left Euston Station, London, by the five o'clock mail train. We were put into a first-class carriage. We took the handcuffs off the prisoner. About half an hour after leaving Rugby, the first stop, he took hold of the strap of the window and dropped it down, at the same time leaning his foot on the seat and throwing himself out from the train which was running at 45 miles per hour! We had to run on twenty-four miles further before the train stopped. The following day we searched about Tamworth and we got his coat in a pawn-office in Atherstone. There we found him and brought him to Ireland.

On the evening of 6 May when Noonan was expected back in Killarney, 2,000 people gathered at the railway station to greet him. They 'cheered for the Irish Republic' and threw stones at the police. Two windows were also broken at the house of Resident Magistrate Galway after he returned from the station. Noonan was brought directly to Tralee and on 24 July 1867 he was sentenced to seven years' transportation. He was among those recommended for release in 1869 on condition of their not returning to Ireland until the terms of their sentences were expired.

During March and April the telegraph wires were still being cut. When this occurred at Deelis Bridge on a day that crowds of people were on the road to Killorglin Fair and to America, Magistrate Cruice questioned all the travellers without success. Thereafter he was strongly of the opinion that: 'Most of these outrages are perpetuated by persons in the employment of the railway authorities, and thus they may be under double pay – both from the company for minding their property and from the disaffected for destroying it.' However, Sir Thomas Larcom took a different view of the situation and at the end of April he recommended that £100 be distributed to the men employed by the Magnetic Telegraph Company to repair the lines and £50 be given to Mr Tanger, the superintendent of stations, for his special services.

On 2 August Mr C. L. Adderley arrived at Kingstown 'for the shooting' *en route* to the Westorph Arms Hotel in Waterville. He was apparently unaware of the 'shooting' that had occurred in Iveragh some months previously and he was highly annoyed when his three guns were confiscated and he was arrested by Policeman F. 65 on the charge of intending to carry arms in a proclaimed district. He was not a man to put up with 'being deprived of his first three or four days' shooting', and though, he said, he had not been introduced formally to Lord Abercorn, the Lord Lieutenant, he had no compunction about writing to him to order the return of his guns. Adderley was perfectly certain that Lord Abercorn 'must know my father or if not you know my uncle, Chandos Leigh'. The guns were forwarded immediately.

Cahersiveen was not the only place where the rebels were being actively pursued. In County Cork, at the end of March 1867, fifteen men had been arrested in Millstreet and lodged in Cork gaol. One was Bartholomew Moriarty, a stonemason from Rathmore, County Kerry. At their trial it was stated that the men had entered Mount Leader, the house of Eustace Leader, JP, on the night of 5 March and, having found 'a five-barrelled revolver between the tick [mattress] and the paliass' in Mr Leader's bedroom, they began to search the house for arms in the name of the Irish Republic. As Mr Leader attempted to rise from his bed Moriarty 'violently assaulted him with a poker', striking him on the head. The intruders took a double-barrelled gun, two single-barrelled guns, a needle rifle and three swords from the house. They then attacked the local railway station, broke the telegraph machine, cut the wires and tried to raise the rails.

Moriarty offered to give information about the raid and Magistrate O'Connell reported: 'As a result several arrests were made, but the attorney-general would not allow Moriarty to be sworn as a crown witness.' Moriarty was described as a young man of slender build, five feet eight inches in height, gifted with a half-pleasing reckless sort of manner. The *Tralee Chronicle* wrote: 'Crowds of women and boys crowded round the barracks [at Millstreet] vowing vengeance on the blackguard informer.' It later transpired that Moriarty was the leader of a Fenian circle and the information he lodged was an effort to divert suspicion from himself.

Most of the fifteen were released, though two at least – James Lucy and Timothy Ring – spent four months in Cork and

Mountjoy gaols, Ring being freed on bail and Lucy being released on condition he went to America. Moriarty was tried before Judge Keogh at the Cork special commission. He pleaded guilty and was sentenced to seven years' penal servitude even though the local magistrates, including Mr Leader's son Henry, petitioned for his release, on the grounds that his testimony meant that 'many persons of known Fenian proclivities have emigrated from Millstreet and its deterrent effect on the minds of others had led to the present decrease in Fenianism in the town'. In October 1867, Moriarty was transported to Western Australia on the *Hougoumont*. He was freed on 9 July 1868 on condition of his not returning to the United Kingdom. There is no official record of his departure from the colony and he may have thought it wiser to remove himself quietly to another part of that continent. Bartholomew Moriarty was lucky to be in Australia, as Eustace Leader was dead – possibly from the effects of the blow of the poker – by April 1868.

Another Moriarty – Captain Mortimer Moriarty – was arrested in Killarney on the morning of the rising and held in Naas gaol in County Kildare. On 10 July 1867 the informer Corydon, who knew him in America, identified Mortimer Moriarty as one of the Fenian leaders. Corydon also said his real name was not Moriarty but O'Shea. (In fact, his mother was O'Shea, and when she died in 1890 she was said to be 110 years of age.) On 24 July Captain Moriarty was tried in Tralee. (Thomas Hill, the leader of the Tarbert Methodist community, was one of the few jurors that the defence did not challenge.) The authorities made sure that there would be no repetition of what had happened in Killarney when the Fenian prisoner, Noonan, was expected to be brought by railway to the town and Magistrate Cruice had posted strong forces of police at the principal points to prevent any disturbance or violence. On 31 July a detachment of the 6th Dragoons were withdrawn to

Limerick, but as soon as the Castle heard this they were ordered to return, 'the prisoners not yet being sentenced in Tralee'.

Colonel Massey was also brought to Tralee for the trial, 'on the 10 p.m. train from Kingsbridge', escorted 'at his own wish' by Inspectors Clarke and McGee, in plain clothes, 'rather than by a detachment of Constabulary'. In a letter, written on 12 August 1867, Massey complained about 'the conduct of the Guard named Hoey, on the train running from Mallow to Tralee, who pointed him out to the people at every station on the line'. Massey described Hoey as being about thirty-four years old, five feet nine inches high, with fair curling hair, ruddy features and a brown beard worn all round and under the chin, and wearing the uniform of the Great Southern & Western Railway. Hoey was suspended until 31 August but it emerged that Massey had been recognised by several people when he changed trains in Mallow, and in Killarney he had been pointed out to the people by Mr F. H. Dowling, a solicitor and 'a gentleman of respectability who will prove if required that Hoey never mentioned Massey's name in Tralee, Farranfore or Killarney'.

In Corydon's evidence against Captain Moriarty he stated that he (Corydon) had been born in Ballyheigue, and that some gentlemen present knew his parents, to which the counsel for the prisoners, Mr FitzGibbon, replied: 'They ought to be proud of the honour.' Before sentencing Moriarty, Judge Keogh addressed him: 'You and desperadoes of your character, who come from foreign shores to disturb the tranquillity of this country and to delude the unfortunate people who are seduced by your words, must be deterred from your enterprises and adequately punished.' On 8 August 1867 Moriarty was sentenced to ten years' penal servitude.

Despite not having taken part in the February rising, the Fenians appear to have been well organised in Milltown and Killorglin.

'Information' taken from Maurice Heffernan is found in the police reports:

On the night of 17 March 1867 I was standing near my own gate at Abbeylands in the parish of Kilcolman about 10 p.m. I saw about fifty men in what is called the Black Field in the Kilcolman demesne. These men were in two parties – in the party nearest to me there were about fifty men walking in a bulk, they were about a hundred yards away from me. In the other party, which I saw about the same time there were about fifteen men. They were about forty yards beyond the first mentioned party, about 150 yards from me and at the time the small party were about 150 yards behind the rest. They were also in a bulk but not so bulky as the first. I could not say if any of the men were armed. I could not say if they had anything at all in their hands. It was a fine moonlit night and the moon was very bright. I watched them for a few minutes and then I went into my house. I told Tom Eager that I saw them – he is a farmer who lives in Milltown. I also told him he would hear some news before morning. Eager told Maurice McKenna and we then came to Kilcolman and told Mr Godfrey. I have it my mind that they were Fenians. I am a tenant to Mr Godfrey. I used to have thirty cows; I have only nineteen now. I lost a good few through disease.

## Mr Godfrey wrote to Sub-Inspector Columb in Killarney:

Some of my tenants have just fallen in to report that at this moment a large body of Fenians are within the walls of my place. I am not an alarmist but I cannot refuse to believe what I have heard. Unfortunately my garrison is too weak to meet them and if they threaten to burn me out they will succeed. The police here number six; they are holding their own in their barracks. If we are obliged to [surrender] I cannot help it although I would like to make a stand if possible. Perhaps notwithstanding the scarcity of the British army you will spare me twenty-five men to meet an emergency.

In haste

J. F. Godfrey.

## Sub-Inspector Columb replied:

[I] received this letter at about twelve midnight on 18 March. I knocked up the adjutant of the 14th Regiment and introduced the bearer, Lieutenant Alfred Godfrey, and showed him Mr Godfrey's letter. It was decided that I should start at once for Kilcolman Abbey (Mr Godfrey's house) with twenty policemen and send back a message to the adjutant should I require reinforcements. I arrived in Milltown at about 2.30 a.m. when to the surprise of my men, and also I might add, to our disappointment we found all quiet. We travelled to Castlemaine where we hoped to find the body of men but no trace of men could be found in that direction. We returned to Kilcolman and when the men had breakfasted we made a further search. It was conjectured that the men had crossed the deep river in a small boat of Mr Godfrey's which was on the north side yesterday and found on the south side today. There was no boat available to examine the opposite bank. This was borne out by Mr Godfrey and the intelligent Head Constable of Milltown. As for Heffernan I believe he had a motive in swearing a false oath. He might wish to have troops quartered near him in order to dispose of his remaining stock to a government contractor.

However, a respectable farmer, Tom Kelliher, said he was walking through Kilderry Wood, when on each side of the road he saw a number of men lined up, some of whom were standing on the ditch and the rest partially concealed in the covert. After he had passed them he heard a gun cocked by one of them. Unfortunately

Mr Godfrey's party was too weak to follow the supposed Fenians. Before I reinforced him, himself and one of his brothers and a retired gamekeeper were the only force he had to depend on. It was decided before I left Milltown that the Clounwilliam police comprising five in number were to be brought to Milltown station.

On 2 July 1868, the Killorglin magistrates requested instructions as to what steps they should take about 'some parties arrested on the previous night for marching and singing seditious songs'. They had remanded them for a week in the Milltown bridewell on the information of Head Constable McClean who 'on hearing them marching and keeping regular step' had sent for reinforcements. Sub-Constables Hutchinson, Connelly and Shummacher came from the barracks and, while sitting down on the fence near Mr Eager's house at Farrantoreen, heard the Fenians singing words from the 'Sean Van Vocht' and the 'Green Above the Red'. They then heard the word 'police' from one of the party which broke up and attempted to get over the fences. The head constable attempted to arrest one but he got away. The sub-constables had better luck and captured Michael Ryan, John McKenna and John Flynn. The matter was referred to the attorney-general for his opinion. The complaint was made that 'no persons could be found on whom we could rely to procure reliable information on the certainty of reward'.

In January 1869 a full review took place of the cases of the 118 Fenian prisoners still in custody. James Reilly and John Golden, sentenced to five years' penal servitude in July and August 1867, were among the thirty-three civilian prisoners held in Australia. Together with Thomas Fennell of Clare, who had been sentenced to ten years for leading the attack on Kilbaha coastguard station, they were recommended for release on condition that they would not return to Ireland until the expiration of their term. There is an interesting note on the police file for the Cahersiveen men: 'Murphy (crown solicitor) says "they might be got at". However, Mortimer Shea (Moriarty), O'Donovan Rossa, Captain McCafferty, John Devoy, 'Pagan' O'Leary and William Rountree "should not on any account be discharged and were deserving of no clemency".'

*Reinforcing the Pigeon House Fort in case of Fenian attack.*

This view changed within a few years, encouraged by the amnesty movement led by John 'Amnesty' Nolan, which held mass meetings all over Britain and Ireland, and also by reaction to the Devon Report on the treatment of the prisoners in Millbank gaol. At the Tralee amnesty meeting on 24 October 1869 there were more than a hundred men from the Listowel area 'composed chiefly of the lower orders' and 'wearing the colours usual on such occasions, orange being mixed with the green'. Three to four thousand people were present at the meeting. A police report of November 1869 lists thirty-three Roman Catholic clergy who either wrote or spoke in 'strong and indiscreet language' in favour of amnesty for the Fenian prisoners – though none of the clergy was from Kerry. The strength of public feeling was shown by the election of O'Donovan Rossa as a Member of Parliament for Tipperary in December 1869. He was immediately disqualified (because he was a convicted felon), though not before he had asked to be transferred from Chatham gaol to Millbank, as being more convenient for Westminster.

Even in England there was great disquiet among Liberal circles about the conditions in which the convicts were held and in January 1870 sixty respectable inhabitants of Birmingham, headed by Reverend Arthur O'Neill, Baptist minister, protested to the Home Office: 'Their treatment was calculated to discredit the character of England in the estimation of other nations.'

These prisoners were released in 1871, in most cases on the understanding that they would not return to Ireland until the expiration of their sentences. Captain Mortimer Moriarty was among them, sailing from Liverpool on 14 February 1871 to New York on the SS *Parthia* of the Cunard line. He returned to Canada and worked in Toronto as a carpenter until his death in 1875. Stephen Edward de Vere of Foynes and Dr Robert Lyons from Cork also took a prominent part in the amnesty movement. Dr Lyons had his hands handcuffed behind his back to find out how it felt to suffer such a punishment, which O'Donovan Rossa had undergone for twenty-four days. He was so shocked he had to have a glass of whiskey and he gave another to Rossa, who remarked that the whiskey 'was the first he had ever taken'. However, the one group who were shown no mercy were the British soldiers who had been convicted of being Fenians.

The following interesting verse had been sent to Larcom (according to his own account) in Dublin Castle on 1 November 1866:

> Codhéshin, codhésin codhésin go deo
> Codhésin goon thé sin ná bock leish Judge Keogh
> And if had him in a place that we know
> We'd make him repint [sic] of his hangings, ohone,
> And if we had only one shot at Judge Keogh,
> We'd powder his wig with nice swandrops, oh ho!

It was supposed to have been found on the Dublin pikemaker Patrick Kearney when he was arrested, but it may well have had its origin much nearer the Castle. At one time Larcom had taken lessons in Irish from the Gaelic scholar John O'Donovan. When he discovered John's son Edmond, a medical student, was leader of a Fenian circle, Larcom did his best to obtain Edmond's release after his arrest on 14 March 1866, at 5 Nelson Street, Tralee. Edmond O'Donovan was re-arrested in Limerick in November 1867 and again released after six months. In February 1868, at the trial of those who were charged with the Clerkenwell explosion, the informer Nicholas English said:

> Edmond O'Donovan is a very clever fellow. He was educated at Trinity College, Dublin and had £100 a year out of it. He used to mix Greek Fire (phosphorus explosive) at our house. He is a Tipperary man who was taken prisoner last year with Colonel Healy in Limerick. A sash and a sword were found on him. He was liberated through the influence of some high man in Ireland called Larkin or Larcom or some such name.

Edmond O'Donovan went to America on his release and in 1870 enlisted in the French Foreign Legion. On 3 October 1871, a Castle note on his file stated:

His [police] photo would hardly assist a person to recognise him, the hardships of the French war have completely changed him. His face is a great deal thinner and more hollow and he has a wound on the crown of his head from the explosion of a shell at the Battle of Orleans and a bullet wound in his knee received at the same battle.

In 1883 O'Donovan went to the Sudan as a war correspondent and was killed at the defeat of Hicks-Pasha by the Arabs. He must be the only Fenian to be commemorated by a plaque in St Paul's Cathedral, London.

In Kerry in 1868 rumours were rife about another rising. The rector of Kilflynn complained that when the mail car was an hour late the previous Sunday, the driver gave as a reason that the Fenians had risen from Limerick to Tarbert, destroyed the telegraph wires and derailed a train on the Limerick–Foynes line by pulling up the rails. Therefore thirteen magistrates met in Killarney and decided to place the workhouse at the disposal of the military so that two companies of soldiers could be sent there in case of a renewed outbreak. At the meeting of the Board of Guardians (who were in charge of the workhouse), it was mentioned that this arrangement would be a great boon to the proprietor of the Railway Hotel (where the troops had been stationed). It would enable him to get the building into shape for the forthcoming tourist season.

Even in January 1869, the Castle was still very worried about the strength of the Fenian movement in Killarney. Constable Thomas O'Brien was promoted to the rank of a 'disposable [plain clothes] constable' and dispatched from Cork to Killarney. 'He can speak Irish well. The five disposable men in this county [Cork] who can speak Irish are natives of Kerry and I did not wish to send them to their own county on the duty in question.' Shortly afterwards Constable O'Brien reported:

I have gone several times into the country districts round about here and conversed freely with men, young and old. From what I have seen and what I have learned I do believe Fenianism to be as rife in this locality and the members as enthusiastic in their ideas as they had been for the last two years, but at present the same activity undoubtedly does not exist. I have never seen in Cork or elsewhere the Fenian element so general and so remarkable as in the young men of this town and the surrounding districts. All of whom wear the Fenian sloughed [*sic*] hat and green neck-ties, with a sort of military appearance which is remarkable in such a backward locality.

In September 1869 considerable correspondence was generated by the arrival in Queenstown on the SS *France* of two brothers, Bartholomew and William O'Leary, after two years in America. The police were highly suspicious of them as they had returned to Drummore, Kenmare via Portarlington, County Laois, having with them a cane sword, a drill book and five copies of the book *Fenian Heroes and Martyrs*, by John Savage. They were under constant supervision until their return to the United States.

In 1967, Professor Seán Pinder of University College Cork (UCC) commented:

It may be that Fenian principles are no longer popular in the best political circles. Today they are regarded in the same light as the Fenians themselves were regarded by church and state in the 1860s and 1870s. In any case it is evident that our public men today are not prepared to number Fenian golden jubilees or Fenian centenaries among what the poet calls the pleasures of memory.

# CHAPTER 5

# THE FENIANS IN LISTOWEL AND TARBERT

No one ever ventured to impugn the name or moral character of Lord Edward FitzGerald, or to unite his memory with any imputation of immorality or dishonesty; and no one ever suggested that he had done anything to make a man blush in the face of his fellow men, so far as regards his moral character or conduct; but still we know that he too (like the Fenians) was engaged in a rebellion against the constitution of the country.

*Judge Keogh at the Kerry assizes 27 July 1867*

## LISTOWEL

Listowel and Tarbert were the centres of Fenian activity in north Kerry. In early February 1867 the police took shotguns from the local farmers for fear they might be seized by the Fenians and the farmers complained to the magistrates that the crows were destroying their crops. On 16 February the magistrates in turn demanded that a company of soldiers be sent to Listowel 'lest the 250 guns in the custody of the police be taken by the rebels from Glin and Abbeyfeale'. Resident Magistrate Ball reported:

In November 1866 at the Listowel races, a respectable-looking farmer told me that Fenianism and its objects were now a constant subject of discussion among the lower orders. The reports that have been published of the Fenian proceedings and speeches in America have created a state of feverish excitement and an expectation similar to what existed last year that some disturbance will take place shortly, and it will take place after Stephens' return to this country.

The local Fenians were aware that there were informers in the locality and when an English tourist who was on a walking tour stopped to question some people on the bridge over the Feale they threatened to throw him into the river, thinking he was a police spy. However, it was a native of Listowel who wrote this letter to Dublin Castle in March 1867:

Dear Sir,

I am bound to inform you with regard to the Fenians in Listowel. They are but a few as yet but if not put down they will increase rapid. The head senter [sic] in Listowel is David Spillane, a shopkeeper. This man has taken a corner house with a storey underground for the purpose of shooting Mr George Hewson who is the only good gentlemen around Listowel but too much against the Fenians and for that will not agree with David Spillane. He is sworn to put an end to his days and with him more of the magistrates. Spillane is a confidential friend of the Head Constable and a meeting house for all constables stationed here for certainly some of them must be aware that he has learned the use of arms from those persons or police. He has arms in his house and the portion underground to drill men there. His father and mother live in Newcastle near Limerick. This is where he gets pistols and firearms and if he is not sent from Listowel he will certainly commit murder and increase the Fenians. He will head a great party with his two brothers.

These are some of his party. John Enright (his brother-in-law, of Church Street, Listowel), William Kirby (publican, The Square), Batt McCarthy (school teacher and publican), George Church (baker), Frank Healy (publican), Dennis Lyons (draper), Ger Enright (draper), Mossy Quille and brother (cart makers, Church Street). David Spillane is the first and has all those to command.

Your obedient servant

I'll give my name when I'll hook the rest of the party.

I am a Queen's man to serve Her Majesty at the sound of the bugle.

Dennis McNamara, the centre leader for Listowel, is not mentioned in the above list of names. He was the teacher in a 'pay school' in William Street and later in St Michael's College. He taught Irish, English, Mathematics, Latin, Greek and Irish music on the violin.

The authorities took no chances, the police were withdrawn from the barracks in the surrounding villages and between eighty and ninety men concentrated in Listowel. On the Wednesday following the Cahersiveen rising on 11/12 February 1867, the horse of a police dispatch constable was found saddled and bridled and without a rider near Banemore on the Tralee Road, so the *Kerry Evening Post* reported it was feared that 'like the unfortunate Duggan (who had been shot by the Cahersiveen rebels), he had fallen victim to a Fenian bullet'. However, it transpired that the rider had dismounted and his horse bolted, so he then continued on foot to his home station, Tralee.

The following day a young man and woman, who had arrived in Listowel in a covered car, were detained by the police on suspicion of being Fenian emissaries. It turned out that the young lady was the daughter of a large farmer near Ballyheigue who had eloped with one of her father's servants.

When the local petty sessions court assembled on 9 March

1867 the entrance was guarded by armed policemen. The *Tralee Chronicle* reported: 'This was said to be a precautionary measure, considered by the authorities highly expedient and judicious in these days when daring and reckless individuals as Fenians have sprung into something more than imaginary existence.'

In the same month the local magistrates – Murray Home, Alexander Elliot and George Hewson – looked for a military force to be stationed in the town: 'There are fifty-one householders, four of whom are ladies, asking for this. The town offers a strong temptation to insurgents to attack it and we are of the opinion that too great precautions cannot be taken against the rebellious propensities which have been evinced in a neighbouring locality.' A polite answer from the Castle spoke of 'the more pressing response of other claims that prevents the Lord-Lieutenant's complying with your request'. In April, a further letter from 'A friend to the government but a true Roman Catholic' stated that 'two hundred men will attack the town of Listowel on Saturday 11 April, kill all who'll oppose them and plunder all the shops in the town'. However, Resident Magistrate Ball said that he did not believe the information to be correct.

John Cleary, described by the police as a labourer from the Listowel area – tall, thin and with a dark complexion – was arrested in Athlone on 11 March 1867 and removed from the local bridewell to Roscommon gaol on 5 April. He claimed to be a 'poor scholar' who had travelled all over Ireland with his late mother, an itinerant mendicant. He said he was from Clounlehard near Athea and he accounted for the £2 13*s.* 4 ½*d.* found on him by stating that he had worked for a farmer named Jeremiah Mulvihill from Saleen near Ballylongford in County Kerry. Constable Doyle from Ballylongford reported that there was a John Mulvihill living near Saleen, but he had never employed a servant boy and knew nothing about Cleary. The police were certain he was the leader of a Fenian circle and had helped to organise the Cahersiveen rising, but they could prove nothing against him even though Sub-Constable Wallace from Kerry and Sub-Constable Dawson from Kilmallock, County Limerick were brought in to identify him. He was released on 5 May 1867.

In the same month, David Nagle, a harness-maker aged twenty-three who was a native of Listowel and suspected leader of 'the Fenian circle in the town', was arrested in Charleville, County Cork. John Drummond, the police sub-inspector in Listowel, reported on 9 May 1867:

> On the ten days previous an unusual number of peddlers have made their appearance in the town. Each man is accompanied by another by way of an assistant and in a horse and tax cart they drive into the countryside in the morning and return in the evening taking with them clothes, tweeds etc. which they are supposed to be selling. They stay in the ordinary lodging houses at night, spending money very freely. From the fact of their remaining in town so long I suspect they may be agents of the Fenian Brotherhood.

After masses in Listowel on Sunday 12 May hundreds signed the petition for the commutation of sentence on all the Fenian prisoners arrested since 1866. The *Tralee Chronicle* of 18 May 1867 reported: 'It was signed by all the respectable inhabitants of the town, except a few Protestants, who said they had no sympathy with traitors.' The local correspondent remarked: 'This uncharitable feeling is not shared by the majority of that religion.'

The previous day Gilsenan, head constable of Listowel, had visited one of the lodging houses in the town. He initiated a conversation with one of the peddlers named John Dobbyn who, he said, openly avowed himself a Fenian:

This man was still in Listowel on 16 May and was watched by the police of several stations. He has made numerous sales of tweed and stuffs to the country people. The receipts don't seem to match the expenses. On his arrest prisoner denies all knowledge of Fenianism. Says that when he made the statements alleged by the police he was drunk. He is only nineteen years old and (he says) the sole support of his widowed mother.

After a conference with Sub-Inspector Egan, the resident magistrate recommended release without independent bail and the prisoner was discharged on his own surety of £20.

On 15 November 1869, Gilsenan wrote to the Castle:

Head Constable Bruen found two Fenian documents posted at a gate at the entrance to this town on the Feale Road. On seeing them he immediately took them down and handed them to me. The names Reidy, Hayes and Charles Egan at the foot of Document No. 1 are respectable shopkeepers in this town who protested against the holding of the Amnesty Indignation meeting [organised to seek release of the prisoners sentenced after the rising] on Sunday last.

The second poster was a verse from a song, 'The Bold Fenian Men', written by Limerick man Michael Scanlan:

Erin go Breagh –
God save the Fenians and dear old Ireland
Now is the time now is the hour to prepare against English tyranny
Let all who love their country prepare to meet the Saxon foe
Let all Fenians throughout the land prepare
Let every man be for the Fenians. I am one.
Hayes, Reidy and Chas. Egan boo.

## TARBERT

When the police were withdrawn from Tarbert, the local magistrates – Thomas Sandes, Stephen Collis and William Sandes – notified Dublin Castle on 16 February 1867 that:

> Four men have been appointed as special constables under the Peace Preservation Act for the parish of Kilnaughtin (Tarbert). This is necessary in consequence of the withdrawal of the police from this town and to guard against the proclamation received and posted this day in Tarbert being removed and defaced.

The proclamation called for the surrender of arms. A further communication from the magistrates was received a few days later:

> We this day received a proclamation requiring all parties to deliver up firearms at the next police station. As the police have been withdrawn from Tarbert we beg to ask your instructions as to where the arms should be delivered as it would not be a prudent course to bring them to Listowel from the distance one would have to travel.

It would seem that unlike Britain, where thousands of special constables were enrolled to combat the Fenian threat, Dublin Castle was not particularly enthusiastic about appointing such officers. The magistrates were told that the constabulary would speedily return to Tarbert and they might then consider the nomination of special constables no longer necessary.

The leader of the Tarbert Fenians was a shoemaker called Murty Duane (Divane), and he was assisted by a teacher in the local national school, Master Dillon or Dillane. According to *The Irish People*: 'Edward Dillon, assistant teacher, Tarbert was dismissed by Father Foley, parish priest, for reading this newspaper.' John Ryan of Tarbert wrote to *The Irish People* proposing to set up a fund for Dillon so that he would not have to emigrate: 'Mr Dillon's father, through the influence of the clergy, is trying to send him to America. He refuses going even though he has no chance of a situation. He is worth too much at home.' O'Donovan Rossa was proposed as treasurer of the fund, and on 26 June 1865 Michael McInerny of Kilrush forwarded a subscription of five shillings.

Edward Dillon was more than a mere reader of the Fenian newspaper. He was a native of Mahoonagh (Castlemahon), County Limerick and was arrested in October 1865 for attending a Fenian meeting but subsequently released. Dillon was then re-arrested as a Fenian suspect in April 1866, when the police reported that he had no means of support except that he occasionally taught in local farmers' houses. Released on 27 December he was again re-arrested, this time by Head Constable Jeremiah Sullivan, on 1 January 1867. When Dillon petitioned for his release in April 1867 the sub-inspector in Newcastle West wrote:

> I would deem it highly imprudent to release from custody a person like him who took much trouble in bringing to maturity the plans for the late outbreak unless he would engage to leave the county at once for America or some of the colonies. A person of his education and knowledge in mixing among the lower classes of society might (if allowed to go at large) be the means of again stirring up the spirit of disaffection which may still be mouldering among the people.

Dillon was finally discharged on bail on 17 September 1867 and it seems he was never subsequently brought to trial.

Information was received from Sub-Inspector Kennedy in Kilrush in December 1866: 'A ticket-of-leave convict named Garrett Mahony was arrested here. He stated he was a Fenian agent and that he had sworn in the following in Tarbert, viz. James Connor and Michael McCarthy, tailors, and Murty Duane and Robert Walsh, shoemakers.' The police were certain that large stores of pikes and ammunition were being held in Glin and Tarbert, and that Duane, together with Walsh and Richard Murray, was organising football matches 'for the purpose of bringing the disaffected together without attracting the notice of the police'. Sub-Inspector Egan from Listowel reported 'a large number of men assembled at Kilpadogue to play a game of football and all the Fenian sympathisers attended'. In January 1866 Resident Magistrate Ball in Listowel reported that his area was very peaceable:

> There are no doubt some people who sympathise with what is called the Fenian movement, but they are few in number. Of those who actually joined the society, some have gone to America and others have totally renounced any connection with it. Drilling is not carried on here but it was at one period by a few young men from Tarbert.

Duane was apprehended at a house half a mile from Tarbert on 19 February 1867, together with 'two suspicious-looking characters found at the house of James FitzGerald, publican, viz. John Mannix, plasterer and Dennis Lynch, cabinet-turner, both natives of Tralee'. They were held first in the local bridewell and later in Tralee gaol. Mannix was reported to have £10 14s. 6d. in his possession while Lynch had only one halfpenny. Coastguards from Kells failed to identify the men who, it was believed, had taken part in the Cahersiveen rising a week earlier. In April 1867 a petition was received from Duane's uncle, Thomas FitzGerald, 'an old member of the Tarbert Corps of Yeomanry', seeking his release and stating that he (the uncle) was a former soldier and had a son serving in the Royal Horse Guards in London, and had served as a non-commissioned officer in the Royal Artillery during the Crimean War. Duane was released on bail on 17 May 1867. Local tradition has it that on the day of his arrest Father Foley rushed down to McAuliffe's shoemaker's shop, where Robert Walsh was employed. He threw all the Fenian documents that he found in the house into the fire. That very night the police raided the shop looking for the names of the local Fenians. As local historian Patrick Lynch remarked: 'If this is true, it shows Father Foley's concern for his parishioners rather than any sympathy he might have for Fenianism.'

The Dublin Castle government had been well aware of the strategic importance of Tarbert in the event of an expected Fenian rebellion. In the draft report of a high-powered committee set up in November 1860 to consider the defences of Ireland it had been stated:

> The area of the Lower Shannon has engaged the anxious attention of the members as being of second importance to none in Ireland, opening, as this magnificent river does, a navigation into the very heart of the country. The six forts are of nearly all the same construction and carry the same armaments, a battery of five or six guns and a tower or keep surmounted by a couple of twenty-four-pound howitzers, on traversing carriages and the whole surrounded by an insignificant ditch.
>
> Tarbert and its opposite redoubt at Kilkerrin deserve the most attention as commanding a pass of 2,000 yards wide which may be considered the nexus of the river. In point of military importance these works cannot be overestimated; once forced, an enemy has no further impediment to his penetrating to Limerick, the heart of the country.
>
> The works should be enlarged and strengthened – not only should

they be improved in all respects but a powerful fort or redoubt with the heaviest armament should be constructed on Massey's Hill, within 800 yards of, and commanding, Tarbert, which would effectively support that harbour and sweep the whole channel with its fire. A blockade ship might be established for the support of the batteries.

There is no record of the completion of the proposed improvements to the defences, but the blockade ship did appear to a great welcome from the people of Tarbert, according to Mr Beale Brown, landlord of Ballygoughlin and Crotta: 'They have now a market for their poultry, eggs &c. and the butchers are slaughtering as never before.' However, in February 1866 the *Irishman* reported:

On Saturday a number of sailors belonging to HMS *Prince Consort* stationed at Tarbert came to Limerick to enjoy themselves having been given leave of absence by their commander and, as is usual with tars, they frequented public houses and houses of refreshment in that city. They were saluted with cries of 'Success to the Fenians' as they passed through the streets and in a public house in George's Street some expressions distasteful to men who had sworn allegiance to the queen were uttered and the respectable proprietor in his anxiety to suppress the row was struck a desperate blow by one of the sailors who cut him over and under the left eye which left it bleeding and swollen. A civilian from Patrick's Well entered the house and intruded upon their company. He began to espouse the cause of the Fenian Brotherhood and spoke of the injustice done to O'Donovan Rossa in whose cause he came out strong. One sailor remonstrated with the disloyal subject and words led to blows and the other sailors who had left the house being summoned rushed back to punish the aggressor. This was when the landlord received the blow described above at which he at once sent for the police and had the sailor detained at the lock up until yesterday (Sunday) morning. The trader then withdrew the charge and the sailor was discharged by Mr Collins, RM. He gave orders that a close watch should be kept after the movements of the Fenian sympathiser, who is well known.

There are no further reports of active Fenianism in Listowel and Tarbert. Nevertheless, when the separatist struggle was united with the demand for 'the land for the people' both parishes had very active branches of the Land League and many of the same names occur in the police reports for that era.

# CHAPTER 6

# THE RISING ELSEWHERE IN IRELAND

Despite the failure of the outbreak in Kerry in February, the Fenian rising proceeded as planned in the rest of the country in March. In January 1867 Colonel Thomas Kelly had arrived in England where it was much easier to develop the plans for a rising without rousing police suspicions and where there was less danger of immediate detection. Over the succeeding weeks about 150 other ex-American army officers also travelled across the Atlantic. Kelly saw a need for professional military expertise. He engaged the services of General Gustave Cluseret, who had served with distinction in the French army and wore the ribbon of the Legion of Honour (and incidentally had fought with Garibaldi in Italy). In the American Civil War Cluseret had served as a colonel on the staff of General Fremont and later as brigadier-general in the Union army. Cluseret in turn recruited Octavio Louis Fariola, a young Belgio-Italian who had served with distinction as a colonel of engineers in the Union army and was now a county surveyor. He again in turn recruited an associate of his in the Belgian military academy named Vifquain, who had also been appointed to the rank of colonel in the Union army. It was understood that these professional soldiers would not travel to Ireland until the

Fenians took the field. On 12 July 1867, Fariola, who had stayed in London after the failed rising in March in the hopes that another insurrection would occur, was arrested in Regent Street in London on a charge of treason felony. He pleaded guilty and was released on condition that he would leave for Queensland.

On Shrove Tuesday night, 5 March 1867, the Fenians assembled in the counties of Dublin, Cork, Tipperary, Kilkenny, Clare, Limerick, Laois and Louth. In Dublin, 1,000 men gathered and marched out of the city in tens, twelves and twenties to the village of Tallaght, capturing some police barracks as they went, but they were soon dispersed by the police and military. Lord Strathnairn reported:

> I directed a flying column from Newbridge under Major Green, RHA [Royal Horse Artillery] and another of three companies of the 52nd Light Infantry from Dublin, which I accompanied. The night was extremely dark which delayed the Fenians and they were in broken bands. We succeeded in arresting ninety-three of them. They were well supplied with arms and ammunition. The flying columns returned to Dublin at twelve noon after a long and continuous night march under rain and snow with all of 153 prisoners. Nothing could be more soldier-like, energetic or zealous than their conduct. Great crowds assembled as the prisoners were marched from the Castle to the gaol, cheering and displaying great sympathy with them.

But one group stayed aloof from the rebellion. That unlikely supporter of social reform, Lord Strathnairn, reported: 'Only eight of the 540 workmen in Sir Benjamin Guinness' brewery joined the rising. This is because of the excellent wages, the careful attention paid to the sick, the liberal pensions paid to the old servants and the good conduct of the workers strictly looked after.'

Also on 5 March 1867 the Cork Fenians gathered to march on Limerick Junction and attacked a number of police barracks to obtain arms. Constable John Brown of Ballyknockane near Mallow, gave evidence at the trial of Thomas Burke and John McCafferty, two of the American army officers who had returned to Ireland to lead the rising, in April 1867. He said he saw 150 men marching past the barracks in military array, armed with guns, pikes and pistols, carrying knapsacks and haversacks. They called on the barracks to surrender in the name of the Irish Republic and when their demand was refused they broke in the door and set the lower part on fire. When the fire became severe Brown asked the insurgents to let his daughter, who was inside the barracks, out and they did so. When the garrison could not stand the smoke and fire, they surrendered and the insurgents procured a ladder, which the police had to descend or 'perish in the flames'. As each descended their arms were taken from them and they heard one of their attackers say: 'This is the day of the general rising. Cork is not attacked yet but will be taken in a week.' They were then allowed to leave and went to Mallow. One of the Fenians, John Coughlin, was shot in the shoulder by what we would now call friendly fire.

Castlemartyr barracks was also attacked. A rick of straw was fired to draw out the police, and in the sharp exchange that followed Captain Tim Daly, a former soldier in the Union army, was killed. In Midleton, the police left the barracks and in the ensuing fight one man was killed and one wounded. Peter O'Neill Crowley led out the Fenians of Ballymacoda in County Cork. One hundred men took eight rifles from the local coastguard station at Knockadoon. Ancestors of many of O'Neill Crowley's soldiers had taken part in the rising of 1798, when their parish priest – Peter's great-uncle, Father O'Neill – had been transported to Australia. However, when it became clear that there was no general rising throughout the country, O'Neill Crowley sent his men home. Then with John McClure, an American officer, and Edward Kelly of Youghal, who was one of the few Fenians to belong to the Church of Ireland, Peter O'Neill Crowley took to the hills of south Tipperary.

Flying columns of police and soldiers searched the hills and mountains for the Fenians. Eight of these columns were based in Thurles, County Tipperary. Lord Strathnairn, commander-in-chief, wrote: 'The ubiquity and rapidity of the columns produced an excellent effect, forcing the insurgents to humiliating concealment and flight. All the guilty were as much in dread of, as the loyal were pleased by, their sudden visits, evidently quite unexpected, in the extensive districts and mountains they traversed.' At the same time Constable Joseph Murphy was sent round the county as a peddler of boots, being instructed to assume 'an awkward gait' to disguise any sort of semi-military bearing. He reported: 'It is remarkable to note the political sagacity and shrewdness of the small farmers. They expect Russia and the United States to become firm allies against England, whose difficulties will aid the Irish cause.' The local resident magistrate recorded: 'Contrasted with other places, Kilcommon [where the local teacher had led out the Young Ireland men in 1848] is a nest of Fenians!' On 9 March 1867, Lord Strathnairn wrote: 'From all I hear, the beat or route of the Tipperary flying column should be the slopes of the Galtees, which harbour certainly Fenian fugitives. The whole thing has turned out as I always predicted a *tempête dans un verre d'eau*.'

On 31 March O'Neill Crowley and the other fugitives were surrounded by police and the Waterford flying column under William Redmond, who was a resident magistrate in that city. After a fierce fight in the wood of Kilclooney, O'Neill Crowley was killed and his companions surrendered. At the risk of his own life from friendly fire, Redmond pulled McClure from the swollen river, where he might well have been swept away and drowned as he tried to escape. He was disgusted that McClure then tried to shoot him.

Canon Sheehan described O'Neill Crowley's funeral in his essay 'Moonlight and Memory':

> I remember well the evening on which that remarkable funeral took place. The men shouldered the coffin of the dead patriot over mountain and valley and river to the churchyard at Ballymacoda. I remember how a group of us, young lads, shivered in the cold March wind there on the College Terrace at Fermoy, and watched the dark masses of men swaying over the bridge, the yellow coffin conspicuous in their midst and then we turned away with tears of sorrow and anger in our eyes.

David Joyce, from Ballymacoda, was one of those subsequently tried with McClure. When asked if he had anything to say as to why sentence of death should not be passed against him, Joyce replied, 'What I have to say, I could not speak in English.' John McClure and Edward Kelly were sentenced to death at the Cork assizes on 2 May 1867. The sentences were commuted to transportation for life.

To make the Fenian rebellion still more hopeless, twelve days and twelve nights of snow followed the rising. It was the worst snowstorm in Ireland in twenty years, and it put an end to any thoughts of maintaining a guerrilla war from the hills. Larcom remarked: 'The weather was enough to kill Hercules.' In '67 *Retrospection*, his short account of the Tipperary rising, William Rutherford said: 'Hardly had the insurgents left their homes when the clear March weather gave way to the hail and snow of midwinter. The howling storms edged by the frost and hail, swept over mountain and valley, rendering life in the open air impossible to man.' The War Diary of the flying column of the King's Royal Rifle Corps, which was based in Mallow, County Cork read: 'Night patrolling was constant and concurrently with the insurrection came a heavy storm of snow, which both melted away after a short period.' Lord Derby, the prime minister, was well pleased: 'There are many dangers that spring from guerrilla warfare, plunder takes place, it is very harrowing to the troops, and utterly destructive of private property.'

The informers struck again on the night of the March 1867 rising and, acting on information received from J. J. Corydon, Constables Joshua Gardiner and James Kelly arrested Geoffrey Massey on the platform at Limerick Junction as he arrived to take charge of the rising in Munster. Such was the shock Massey received that he fainted on the platform. When Massey arrived at Dublin Castle, Robert Anderson was sent to interrogate him. He found Massey so disgusted with the failure of the arrangements for the rising that 'after six hours, he had the whole story'. He arranged for Massey 'to be transferred to a comfortable bedroom' and after he had given evidence at the later trials of his former comrades he was 'well paid and passage was arranged for his relatives [and probably himself later on] to Australia at a total cost of £86'. In fact, there is a note from Samuel Lee Anderson in Massey's police file stating: 'Even though the prisoner is one of the most prominent of the Fenian Brotherhood, if not the leader in Ireland, yet there is no evidence on which he could be committed for trial, though his discharge would be dangerous in the extreme.' At his trial in April 1867, Colonel Thomas Burke, who had led the rising in Tipperary, said:

I deny that Massey ever wore the stars of colonel in the Confederate army. Him I shall let rest in the words of the poet:
'May the grass wither from his feet,

May the woods deny him shelter – earth, a home,
The ashes, a grave, the sun, his light,
And heaven, its God.'

A reporter who gave an account of Burke's trial in *All the Year Round* wrote: 'Once, when the very man who was to lead the rebel forces in the south rose like a spectre to the witness chair, one of the accused changed his position with the other and fixed a stern gaze on the informer for hours.' This may have been the moment when Massey is alleged to have said, 'if I swooned, would to God I had never revived'.

On 10 March, Lord Naas reported from Dublin Castle:

Thirteen police barracks were attacked, two unoccupied ones burnt, three taken and the remainder successfully defended by the police. The troops under Lord Strathnairn and the Metropolitan Police have taken upwards of 250 prisoners supposed to have been concerned in the Tallaght Outrages and Mr De Gresson, RM, and the military have on two occasions dispersed a large body of insurgents in Tipperary.

Considerable alarm still exists throughout the country, several coastguard stations have been attacked, bodies of armed men are still roaming about, robbing the gentry and farmers of their arms, taking horses and forcing many of the young men to join them. The Pensioners [Reserve Forces] have been called up and small removable columns of troops have been established up in various parts of the country for the suppression of unlawful assemblies and for the protection of life and property. In all cases where numbers of men have collected it is manifest their movements have been directed by strange [i.e. foreign] persons who had been in America and who had come to this country for the purpose of insurrection, but no person of property, position or intelligence has joined the movement.

When the Dublin magistrates demanded a force of cavalry to escort the prisoners to and from court, Lord Strathnairn wrote:

> The use of cavalry in Dublin city is an old custom because the authorities conceive that the people are afraid of cavalry, and so they are! But their fears would prove groundless if desperate American leaders shot down a few horses, their riders lying helpless under them, in front and rear of the prison van obstructing its movement and then confusion would ensue. Cavalry can be neutralised by a couple of carts drawn across a street.

There had been a change of government in 1866 and Lord Naas (later Lord Mayo) became chief secretary, a post he previously held at the time of the 1848 rebellion. In May 1867 he directed Solicitor-General Samuel Lee Anderson to prepare a report of the 'recent insurrectionary movement'. Because of the pressure of work and the fact (familiar to all researchers of the period) that many of the documents required 'were mixed up with thousands of others in the registry of the office', the solicitor-general asked his younger brother, Robert Anderson, a Dublin barrister (later the British spymaster), to assist Lord Naas in mastering the details of the Fenian conspiracy. Robert efficiently prepared the *Narrative of the Origins and Proceedings of the Conspiracy*, which is still extant among the Larcom papers, and by 1868, following the Clerkenwell explosion, he found himself in London as adviser to the Home Office in materials relating to the Fenians and to Ireland generally. He served as assistant commissioner in Scotland Yard for thirteen years and became head of what we would now call the British Special Branch.

Despite the failure of the rising, in Cork, Captain Mackey, whose real name was William F. Lomasney (his mother was Mackey), kept to the original plan of acquiring firearms and conducting guerrilla warfare. A police report stated that a Limerick gunsmith named Joseph Delany had supplied arms to the Fenians and, as a result, lost his licence. He moved to Cork and began to work at Richardson's gunsmith's shop. One hundred and twenty revolvers and five rifles were taken from these premises on 28 November 1867. On 26 December Captain Mackey led an attack on the Martello tower at Fota, near Cobh, taking 300 pounds of gunpowder and the small arms that were held there. Among those arrested in the police swoop that followed was Thomas Allen, a brother of one of those who later became famous as the Manchester Martyrs, but he was released when the artillerymen from the tower failed to identify him. A daylight raid by eight Fenians followed this on Allport's, a gunmaker's in Patrick Street; the shop was stripped and eighty new revolvers taken. Police reports stated that: 'Captain Mackey was the leader in these outrages, but because of the sympathy of the lower orders and the fear of those better disposed, including some of those who suffered from the raids, the man continued at large.'

On Friday 3 January, 1868, ten hundredweight of gunpowder (used for blasting stone in quarries) was removed from the magazine of Murray's of Ballincollig, agents for Curtis & Harvey, gunpowder manufacturers: 'Three doors, one of iron, one of wood and one of copper, were forced at the premises.' A police file on Charles O'Connell, a schoolmaster in Macroom, contains a letter to him in January 1869 from a William Coveney: 'Since Allport's affair the house was searched eight times and on one occasion they searched five of the boys that were in. We got as much powder from the tunnel as would blow up Cork barracks.' On Tuesday 28 January, 1868, a Martello tower near Duncannon fort in Waterford harbour was attacked. The signalmen fired rockets and a reinforcement of military from the fort engaged the insurgents, who were driven off.

After the arrest of Captain Mackey on Friday 7 February 1868, the police had to fix bayonets and charge the crowd to get their prisoner to the Cork bridewell. He was sentenced to twelve years' penal servitude at the Cork assizes on 9 March 1868.

Mackey's capture did not stop Fenian activity in the area. On 20 July Morton's gun shop was raided and eighteen guns taken. Fifty Fenians, some in uniform, were seen in Millstreet in September. Shotguns were taken from Mount Justice House and the leader of the party wore a forage cap, trimmed in green and gold: 'The inhabitants of the district were unwilling to give any assistance to the police.'

In *Story of Ireland* A. M. Sullivan wrote of the rising:

> The inmates of a lunatic asylum could scarcely have produced a more impossible scheme. The most extravagant of the ancient Fenian tales supplies nothing more absurd. The one redeeming feature in the whole proceeding was the conduct of the hapless men who engaged in it. Nothing could surpass their courage in responding to the summons, unarmed and unaided as they were, their intense religious feeling which saw them crowd the churches on the days preceding the rising and their humanity to their prisoners.

On Friday 6 September the prefix 'Royal' was bestowed on the Irish Constabulary because, according to the *Tralee Chronicle*, of 'the battles, sieges and fortunes they had passed and the triumphs they had won'.

On 11 September Colonel Thomas Kelly, who had as we have seen taken Stephens' place as chief organiser, was arrested in Manchester on J. J. Corydon's identification. According to the police reports, Corydon and another informer, Devany, 'patrolled from 7.00 p.m. to 1.00 a.m. such neighbourhoods as Kelly might lodge in'.

*The arrest of the Fenians at Manchester.*

A week later Kelly was rescued from his prison van. A policeman, Sergeant Brett, was killed during the attempt and as a result William Allen, Michael Larkin and Michael O'Brien, three of the Fenians involved in the rescue, were hanged on 21 November 1867. Their last words before they were sentenced became the chorus of a song, ironically written by A. M. Sullivan's brother, which became the unofficial Irish national anthem:

'God Save Ireland,' said the heroes,
'God Save Ireland,' say we all,
Whether on the scaffold high or the battlefield we die,
O, what matter when for Erin dear we fall.

Father Gadd, the English-born prison chaplain, paid this tribute to the Manchester Martyrs, as they quickly became known in

*The escape of the Fenian prisoners at Manchester.*

Ireland: 'I never had more devotional penitents in my life than the condemned Irishmen in Salford gaol. My poor boys, how they did pray!' Denying reports that he presided at a memorial mass, Bishop Moriarty of Kerry, a fierce opponent of the Fenians, wrote:

> We prayed for them in secret and asked the Almighty to take them to His eternal rest. Their crime was not perpetrated through hatred or revenge or for sordid gain and many are of the opinion that their trial was not a fair trial. They met their doom in a manner both edifying and Christ-like.

Any policeman or magistrate who referred to the 'Manchester Martyrs' soon found themselves in very hot water. In February 1868 a number of soldiers in Cork were court-martialled 'for attending the procession in honour of the Manchester Fenian criminals'.

In revenge for their death, as he claimed, William Farrell shot and wounded Queen Victoria's son, the Duke of Edinburgh, on 12 March 1868 as he visited Australia. Farrell, who said that he was a Fenian but seems to have been working on his own, was executed for his crime, even though the Duke asked that his life be spared. The following month the

*Queen Victoria's son – target of a Fenian assassination attempt.*

police reported the following rhyme posted on the Dublin pillar-boxes:

'A Real Live Prince'
They say that kings can do no wrong
Their murderous deeds denied
But since from us their power has sprung
The starving wretch who robs for bread
He seldom meets compassion
And why should a crown preserve the head
Of one that robs a nation.

At the end of September 1868, when Monsieur Laubert D'Arc's

exhibition of waxworks at the Rotunda featured the execution of the Manchester Martyrs – Allen, Larkin and O'Brien – a band of Fenians rushed in and broke the figures to pieces. At a confirmation ceremony in Listowel, Bishop Moriarty asked, 'Who were the martyrs of the early church?' and was very surprised when he received the response, 'Allen, Larkin and O'Brien!' For the next thirty years memorials were erected in their honour in towns all over Ireland. In Listowel graveyard there is a fine Celtic cross, which was unveiled in July 1883. The attempts of the local resident magistrate, C. P. Crane, to prevent the unveiling led to a very serious riot and many people from all over north Kerry were injured in the police baton charges. People would have been killed but for the fact that the officer in charge of the British soldiers in the town refused to allow his men to fire on the crowds.

# CHAPTER 7

# KILMALLOCK BARRACKS AND THE RISING IN LIMERICK

I was down there in Kilmallock, the hottest fight of all,

And you see – he bared his arm – there's the mark there of the ball,

I hope the lads a-growing now will hold the ground we won,

And not disgrace the cause in which I held the Fenian gun.

*Traditional ballad*

There is a monument in Kilmallock, Co. Limerick, to the Fenians who died in the attack on the police barracks there on 6 March 1867 and those who were captured and died in prison afterwards. Fifty-four years later history was to repeat itself when the Irish Republican Army attacked the barracks on the night of 28 May 1921. Though the barracks was not captured, it was destroyed and one Irish Volunteer killed in the attack. He was Liam Scully, a teacher of Irish and a native of Glencar, County Kerry.

The Fenian rising had been planned for the night of 5/6 March 1867. The leader of the rising in Kilmallock was Captain John Dunne, a native of the nearby town of Charleville, who had fought in the Union army during the American Civil War. The Fenians in the surrounding villages were to capture guns at the local police posts and then march to Kilmallock. On the way they were to pull up the railway lines and tear down the telegraph wires.

The Kilmallock Fenians gathered that night at Gabbett's Field near the town and at the house of Christopher Hawthorne, a leading Fenian in Kilmallock.* As the Fenians waited, parties of men were sent to seize guns in the neighbourhood. Charles Bourne, the manager of the Union Bank, had a six-chambered revolver, which he refused to give up. Thomas Orr (Reverend James Gabbett's caretaker) later gave evidence as to what happened next: 'The man in green [Captain Dunne] said he should give it up, but he said, "Death first!" The man in green repeated the same words and immediately shot him in the neck, the pistol was about ten inches from him.' Mr Bourne survived to be a witness at the subsequent trials and his revolver was found, when 'Daniel Bradley, one of the Fenians, was arrested at the house of Thade McCarthy of Kilmallock, hiding between two ticks [mattresses]'.

Back at the Hawthornes', the Fenians heard the sound of the mail train. Captain Dunne, in his green uniform, with a green plume in his hat, realised that something was wrong, since the tracks had not been torn up. 'Boys,' he is reputed to have said, 'the pass is sold!' It appears he was right and that the police were expecting an attack on the barracks. Sub-Constable McSherry reported: 'The police remained up until five in the morning and the lights were not quenched until 5 a.m., when all the men went to bed except three.' In the barracks were a sergeant, thirteen constables, four of their wives and eleven children. As soon as the lights went out in the barracks, the Fenians fell in, four deep, and marched towards

---

* The family had come to Kilmallock at the beginning of the eighteenth century as linen weavers. They were originally Presbyterians but became Catholics and had been active in the United Irishmen of 1798.

the building. They had already captured Sub-Constable Michael Connor from Bruff barracks and placed him five paces in front of the ranks with a heavy pike in his hand. He wrote in his report:

> I heard a voice behind me crying out: 'Ireland will be free this night.' On my hesitating to take the pike the colonel told me he would shoot me and I would be sleeping with the men in the barracks after a short time. A man called Patrick Walsh walked over to the porch of the door. I saw him strike matches against the door and fire up at the top windows.

Head Constable Richard Adams confirmed this: 'A shot was fired and then a volley, the police returned the fire through the windows broken by the fire of the attacking party.' He identified John Sheahan, a militia man: 'He could see me, at my bedroom window, I could see him, he appeared to be trying to shoot me and I to shoot him, this lasted nearly three hours.'

Two quarrymen tried to drill holes with a pickaxe and crowbar in the gable of the barracks to blow it up with dynamite, and they also attempted to set fire to the door with a barrel of blazing tar, but they did not succeed. Afterwards the police found a small hole in one of the quoin stones of the barracks about two feet from the ground and found a canister of blasting powder and two parcels of blasting fuse in the water under the arch of the nearby bridge.

Daybreak came and still the fight continued. Reinforcements arrived for the police – ten constables from Kilfinane led by Sub-Inspector Milling who went 'in a lively pace towards Kilmallock', observed by Sub-Constable Connor. By this time Sub-Constable Connor had got away, firing a shot at Patrick Walsh in the process, but 'he [Walsh] hopped over by the porch of the door'. Having escaped being killed, either by the Fenians or the police in the barracks, Sub-Constable Connor took no chances: 'As I was a stranger and in plain clothes I did not go to them.'

By ten o'clock in the morning the Fenians found themselves caught in cross-fire. The pikemen retreated and about a dozen riflemen fought their way down to the crossroads at the centre of the town, by the bridge and the hotel. Here a brief council of war was held. The men wished to fight to a finish but Captain Dunne advised them to scatter and avoid capture. 'Now you have fought,' he said, 'you will be even more ready to fight on another day.' He mounted Sub-Constable Connor's horse and rode away. After many adventures and helped by Father Ned Clifford of Loghill, Captain Dunne succeeded in escaping to America by ship from Foynes.

Head Constable Adams reported that the police found seventeen guns, two swords, a stone weight of bullets, boxes of caps, several crowbars, a drill and a pickaxe, two sledges, about thirty-seven pikes and 'three dead Fenians' on the streets of Kilmallock. Two of these were Daniel Blake (a cobbler from Bruree, aged twenty) and the local doctor, Michael Cleary (aged twenty-five), who was a sworn Fenian and had joined them as they began the attack.

The third man was not identified at the time and has ever since been referred to as the Unknown Fenian:

> Who was he at Kilmallock, that brave-hearted stranger,
> Who daringly breasted the fire of the foe,
> Like a veteran inured to the battle's grim danger;
> He fought till the red hail of death laid him low.

It is now known, thanks to the late Mainichin Seoighe, that this man was Patrick Hassett, whose father owned a public house in the village of Bulgaden. When his sister went to call him on that Ash

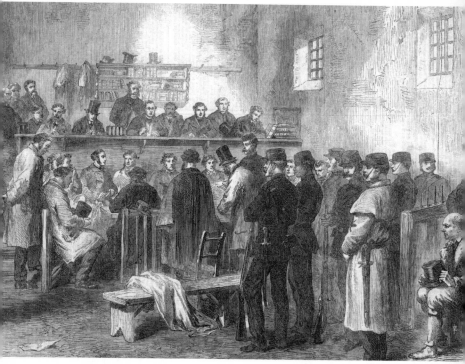

*Inquest on Dr Cleary, who died in the attack on Kilmallock barracks.*

Wednesday morning she found that his bed had not been slept in. His family knew that he was a Fenian and hoped that he had survived the rising and escaped out of the country but they never saw him again. Why did his father not go to the barracks to check if the body was his? Perhaps he was afraid of losing his licence and he would have no way of supporting his wife and family, as happened to another Limerick publican, William Costelloe of Rathkeale, as soon as the government discovered that his son had been one of the Fenian leaders.

According to the *Limerick Chronicle*'s report about the Kilmallock attack:

The police found two of the attacking party lying dead outside the barracks, one of whom was pierced by a bullet through the side and the other had a bullet wound passing from the left shoulder through the body. Their names are unknown, they were strangers in the locality and they are believed to have been natives of Kerry, from the peculiar make and cut of their clothes, which consisted of black frieze jackets and trousers of the same material, peculiar to those worn in western and southern parts of Kerry bordering on Cork. Their flannel shirts have the same tie of ribbon in front which Kerrymen wear. Their head covering was caps and on their feet brogues and worsted socks. Their faces were pale from the loss of blood and it appeared as if the unfortunate wretches died in great agony.

Head Constable Adams was awarded the Queen's Medal for gallantry and received £20 reward from Dublin Castle for 'his sterling defence of the barracks' and another £50 from private subscriptions.

Meanwhile those Fenians who were captured were brought to trial on 6 May 1867. A police report stated: 'Twenty men gathered at Bruree – to attack the barracks at Garryfine – under Richard Birmingham, all armed with pikes.' Colonel Massey also gave evidence that, according to the Cork Fenian circles, 20,000 men were ready to fight, but they had only 1,500 weapons and these were mostly pikes.

Sentences of from five to fifteen years were passed. Some Fenians were transported to Australia and some of those who gave information against them ended up on the same continent. It took some time to assemble these latter but they were eventually persuaded into the witness box – fed, found *and* supplied with clothing by the Castle. 'If they [the witnesses] are likely to emigrate soon the purchase of clothing might be deferred until they are about to sail.' Each male witness was supplied with a coat, hat, trousers, vest (i.e. waistcoat), three shirts, three pairs of socks and a pair of shoes. Each female witness received a dress, shawl, two petticoats, three chemises, three pairs of stockings, two aprons, two p(lain?) handkerchiefs, two collars, a bonnet and a pair of boots. They all finally set sail for Brisbane in eastern Australia, in the *Flying Cloud*, leaving London on 10 October 1867.

At a court martial in Limerick on 3 April 1867 James Healy, a gunner in the 13th Brigade, Royal Artillery, was sentenced to two years' hard labour and dishonourable discharge, having been charged with desertion and sedition and being engaged in the rising on the night of the attack on Kilmallock barracks. Healy had been arrested by Constables Gormley and Dalton on 7 March at the railway terminus in Cork.

Tim Pat Cleary of Ballycullane wanted to take part in the fight, but because he was only sixteen years old his parents locked him in his room. He kicked the door down during the night and joined his two brothers – one of whom (Michael) was killed – in the attack on the barracks. The police said Tim Pat Cleary was wearing a Glengarry cap with ribbons and carrying a gun. After the rising he was arrested on 25 April and detained in Limerick gaol until the end of August 1867. It proved impossible to convict him – 'the witness on whom the police placed most reliance having gone out of the way' (i.e. could not be found). When released on bail Cleary went to America but he returned to Ireland in his old age. He had great pain in one of his big toes and he told a doctor: 'This is my Fenian toe.' It was no lie, for Cleary had injured it in breaking down the door so many years before.

The strangest story of all those related about the Fenians of Kilmallock is of Edmond Houlihan of Darnstown who lost his sight when his gun exploded during the fight. He could speak Irish as fluently as English and he was a fine musician. For more than fifty years he walked the roads of Ireland playing Irish airs and singing rebel songs. His voice and his violin were his weapons in the cause of Ireland. When Jeremiah O'Donovan Rossa was buried in Dublin in 1912, Houlihan walked there and heard Pádraig Pearse speak at the funeral. Houlihan died peacefully at home on 27 December 1931, at the age of ninety-two. He wished to have his coffin wrapped in the Fenian flag. But so many years had passed that no one was quite sure what this flag was, so they used the Irish Tricolour, which had first been brought to Ireland from France by Thomas Francis Meagher in 1848 when Houlihan was a young boy of nine years old.

In autumn 1868, a year and a half after the attack on the barracks, Head Constable Adams reported on the arrival of 'Walsh, the ballad singer' in Kilmallock:

> Large groups of people group round him in the street at night, all eager to get possession of his ballads. I respectfully request instructions as to whether the constabulary should arrest persons whom they might find selling or distributing such. I have had Walsh watched as closely as possible to try and catch him singing some of the songs in question but the police were as closely watched! I am of the opinion plainly indicated that the Fenian spirit prevails in this locality and is daily growing worse.

Three sample ballad sheets were enclosed with the report. The first was the well-known 'Burke's Dream':

> Slowly but sadly one night in November,
> I lay down my weary head to repose,
> In my pallet of straw which I long will remember

Weary from sleep I fell into a doze
Tired from working hard
Down in the Felons' Yard.

The others were 'The Fenians Welcome to Ireland' and 'A New Song on the Downfall of Heresy', a ballad inspired by Gladstone's Bill, which had been the subject of conversation for some time and was finally passed in 1869, to disestablish the Church of Ireland, and which may well have originated in north Kerry:

He [The Parson] says; Alas! What shall I do?
I'll loose the glebe of Shannon View
Where rent or rates I never paid,
Since the Reformation of Luther.

Kilmallock was not the only area of Limerick where the planned Fenian rising was attempted. In the little west Limerick village of Ardagh, even though there was no American officer to lead them, the Fenians obeyed their orders and attempted to capture the local barracks and obtain the arms that were stored there. On 11 March 1867 the *Limerick Chronicle* reported on the happenings at Ardagh on the night of 5 March:

This dreadful outrage occurred when a number of rebels – one to two hundred – assembled at Ardagh and attacked the barracks, demanding arms. The four men in the barracks under the command of Constable Forsyth immediately proceeded to defend their arms with their lives. They had only time to put on their trousers and put their crossbelts over their shirts, when the door of the barracks was furiously attacked by a man with a hatchet, who smashed in the door under cover of fire from his comrades outside. They rushed in and the guards retiring upstairs were fired on. Some of the wretches attempted to force their way up the stairs, calling on the police to surrender, when they were fired on in self defence and it is supposed one was shot dead and others wounded. They retreated to the street and the police not being daunted, reloaded and followed them and a running fight took place, the rebels finally dispersing, leaving six or eight pikes, a scythe and a hatchet in the yard, and such quantities of blood as showed severe wounds. Head Constable Sullivan from Newcastle was early on the spot this morning and succeeded in arresting six men, one a soldier of the 6th Regiment stationed at Rathkeale, whose coat was on 'inside out'. He also found in a house there a coat with a bullet hole through the arm; but the owner of the coat was gone.

This must have been Stephen Ambrose of Duncanville, whom the informers at the subsequent trial identified as being shot in the right arm as he led the attack on the stairs. One gave evidence as follows:

When he [Stephen Ambrose] had got up three or four steps he fell back into the kitchen, and he said 'Boys, I am shot, but I would as soon be a dead man as a live one. I will lead ye again boys if I get anyone to follow me.' No one followed him. He then said: 'This is the way Irishmen always do.'

Eventually, on 7 April 1870, his father, Thomas Ambrose, applied for the return of the coat, which he said he had purchased himself and claimed it as his own property. The inspector-general of constabulary recommended that the coat be handed back if it was plain clothes and not a uniform, and this was done on 14 April 1870.

Meanwhile on 16 March 1867 Edmond Smith O'Brien, of Cahermoyle House, had received the following letter:

Edmond S. O'Brien

Your becoming a common spy in the arrest and annoyance of your honest neighbours and the public will be the cause of your premature death as soon as an opportunity presents itself so rest assured and be not surprised if such a fate overtakes you.

Signed on behalf of the people

Annomemous [*sic*]

The local sergeant said that:

He [Edmond] had given active assistance to the police in making the arrest of parties suspected of being at the attack on Ardagh police barracks. This caused expressions to be used to him by some parties who said that he was not so active when the police were after his father.

However, the police were of the opinion that there was no need for alarm as O'Brien had gone to meet his family on the continent and the letter had been opened by his brother.

An interesting leader appeared in the *Saturday Review* on the same day (16 March):

The belief that this insurrection is serious seems to be well founded. The movements that were commenced on Wednesday extended across the island and were evidently planned by persons of some military knowledge. But the rebels proved themselves a cowardly mob as soon as they found themselves in collision with a handful of the constabulary. At present it is impossible to judge whether any other portion of the insurgent force is of better quality but there can be no doubt that the American Irish officers who have had experience in war would be formidable opponents if their numbers were considerable.

No foresight could have guarded against a conspiracy, which is in many respects of an unprecedented character. Generals and colonels, who have really served in the grades denoted by their titles, must naturally impress the Irish imagination with confidence and respect. When the present insurrection has been suppressed and punished an interval of tranquillity may perhaps give Ireland a chance of partial and temporary improvement. The removal of the chronic disease of turbulence can only be the object of vague and distant anticipation.

Lord Strathnairn had his own view on the 'Generals and colonels':

There is no devilry, so ingenious an institution is Irish Fenianism, that these men trained in the American Civil War are not prepared to undertake. They will not take the open, the field, but are ready for a torpedo or mining explosion or any treacherous destruction.

In Kilteely, County Limerick, the Fenians had also assembled on the night of the rising. The barracks was unoccupied as the police had been withdrawn to reinforce the Limerick City Division, so the Fenians got the key from Hugh Ryan, the barrack master. They occupied the barracks but dispersed quickly when the alarm was raised. According to Captain O'Donnell, JP: 'Immediately on hearing this news, I myself and 200 of the 74th Highlanders proceeded to Newpallas by special train at 8.30 a.m. and marched without delay to Kilteely but finding no Fenians returned to Limerick at 2 p.m.' In a follow-up search on 23 March, the Tipperary flying column and the Newpallas police discovered thirty-nine pikes, complete, buried deep in a ditch.

Some of the Fenians had a sense of humour. One hundred pikes were found under the floor of Kilteely chapel, much to the chagrin of the parish priest, Father Heaney, who was said by the newspapers to be strongly opposed to the movement. However, this was a view not shared by the local police and Constable Malachy Murphy reported on 24 April 1867 that: 'Father Heaney had said to his congregation that God intended people to increase and multiply, but the British government orders the contrary, it is for thinning the people and multiplying the bullocks in their place.' According to the police, Father Barry, the curate in Kilteely, was a strong supporter of the Fenians. Mr Moriarty, resident magistrate in Limerick City, sent word to the Castle that: 'He [Father Barry] was giving every countenance if not direct encouragement to the Fenian movement.' Moriarty also commented to Dr Leahy, the Catholic bishop of Limerick: 'It gave great satisfaction to the local police when Father Barry was transferred from Kilteely on 2 May.'

Father Barry was supposed to have been given a revolver by Miss Walsh of Tipperary, and the police claimed that: 'He had gone to the house of John Carroll of Killiner [later sentenced to two years' imprisonment for his part in the rising] for the purpose of hearing Fenian confessions on Shrove Tuesday. Mrs Carroll was crying all the time he was there.'

In August, Resident Magistrate de Gernon reported: 'Rocket signals were being fired in Kilteely, which continues to be a hot-bed of disaffection and a renewed rising is expected there as well as in Hospital and Bruff.'

The well-known collector of folklore, Kevin Danaher from Athea, County Limerick, in 1934 wrote down for the Folklore Commission this account from his grandmother, when she was ninety-four years old:

There were Fenians in Rathkeale, Newcastle West, Askeaton and a very strong one in Ardagh – ní nach ionadh, for it was there

[William] Smith O'Brien lived and people still remembered 1848. Captain Guiry came to train them. He was born in Castlemahon but his family had to go to America in the bad times when he was only a child. He fought for the North [*recte* South] and was promoted captain. He came back to Ireland in '64. When the signal came he led the attack on the barracks in Ardagh, but they could not take it for they had only muzzle-loaders and the police had rifles.

There were informers and they [the Fenians] had to go on their keeping. Sergeant Ashe went into the village [Castlemahon] and he met Captain Guiry on the road and fired at him, but Guiry shot him in the shoulder. He went to Newcastle for help and they sent a troop of horse, but when they got to the village he was gone. A priest [Father Nolan of Ardagh] disguised him and he crossed the Shannon to Clare and Galway and Belfast and on to Southampton and he made his way back to the States. He died in 1931 – in June.

Mr Chamney, who was secretary of the Dublin special commission established to try the Fenians in 1867, wrote in an unpublished preface to the official report:

> The government had obtained information from different sources of the Fenian conspiracy and were fully prepared for any emergency, so that when the appointed time arrived, and the outbreak was attempted on the day fixed on, they were enabled to put it down at once and to make prisoners of the principal leaders engaged in it. In and around Dublin nearly 300 persons were arrested and sent for trial and in Cork, Limerick, Clare, Kerry, Louth and other counties, numerous arrests were also made and the parties returned for trial.

On November 1867 the *Daily Express* gave an interesting insight into the diet and conditions of these prisoners in Kilmainham:

*Fenian prisoners before the special commission in Dublin.*

Eight ounces of oatmeal stirabout and a half pint of milk for breakfast. Fourteen ounces of bread and a pint of milk for dinner. Seven ounces of bread and half a pint of milk for supper. On three days a week they get four pounds of potatoes in lieu of bread for dinner and on two other days three-quarters of a pound of beef in a pint of soup. They must keep strict silence in the cells – a provision which to fluent orators like them is a severe privation and at exercise walk from three to four yards apart from one another, which may keep alive some recollection of their drill, but prevents any cordial intercourse.

The Fenian prisoner Con McInerny took a different view of the situation as he described exercise in the 'cage' in Mountjoy gaol in a letter to his sister in Corofin:

You would be surprised to see all the boys promenading the circus during exercise. They all look so gay [i.e. happy], you would hardly take them to be a number of prisoners only for the high iron rails and the warders walking round the outside. They are all allowed to smoke during exercise and two men carry lamps and keep a supply of touch paper to light the pipes. When going in the pipes must be given up. There is a hand basket at the gate of the ring and as each man goes out he places his pipe in it and when he goes in again he takes his own pipe from the basket.

On 3 March 1868, Michael Harnett of Abbeyfeale, formerly a sailor in the Federal (United States) navy was arrested by Head Constable Sullivan while 'ostensibly on his way to visit friends' in his native town. He was committed to the county gaol by Mr Curley, JP, to be detained pending further instructions. No treasonable documents were found on him and he was discharged on an undertaking to return to America within one month. But he did not do this. Head Constable Sullivan stated:

Harnett is doing an immense amount of damage in the district by swearing in the disaffected into the Fenian Brotherhood. He visits Newcastle on market days and appears to feel that he enjoys a sort of immunity in consequence of his being once in custody and being discharged. It seems suspicious that he should come into the district at the critical time when Carey [recte Guiry], the local Fenian centre, who led the attack on Ardagh police barracks, is on the run and could forward the cause no further.

The sub-inspector in Newcastle had advised that Harnett should be arrested: 'He is a dangerous character.'

# CHAPTER 8

# THE *ERIN'S HOPE*

Monuar, a lucht na nDéise, gur lig sibh leis na peelers,
Nuair a gabh said na hOghlaigh, a thainig ar an dtráigh,
Bhi na gunnai in bhur lámha, is nior scaoil sibh na Redcoats,
Is tá meirg ar na pici a shaith sibh thios sa diogh.

*Amhrán na nDaoine*

But what of the Fenians in America? Had they forgotten their promise to send guns and men? Well, the answer is that they had not, but it had taken them much longer than they expected to organise such matters. On 12 April 1867 John Powell, the Fenian 'chief of naval affairs' in the United States, had written to Captain John Kavanagh, an American ex-officer in the Union army:

> You will proceed with the vessel under your command to Sligo Bay and ensure every precaution to ensure the delivery of your cargo and passengers. If possible you will return with your vessel to New York, but if you see no chance of escaping with her, destroy her if practicable.

Although the Fenians in America did not know it, the rising was already over when the *Jacmel*, a brig of 200 tons, left New York on 13 April. Its manifest showed a cargo bound for Cuba, made up of pianos, sewing machines and wine barrels but in fact it was laden with 5,000 rifles – 'Springfields, Spencers, Enfields and Sharps' – and boxes containing 500,000 rounds of ammunition. Off Sandy Hook Point, thirty-eight men came on board from a New York steamer. All were former officers in the American army, led by Captain Kavanagh, and among them were General James Kerrigan (a former member of Congress), Colonels William Nagle and John Warren and Captains Prendergast, Phelan, Dogherty and Tresilian, the last 'an engineer officer of considerable reputation'. When the *Jacmel* was on the ocean she was renamed the *Erin's Hope*, and on 21 April a new Fenian flag, 'The Sunburst' or 'The Rising Sun', was flown from her masthead. Later, from his prison cell in Mountjoy, James Nolan, the cook on the *Jacmel*, graphically described this in a statement he wrote for Solicitor-General Samuel Lee Anderson, and for which he received his freedom, as well as £10 and permission to take passage to Liverpool:

Sir,

I wish to inform you of what I have forgot, the day that we sailed Nagle gave to the officers there commissions and the day the flag was reased, the captain optened the sealed orders and read them to us all on the quarter-deck and told us our destinishon was Sligo Bay and christened the ship and gave her the name 'Erin's Hope' and likewise there was on board three six-pounders of a new patrine called the spider gun that never was fired out of till on board which proved good. He thrw a shell fourteen hundred yards and one man can carry one of them as easy as a rifle with a sling attached to it. We made a raft in case we were attacked and we got the magazine ready to blow up the ship.

They got ready several times to fight the cutters they taught was coming on them and I have heard them say that there was some arms put on shore and also there was fore others landed in Dongarven that was arrested, whose names weur as follows: John Murhihan, Corcoran, Dorning and Horinger. I have no doubt but if I am discharged in a few days afyer you will get one or to others to go to the table and give infermashion. When they will here of me getting out they will suspect that I informed and they will come up and I now too that it would not take much to have them come up if they taught I was discharged. [spelling mistakes from the original have been retained]

The *Erin's Hope* made her landfall at Blackrock, off Eagle Isle at the mouth of Donegal Bay, after a passage of thirty-three days. For six more days they waited for the local Fenians to make contact and finally they sailed into Sligo Bay on 22 May 1867, determined to capture the barracks, take over the town and emulate General Humbert's feats in Castlebar in 1798. It was at this point that a cutter came from the shore with Colonel Ricard O'Sullivan Burke on board to tell them that the rising was over and that it would be useless to go ahead with the planned attack on Sligo barracks.

They set off again and spent the next twenty-four days making their way along the coast, looking for any organised band of Fenians who might join them and a place to land their arms and ammunition to be stored for a future rising. They avoided the British warships that patrolled the Irish coast and came to the mouth of the Shannon. Tradition has it that they contacted the Tarbert Fenians who tried to disable the guns on the British fort on Tarbert Island but were driven off. Resident Magistrate de Gernon reported: 'On 12 June 1867 I proceeded to Foynes to acquaint the commander of the guard ship with particulars respecting the Fenian brigantine, which conveyed the men who were landed in Dungarvan.' They also anchored off Valentia Island and arrived at Toe Head near Skibbereen on 27 May. Colonel D. B. Moylens – presumably a brother of Lord Ventry, who lived on the outskirts of Dingle – complained of the neglect of the coastguard in not boarding the vessel at that point. The Admiralty said that no blame attached to the Kerry coastguards and by way of pointing out the justice of their reply forwarded a forty-page report of what happened in Sligo Bay, where the coastguards did inspect the vessel without realising what she really was! Not only that but they also allowed some of the men to land, who amused themselves 'by pelting jackdaws about the old castle'.

Finally on 1 June the *Erin's Hope* sailed into Helvick Head harbour in Waterford. A heavy mist enveloped the ship and, when they met a fishing boat, twenty-nine men were sent ashore under the command of Colonel Nagle. The mist lifted as they landed on the Cunnigar sandbank near Trá na Rinne, where they were observed by the local coastguards. At once they reported the invaders to Resident Magistrate Redmond who was on the bench in Dungarvan courthouse. With two other magistrates and twelve constables – all he could muster – Redmond set off in pursuit 'on cars', and arrested twenty-two of the Fenian invaders, 'fine able intelligent young men', within a few hours. Before the day was over, twenty-seven of the twenty-nine were captured, Colonels Nagle and Warren having been arrested at the Blackwater bridge in Youghal, where they had been taken by Aindreas de Roiste of An Rinn in his pony and cart.

When examined by the magistrates in Dungarvan, one of the crew, Patrick Wheelan, was very guarded in his description of the Fenians:

I am a fisherman and reside at Baile na nGall. I went out to sea on Saturday last to take up trammel nets. About mid-day I saw a brigantine coming in from the sea and a man asked me what would

I charge to put two men on shore. I said £2 and came alongside. Just
then a number of men, I would say more than twenty, jumped over
the side of the brigantine into my boat. Patrick Browne, one of my
men, gave me three sovereigns but I don't know where he got them. I
landed them at Ring strand outside the pier at Baile na nGall in three
and a half feet of water. They were speaking Irish and English. When
they were leaving the boat one of them gave me a half sovereign.

Many years later, another fisherman, Eamonn Breathnach, gave
this account of the landing of the Fenians:

Bhí hooker ag iascaireacht ar an mbágh – an *St Nicholas*. Páid Mor
Ó Faoilean a bhi mar scipear uirthi. (Chuaigh Liam Toibin ag
iascaireacht ar an 'hooker' sin nuair a d'fhág se an scoil. *The Fenian* a
tugtai uirthi ansin. Nil fagtha anois di ach an crann – tá san le feiscint
ag Cosa an Fhir Mhóir.) Duaradh le Páid gan na fir a thabhairt i dtir
go dti an tráthnóna – bhí ceo trom ann. Bhí an iomarcha sa bháid
agus thug se isteach iad go cée Bhaile na nGall. Ghlan an ceo agus
chonaic George Jones iad. Coast Guard on Helvick ab ea e agus chuir
sé an sceal go dti na Pés (na polini)'.

  Duine eile de chriu an bháid, tharraing se fearg na ndaoine ar fein:
  'A Dhonaill Ui Choileain, ná bhfeice tu Dia
  A Dhonaill Ui Choileain, ná bhfeice tu an ghriain
  Dhearbhaigh tu ar na bhFinini a bhi fliuch go dti a dtuin,
  Agus chuir tu ona ngaolta iad isteach i bpriosúin'.

(Páid Mor Ó Faoilean was the skipper of the *St Nicholas* – the very
same boat on which Liam Toibin went fishing when he left school –
she was called *The Fenian* then – and all that's left of her now is her
mast sticking out below Cosa an Fhir Mhóir. Páid was asked not to
take the men ashore until nightfall, but there was a heavy mist and

the boat was over-laden. So he brought them in to the pier at Baile na nGall. But George Jones, one of the Helvick coastguards spotted them and he sent word to the police.

The people remembered how Donall Ó Coilean, another of the boat's crew, had given evidence against the Fenians at their trial:

'That God and the sun may hide their faces

From the man who swore on the courtroom table,

On misfortunate Fenians, all drowned with spray,

Swept from their friends and sent far o'er the say.')

To be fair to 'Daniel Collins', as he was called in the court report, he identified only one of the Fenians, 'the last man who landed from the boat'.

When Thomas Talbot and J. J. Corydon, the two informers, came to Waterford on 17 June 1867 to identify the prisoners, the *Waterford News* of 21 June 1867 described what happened:

The science of physiognomy appears to have been unknown to the Fenian chiefs, for the very sight of the two wretches should be enough to excite a feeling of loathing in the breast of any intelligent person. When the engine reached the platform Corydon jumped off and with a face of brass walked through the crowd of Fenians who were waiting. One man, by way of a joke, came up and said: 'Morrow, Corydon.' Much to his surprise Corydon put up his hand [to his hat] and replied, 'It is a fine day,' to which he got the reply, 'Yes, for your business!' Talbot, big and burly with his hands grasping the revolvers in his coat pockets jumped out and, getting on a sidecar, they cut over the bridge and saved themselves from the Ferrybank mob.

At the gaol Corydon identified ten or twelve of the Americans as prominent members of the Fenian Brotherhood, many (he said) having held high rank in the North American army. However, he told the governor of the gaol: 'He was disappointed at the class of men he saw, as the officers he had expected from America were of far superior intelligence – he could not conceive how Warren and Nagle could be mixed up with these men.' The *Waterford News* stated that: 'A large crowd threatened the approvers as they left the prison and the ladies especially were determined in their demeanour. They urged the police, who were restraining them, that they [the police] might pretend to be overpowered for two seconds and they would see the rascals were dragged asunder.'

The prisoners were held without charge for some weeks, and it was only when William Mellon, one of the party, had turned queen's evidence that Nagle and Warren were brought before a court. According to the *Cork Herald*:

> The prisoners presented a military and firm look and some wore the unmistakable square-toed boots, clean tufts and luxuriant mustachios of the Union army. When they were brought through Waterford on 13 June on their way to Dublin, an attempt was made to rescue them in which a man named Walsh was killed and there was considerable difficulty in lodging them in Waterford gaol.

When Nagle heard about Mellon, he wrote from his cell in Kilmainham to his solicitor, Mr Collins, South Mall, Cork:

> The breed of the Corydon's is not extinct, in the words of the poet:
> 'May the grass wither from his feet,
> May the woods deny him shelter, earth a home,
> The ashes a grave, the sun his light,
> And heaven its God.'

As a reward for his information Mellon was offered free passage to the colonies. Strangely, he opted to return to New York and two days after his arrival in that city he was shot dead by a son of Michael Doheny, the 1848 leader.

For another full week after the disembarkation on the Cunnigar sandbank near Trá na Rinne on 1 June 1867, Captain Kavanagh had sailed the *Erin's Hope* up and down St George's Channel. Once a British warship stopped him but he was able to fight his corner and as he later wrote (quoted in O'Mullane):

> She hoisted the English ensign and asked the usual questions: What ship? Where from? &c. I ran up the rag of the Britisher, dipped it thrice by way of salutation and answered his questions to my own and his satisfaction. He left me for another – for another ship [*sic*] three miles off, and lest he should return, I tacked ship and stood for the west coast of England.

Finally Captain Kavanagh realised that nothing more could be done and he returned to New York, reaching that port on 1 August after a voyage of 100 days covering 9,000 miles. He reported that he could have landed the arms and ammunition on any part of the coast of Ireland if there had been preparations to receive them. Captain Kavanagh volunteered to lead any further expedition to Ireland, but this was not to be. Almost forty years were to pass before the *Aud* arrived off the Kerry coast where 'Banna was lonely and Casement coming in!'

Dublin Castle found itself in considerable difficulty in bringing the men who were arrested to trial. Many were American citizens and the British government was not anxious to rouse public opinion in America by court cases which would inevitably result in a guilty verdict. After the trials of Colonels Warren and Costello who were sentenced to fifteen and twelve years' penal servitude, respectively, the other Fenians were released by degrees and returned to the United States.

One who was never to cross the Atlantic again had Kerry connections: John Smyth (alias John O'Connor), a sailor on the *Erin's Hope*. Off the coast of Sligo, he had been 'accidentally' wounded by a revolver shot discharged by Captain Daniel Buckley, and was put ashore on Streeda strand on 25 May. His wound was too severe to allow him to be taken to Dublin so he remained in Sligo until 5 August when he was transferred to Mountjoy gaol. He was identified as one of the Fenian party by the same Daniel Buckley who shot him and who had turned informer. After some time, Solicitor-General Samuel Lee Anderson visited him in his cell and advised that as he was regarded 'as merely a private in the expedition' he could obtain his discharge on condition that he went immediately to America. Smyth replied that he did not consider himself well enough to go at that time and would prefer to wait until he was stronger. However, his health took a sudden turn for the worse and he died in the prison hospital at 6.15 p.m. on Sunday 29 December 1867. The inquest, before Coroner Henry Harty, was held the following day and the jury returned the verdict that death was due to haemorrhage caused by congestion of the intestine. As Smyth had some money – sufficient funds to provide a decent interment – he was buried 'in a respectable fashion, at 8 a.m. on 31 December in the parish burial ground in the Richmond Cemetery, Goldenbridge, by the Reverend Donovan, curate of the prison Catholic chaplain, there being no person present but the prison warders'. The news of his death was conveyed to Mr Archibold, the British consul in New York and acknowledged by him on 21 January 1868.

# CHAPTER 9

# THE CLERKENWELL EXPLOSION

On the 13th day of December at four in the afternoon,
Those villains with a barrel of powder, the result will be known soon,
A wretch in the form of a female, with two men was going the way,
He set light to the barrel of powder, in a moment all was fear and
    dismay.
Sixty houses in one mass of ruins, the people they all fled in fear,
Children from shop doors ran crying: 'Where is my poor mother
    dear?'
The murderous villains absconded, but this was their treacherous plan,
To blow up poor innocent people, to rescue but one single man.

*Contemporary ballad 'The Blowing Up of the House of Detention'*

The *London Evening News* of 14 December 1937 reported:

Mr Arthur Abbot, the blind man who stands in Holborn by Gray's
Inn Road, lost an eye in the Clerkenwell explosion. He says: 'It was
directly opposite our house in Corporation Row. My sister Minnie
was one of those killed. My right eye was destroyed and the other
one went when I was twenty-eight. I was a coppersmith, but then I
couldn't work, I was discharged so I came to this [begging] for a living
– in 1890. It was my brother, John, from whom the man borrowed
a light to set fire to the taper.' This account was collaborated in the

*Clerkenwell House of Detention, two hours after the explosion.*

letters of Sir William Jenner, the royal physician, who had written to the queen at the time of the explosion in December 1867: 'A little child, between five and six, has one eye destroyed and the other so injured that there is no hope of preserving it to be entertained.'

*The Illustrated London News* of 21 December 1867 gave a graphic account of the Clerkenwell explosion:

No event for years past has excited greater surprise and indignation than the attempt made by the Fenians to effect the escape of Ricard Burke and [James] Joseph Casey by blowing down the outer wall of the House of Detention in Clerkenwell with a barrel of gunpowder. The wall was two feet thick and twenty-five feet high. This mad and wicked scheme has failed in its object but has done terrible mischief to the innocent. The authorities had received word from Dublin that an attempt to rescue the Fenians would be made, and as a result the police had undertaken to have a large body of men perambulating the prison. At twelve o'clock three police officers saw three men and a woman of suspicious appearance reconnoitring the prison. There followed a series of manoeuvres on both sides, one party being eager to throw the other off the scent, the other just as determined to keep the game in view. At 3.30 the officers saw the Fenians turn into St James' Passage and as two of them followed they met two of the men and the woman running at full speed up the passage, with such an expression of anxiety and alarm that they at once arrested them. At that moment a tremendous explosion occurred which almost prostrated the struggling group, followed by a shower of dust the crashing of houses and the shrieks and wails of the wounded.

The married daughter of Mrs Thomas Young, 5 Corporation Lane, saw a man rolling a large barrel, about three feet in length along the road. She saw him place it on one end and cover it with a large piece of oil-cloth, oak grained. He then took a fuse or piece of paper about eight inches long and stooping down he set one end on fire and thrust the other into the barrel. (This was confirmed by the evidence of a very sensible plain-clothes policeman, named Edward Moriarty, who explained that when he saw the burning fuse he 'stepped back eight to ten yards to see what would happen next'.) Mrs Young wondered: 'Whatever it was for?' When the explosion took place she was struck by fragments of iron and glass from the windows and sent reeling to the other side of the kitchen, where she fell senseless to the ground. When she came to herself she was weltering in blood, being frightfully cut about the head and face. A triangular section of the wall was blown in twenty feet at the base, sixty or seventy at the summit, the house immediately opposite was utterly destroyed, burying all within under the ruins and demolishing a great part of the houses right and left. The houses damaged were in Corporation Lane, Coburg Street, Rosoman Street, Woodbridge Street, Short's Building, Sekforde Street, St James' Walk, Plumber's Place and St James' Building. Not a window was to be seen in ten or eleven houses while in some not a trace of furniture could be seen. In some cases it had been shot out the windows at the back by the force of the concussion, but generally speaking it was to be found in heaps of atoms in the corner of the rooms. Thirty-six of the sufferers were removed to St Bartholomew's Hospital and six to the Royal Free Hospital, Gray's Inn Road. Those who died were Sarah Hodgkinson (aged thirty-five), William Clutton (fifty-five) and Minnie Julia Abbott (eight years old). The mother of this child, Maria Abbott, and three others of her children, John (thirteen), William (eleven) and Anne (two) are also patients in St Bart's, while a fourth, Arthur, is in a dangerous condition in the Royal Free Hospital. A large body of police of the 'A' Reserve division, armed with cutlasses, were stationed within the prison, making, it is said, with the force outside, 1,500 men under the direction of Captain Labelmondière, assistant commissioner of police, and supported by a detachment of the Guards [i.e. cavalry].

On the following day, the chancellor of the exchequer dispatched his private secretary, Mr Montague Corry, to make enquiries on the spot and to relieve the destitute at his discretion, at once visiting the poor homeless people in the neighbourhood, carrying a leather bag containing money.

During the following week, Martha Evans (sixty-seven) died from her injuries as did Martha Thompson (eight), Humphrey Evans (sixty-six) and Elizabeth Leland, otherwise known as Harriet Balzawi (fifty-four). By command of the queen, Dr Jenner visited both hospitals and satisfied himself that the parties were receiving all due care and every comfort. Her majesty caused large supplies of hothouse grapes and other fruits, toys and beds to be forwarded for their use. More than £3,000 has been received by the relief committee.

Jeremiah O'Sullivan from Caherdaniel, County Kerry, took a leading part in this attempt to free Colonel Ricard O'Sullivan Burke and James Joseph Casey, who was a nephew of James Stephens, from the Clerkenwell House of Detention on 13 December 1867. They had been arrested the previous month, after a scuffle with the police. It seems clear that too much explosive material was used because not only was the wall of the prison blown up but also a large part of the neighbouring street. Seven people were killed, eleven died later and 120 were injured. Indeed Burke himself would have been killed had he been in the prison yard at the time, as was planned. A white ball had been thrown over the wall as a signal and the police report stated: 'It was later found by William Scott, painter, as he walked over the rubbish of the fallen prison wall.' Jeremiah O'Sullivan had brought up the barrel of gunpowder to the wall of the gaol on a handcart. He escaped the police hunt after the explosion and eventually reached New York where he was involved in Irish-American politics until his death in 1922 at the age of seventy-seven.

Burke and Casey (under the name 'Egan') were immortalised in the pages of James Joyce's *Ulysses*:

> Raw-boned face under his peep of day boy's hat ... he prowled with Colonel Ricard Burke, tanist of his sept, under the walls of Clerkenwell and, crouching, saw a flame of vengeance hurl them upward in the fog ... In gay Paree he hides, Egan of Paris unsought by any save by me ... loveless, landless, wifeless ... They have forgotten Kevin Egan, not he them. Remembering thee, O Sion!

The three people mentioned in *The Illustrated London News* report as being captured at the site of the explosion were Timothy Desmond (tailor; forty-six), Jeremiah Allen (bootmaker; thirty-six) and Ann Justice (thirty). All were charged with wilful murder, as was Michael Barrett, a native of Drumkeeran in County Fermanagh, who had been involved in planning the escape. Evidence provided by informers during the trial was so contradictory that Barrett alone was sentenced to death, with Lord Chief Justice Cockbourn remarking: 'I cannot suppose that these two witnesses [Nicholas English and Patrick Mullaly] can have knowingly sworn what was false.' Barrett was hanged outside Newgate Prison on 26 May 1868, convicted, as he wrote himself, on 6 May, 'by the paid witnesses of the crown, with the gold of the government jingling in their pockets'. He was the last person to be publicly executed in Britain. Evidence had been given that he had been in Glasgow at the time of the explosion and *The Times* (London) on 14 December 1868 stated that 'Barrett was convicted on false evidence', and reiterated this view in its *On This Day* column on 27 May 1895. 'It has been said that Barrett was speaking the truth and was not guilty of the crime.' Even the home secretary seems to have had doubts about the case as the documents preserved in the United Kingdom national archives show that the execution was postponed on two occasions. Also in the file is a copy of a letter by Barrett to his friend in Glasgow, Charles McManus, from 29 January 1868:

> We are in a miserable enough condition, being without friends or acquaintances to do anything for us – Please send me my red Crimean shirt, a change of underclothing – vests and drawers are what I need most, also a few collars.

There had been radical and working-class support in England for the Fenian aims. A great part of this sympathy was lost as a result of what happened at Clerkenwell and Head Constable Meagher reported from Liverpool on 27 September 1868: 'Since this outrage, Fenians have fallen in the estimation of many of the old Chartists who had till then sympathised with them.' Some 166,000 special constables were sworn in to combat the renewed Fenian threat – more than were enrolled in either of the two world wars. Among them was Isaac Jefferson, known as 'Wat Tyler', who had been imprisoned in York Castle in 1848 for making pikes in preparation for the Chartist Revolution. In January 1868, 500 London-Irish Rifle Volunteers (somewhat similar to a militia regiment in Ireland) were also sworn in. The Metropolitan Police report stated:

Major Ward, commanding officer, called for three cheers for the queen and three for Ireland. He was the first to be sworn with Captains O'Connor, Purcell, Fowler, Tate, Dr West and Captain Daubney. They were supplied with truncheons, armlets of red and white (the colours of the City of Westminster). They then marched from St Martin's schoolrooms to Somerset House where they were dismissed.

Such was the impression the Fenians had made that in January 1868, when Patrick O'Hara was charged at the Old Bailey Court in London with stealing a watch and chain from John Shepherd, he was identified by Charles Carpenter because he wore a grey coat with a velvet collar and 'what they call a Fenian hat – a black hat with a crowned head'.

According to the *Evangelical Mission*, Fenians in London had a novel method of fundraising:

*Swearing in special constables in London.*

Wherefore have the Roman Catholic priests had so many raffles lately? What has been their number? Ostensibly they have been for the Hatton Garden church and schools, the Homer Row schools and numerous others. How many Protestants have been induced by the prizes offered to purchase tickets and thus aid in supporting a system, which we have every reason to abhor!

Have these large sums raised not been devoted to another purpose?

The explosion at Clerkenwell had results that the Fenians could never have expected. Because of the 'intensity of Fenianism', William Gladstone – temporarily on the back benches and for long completely opposed to Irish claims for self-government – began to move to the position that would see him disestablish the Church of Ireland, make a start on land reform and finally make every effort to give Ireland Home Rule. Gladstone later said: 'The Fenian outrages had a very important influence on the time for moving upon the great questions of policy for Ireland.' Or as John Devoy wrote in *Recollections of an Irish Rebel*: 'He [Gladstone] was driven to disestablishmentarianism by the intensity of Fenianism; he was led to do justice to Ireland by the rising of '67, the Manchester rescue and the Clerkenwell explosion.'

*Preparing for the Fenians – London police at sabre practice.*

# CONCLUSION

When the Kilkenny Fenian Commemoration Committee unveiled a plaque in memory of James Stephens, they described that native of the Marble City in terms that would have pleased him – as 'a patriot and a scholar'. But Martha Ramón perhaps came closer to the truth when she entitled her magnificent biography of Stephens *A Provisional Dictator*. Stephens was an organiser *par excellence* and though, as we have seen, he was not alone in recruiting members to the Irish Republican Brotherhood, there can be no doubt that directly or indirectly he was responsible for the fact that some 50,000 men joined a secret oath-bound organisation, dedicated to securing Irish Freedom. But 'dictator', he would be, something that was not acceptable to the American Fenians who were bankrolling the movement and many of whom had fought through a terrible civil war, a war fought on both sides to establish freedom from what was seen as that tyranny of dictatorship.

The disagreement between Stephens and the American Fenians led to confusion in setting the date for the rising and it also meant that many of the American officers who were to lead the men of Ireland into battle failed to do so. But in Kerry and Limerick the rebellion did happen, though only in an isolated and sporadic fashion. While in other counties there were numerous Fenians ready to rebel, the absence of professional leadership meant that in contrast to the two Munster counties, there was no actual rising in much of the rest of Ireland.

Despite their failure in 1867, the Fenians did not disappear. Just as happened many times since over the last 140 years, some moved into politics and joined Parnell, while others followed O'Donovan Rossa's lead and took part in various attacks on English cities. The 'die-hards' and the 'hillside men' of Kerry and Limerick kept alive the Fenian ideal, which inspired future generations to continue the fight for Irish independence.

# APPENDICES

The appendices show at once the strength and weakness of the Fenian movement in Kerry and Limerick. There were a large number of committed activists in certain areas of both counties, but only in those areas. As was to happen again in 1916, the absence of firearms and even more to the point the absence of trained soldiers as leaders prevented a more general outbreak. If the rising had taken place in 1865, these might have come from the British army. However, in 1867 they were to be the veterans of the American Civil War. Too thinly spread over the country to render a widespread rising possible, the veterans did their duty and were ready to face death as a result. But the shade of Robert Emmet had made the Westminster government very unwilling to add to the pantheon of Irish martyrs and, were it not for the killing of Sergeant Brett in Manchester and the slaughter of Clerkenwell, 1867 might have gone into history as yet another rebellion in the mode of 1848. As we have seen it was only at Cahersiveen, Kilmallock, Kilteely and Ardagh that the Kerry and Limerick Fenians took the field but because they did they too 'were spoken of among their people' – they too were 'faithful and they fought'.

# APPENDIX 1

## FENIAN SUSPECTS

*List of warrants issued against persons in Limerick and Kerry suspected of treasonable practice, those detained under the Act to Suspend the Right of Habeas Corpus 1866 and those sentenced to terms of penal servitude.*

| Name | Date of Issue of Warrant/ Date of Arrest | To Whom Issued | Details | Warrant/ File No. | Where Detained and What Action Taken |
|------|------|------|------|------|------|
| Aherne, Michael | 19/2/1866 | County Inspector, Kerry | Foreman in Lunham's Provision Store, Tralee, Co. Kerry; 'Chairman of the Fenian Rooms' | F412 | Warrant suspended, no action taken |
| Allen, Jonathan | 5/2/1868 (already in custody; arrested 25/1/1868) | Governor, Limerick gaol | Schoolmaster, former soldier Limerick City | | Limerick gaol; removed to Mountjoy 13/4/1868; Kilmainham 4/6/1868; discharged on bail 22/6/1868 |
| Bailey, Patrick Aged 22 | 22/2/1866 | Governor, Limerick gaol | Engine driver at Russell's Mills, Limerick City; 'Deputy head centre' | 3392 No. 8142 | Limerick gaol 2/4/1866; removed to Mountjoy 27/4/1866; discharged on bail 3/10/1866 |
| Barry, David | 24/2/1866 | Sub-Inspector, Kilfinane | Farmer's son Ballyshanakin (Kilfinane), Co. Limerick; 'Organiser, Mt Russell' | F2 | Released on bail |

| Name | Date of Issue of Warrant/ Date of Arrest | To Whom Issued | Details | Warrant/ File No. | Where Detained and What Action Taken |
|------|------|------|------|------|------|
| Barry, John O'Gorman Aged 21 | 26/2/1866 | Superinten-dent Ryan, Dublin | Stonecutter, 3 Harold's Cross, Dublin; native of Rathkeale; returned American | 3682 | Kilmainham gaol; discharged on condition of returning to America 17/7/1866 |
| Bradley, Daniel Aged 18 | 16/3/1866 (already in custody; arrested 6/3/1866); re-arrested 6/3/1867 | Sub-Inspector, Kilfinane | Draper's assistant, Kilmaniville, Kilmallock, Co. Limerick | F480 F1123 C. No. 7473 | Limerick gaol 2/4/1866; Mountjoy 15/6/1866; discharged on bail 2/7/1866; Limerick gaol, sentenced to ten years' penal servitude at Limerick special commission 11/6/1867; transported to Australia |
| Brazill, Matthew | 23/2/1866 | Sub-Inspector, Kilfinane | Land surveyor, native of Kilfinane, Co. Limerick; 'Seen with Captain Dunne' | 3377 | Warrant not executed, 'Suspect fled to America' |
| Breen, Peter Aged 19 | 12/3/1866 (first arrested 25/9/1865; committed for trial 16/10/1865) | (Sub-Inspector, Killarney) Governor, Tralee gaol | Post office clerk, Killarney, Co. Kerry | 4629 F1013 | Tralee gaol 2/10/1865; not tried; discharged for America 4/5/1866 |
| Brennan, Matthew Aged 24 | 22/2/1866 | Governor, Limerick gaol | Publican and grocer, Patrick Street, Limerick City | 3392 | Limerick gaol; discharged on bail 12/4/1866 |
| Brown, Thomas | 14/5/1866 | Governor, Limerick gaol | National teacher, Ballingarry, Co. Limerick | 9521 | Papers sent to the attorney-general 16/5/1866 |

| Name | Date of Issue of Warrant/ Date of Arrest | To Whom Issued | Details | Warrant/ File No. | Where Detained and What Action Taken |
|---|---|---|---|---|---|
| Burke, Dennis F. Aged 25 | 17/2/1866 | Superinten-dent Ryan, Dublin | Commercial traveller, 33 Mount Pleasant Square, Dublin; native of Limerick; Colonel in the American army | 3018 | Kilmainham gaol; removed to Mountjoy 23/3/1866; discharged for America 3/8/1866 |
| Burke, Edmond | 5/6/1866 | Sub-Inspector, Cappamore | 'No trade', Kilteely, Co. Limerick | | Limerick gaol 8/6/1867; discharged on bail 13/7/1867 |
| Burke, John | 22/2/1866 | Sub-Inspector, Limerick | Baker, John's Square, Limerick City | 3392 | Warrant suspended, no action taken |
| Butler, Whitwell Aged 21 | 22/3/1867 | Governor, Tralee gaol | Apprentice to Edward Murphy, attorney, Tralee, Co. Kerry; 'Seditious language and treasonable conduct' | | Tralee gaol; discharged on bail at Tralee petty sessions 29/3/1867 |
| Carmody, John | 15/1/1868 | Governor, Limerick gaol | Butter buyer, Anne Street, Limerick City | | Limerick gaol; discharged on bail 13/3/1868 |
| Carty, James | 22/2/1866 | Sub-Inspector, Limerick | At Railway lay-bye, Limerick | | Warrant suspended, no action taken |
| Casey, Maurice Aged 20 | 24/2/1866 | Sub-Inspector, Rathkeale | Whitesmith, Rathkeale, Co. Limerick | F3 3846 | Limerick gaol 2/4/1866; discharged on bail 20/6/1866 |
| Casey, Robert Aged 29 | 24/2/1866 | Sub-Inspector, Rathkeale | Surveyor and acting master of Rathkeale Union Workhouse; 'Arrested twice while on bail – just as bad as ever' | F3 3846 No. 11257 | Limerick gaol 2/4/1866; removed to Mountjoy 9/6/1866; discharged on bail 1/10/1866 |

| Name | Date of Issue of Warrant/ Date of Arrest | To Whom Issued | Details | Warrant/ File No. | Where Detained and What Action Taken |
|---|---|---|---|---|---|
| Cleary, John | 2/4/1867 | Sub-Inspector, Athlone | Labourer; native of Listowel, Co. Kerry | F3402 | Roscommon gaol 6/4/1867; discharged 5/5/1867 |
| Cleary, Joseph Aged 23 | 17/2/1866 (already in custody) | Superintendent Ryan, Dublin | Clerk, 20 Cullinswood, Dublin; native of Limerick, returned American | 3018 | Kilmainham 11/2/1866; discharged for America 26/5/1866 |
| Cleary, Timothy | 14/5/1867 (already in custody; arrested 24/4/1867) | Sub-Inspector, Limerick | Farmer's son Bulgaden, Co. Limerick | 8514 | Limerick gaol 25/4/1867; discharged on bail 27/8/1867 |
| Clifford, John | 14/3/1667 | Governor, Cork gaol | Labourer; native of Limerick | | Discharged |
| Collins, William Aged 20 | 18/2/1867 | Superintendent Ryan, Dublin | Draper's assistant, 27 Lower Sackville St, Dublin; native of Killarney, Co. Kerry | 6567 | Kilmainham gaol; discharged 21/5/1867 |
| Condon, Maurice Aged 21 | 26/2/1866 | Governor, Limerick gaol | Farmer's son, Newcastle West, Co. Limerick | F899 | Limerick gaol; discharged 21/4/1866 |
| Connell, James | 5/6/1867 (already in custody; arrested 30/3/1867) | Governor, Limerick gaol | Labourer, Hospital, Co. Limerick; 'One of the party who attacked Kilteely barracks' | 9814 | Limerick gaol 30/3/1867; discharged on bail 13/8/1867 |
| Connor, John D. | 21/12/1867 | Sub-Inspector, Killarney, and Governor, Tralee gaol | Draper's clerk, High Street, Killarney, Co. Kerry | 21757 823R | Tralee gaol; removed to Mountjoy 29/1/1868; released on bail 1/5/1868 |

| Name | Date of Issue of Warrant/ Date of Arrest | To Whom Issued | Details | Warrant/ File No. | Where Detained and What Action Taken |
|---|---|---|---|---|---|
| Cooke (or Coote), Captain | 22/2/1866 | Sub-Inspector, Limerick | Officer in the American army | 3392 | Warrant not executed |
| Corbet, Nicholas Aged 27 | 22/2/1866; re-arrested 6/7/1867 | Limerick | Writing clerk at the Chamber of Commerce, William Street, Limerick City; native of New-townmahon, Co. Limerick | 3391 No. 8142 | Limerick gaol 2/4/1866; removed to Mountjoy 27/4/1866; discharged on bail 17/9/1866; discharged on bail 19/3/1868 |
| Cormack, Roger | 15/6/1867 (already in custody; arrested 15/4/1867) | Governor, Limerick gaol | Small farmer and shoemaker Cullen, Co. Limerick | | Limerick gaol; discharged on bail 13/8/1867 |
| Costello, Thomas M. Aged 26 | 17/2/1866 | Superinten-dent Ryan, Dublin | 19 Palmerston Place, Dublin; native of Limerick; officer in the American army | 3108 | Kilmainham gaol; discharged for America 21/5/1866 |
| Cussin, Thomas | 28/9/1867 | County Inspector, Louth | Shoemaker; native of Limerick | | Dundalk gaol; discharged 16/10/1867 |
| Daly, Cornelius Aged 19 | 22/2/1866 | Governor, Limerick gaol | Bookmaker in hardware establishment, Thomas Street, Limerick City | 3392 No. 8794 | Limerick gaol; removed to Mountjoy 12/5/1866; discharged on bail 28/7/1866 |
| Daly, Thomas Aged 21 | 13/3/1867 | Governor, Limerick gaol | Tailor, Kilmallock, Co. Limerick | 7487 | Limerick gaol; tried and sentenced to five years' penal servitude at the Limerick special commission 15/6/1867; transported to Australia |

| Name | Date of Issue of Warrant/ Date of Arrest | To Whom Issued | Details | Warrant/ File No. | Where Detained and What Action Taken |
|------|------------------------------------------|----------------|---------|-------------------|--------------------------------------|
| Dee, William Aged 27 | 28/3/1866 | Sub-Inspector, Cappamore | 'Farmed with his brother', Kilnagoneeny, Oola, Co. Limerick | F653 No. 11257 | Limerick gaol 2/4/1866; removed to Mountjoy 9/6/1866; discharged on bail 20/7/1866 |
| Devanny, Patrick Aged 20 | 24/2/1866 (already in custody; arrested 19/2/1866) | Governor, Limerick gaol | Labourer, Meanus/Bruff, Co. Limerick; former soldier in the American army | F4 No. 8142 | Limerick gaol 2/4/1866; removed to Mountjoy 27/4/1866; discharged for America 27/6/1866 |
| Dillon, Edward (aka Edward Dillane) | 14/5/1866 (arrested 1/1/1867; first arrested October 1865) | Governor, Limerick gaol | Mahoonagh (Castlemahon); former national teacher in Tarbert, Co. Kerry | 9521 | Papers sent to the attorney-general 16/5/1866; discharged 27/12/1866; Limerick gaol 11/2/1867; discharged on bail 17/9/1867 |
| Dobbyn, John Aged 22 | 19/5/1866 | Sub-Inspector, Listowel | Agent for Tweed company; arrested in Listowel, Co. Kerry; 'No fixed residence' (native of Newry, Co. Down) | F1035 | Tralee gaol; discharged on bail 3/6/1866 |
| Donegan, Owen | 25/3/1867 | Sub-Inspector, Kilfinane | Car driver for O'Sullivan's Hotel, Kilmallock, Co. Limerick | 3837 | Limerick gaol; discharged on bail 9/7/1867 |
| Donnellan, Francis Aged 27 | 22/2/1866; arrested 5/3/1866 | Governor, Limerick gaol | Publican, Thomondgate, and clerk in Russell's Stores, Limerick City | 3392 No. 8142 | Limerick gaol 2/4/1866; removed to Mountjoy 27/4/1866; discharged on bail 24/8/1866 |

| Name | Date of Issue of Warrant/ Date of Arrest | To Whom Issued | Details | Warrant/ File No. | Where Detained and What Action Taken |
|------|------|------|------|------|------|
| Dowling, Michael Aged 15 | 12/3/1866 | Governor, Limerick gaol | Farmer's son, Mahoonagh, Co. Limerick | F899 | Limerick gaol; discharged on bail 15/6/1866 |
| Dowling, Patrick Aged 64 | 12/3/1866 | Governor, Limerick gaol | Small farmer Mahoonagh, Co. Limerick | F899 | Limerick gaol; discharged on bail 10/5/1866 |
| Dowling, Patrick Junior Aged 18 | 12/3/1866 | Governor, Limerick gaol | Small farmer's son, Mahoonagh, Co. Limerick | F899 | Limerick gaol; discharged on bail 15/6/1866 |
| Duane, Murty (aka Murty Devine) Aged 22 | 12/3/1867 (already in custody; first arrested 19/2/1867) | Sub-Inspector, Listowel | Shoemaker, Tarbert, Co. Kerry | | Tralee gaol; discharged on bail 15/5/1867 (discharged on bail 4/3/1867) |
| FitzGerald, James Aged 21 | 22/2/1867 | Governor, Tralee gaol | Driver of mail car, Cahersiveen, Co. Kerry | | Tralee gaol; removed to Richmond bridewell; removed to Naas gaol July 1867; tried under the Whiteboy Act 1765 at Tralee summer assizes 26/7/1867; acquitted 10/8/1867 |
| FitzGibbon, Maurice Aged 19 | 6/3/1867 | Sub-Inspector, Kilfinane | Clerk in O'Sullivan's Hotel, Kilmallock, Co. Limerick; native of Bulgaden, Co. Limerick | C. No. 7484 | Limerick gaol; tried and sentenced to five years' penal servitude at the Limerick special commission 15/6/1867; transported to Australia |
| Fleming, Robert Aged 18 | 12/3/1866 (first arrested 25/8/1865; committed for trial 21/9/1865) | (Sub-Inspector, Killarney) Governor, Tralee gaol | Clerk in the state solicitor's office, Killarney, Co. Kerry | 5053 F1013 | Tralee gaol 2/10/1865; not tried, discharged for America 15/5/1867 |

| Name | Date of Issue of Warrant/ Date of Arrest | To Whom Issued | Details | Warrant/ File No. | Where Detained and What Action Taken |
|------|------|------|------|------|------|
| Flynn, William | 22/2/1866 | County Inspector, Tralee | Carpenter, Tralee, Co. Kerry; supposed to be an officer in the American army | | Warrant suspended, no action taken |
| Foley, John | 12/12/1867 | Governor, Cork gaol | Blacksmith, Sneem, Co. Kerry | | Cork gaol (no report) |
| Foley, Michael Aged 20 | 22/2/1866 | County Inspector, Tralee | Nailer, Cahersiveen, Co. Kerry | 3841 | Tralee gaol; removed to Richmond bridewell; removed to Naas gaol; tried under the Whiteboy Act 1765 at Kerry summer assizes 26/7/1867; acquitted 8/8/1867 |
| Frewhan, Thomas Aged 22 | 12/6/1867 | Governor, Waterford gaol | Plumber and gasfitter; native of Limerick; *Erin's Hope* prisoner | | Waterford gaol; discharged for America 3/1/1868 |
| Gallivan, John Aged 19 | 22/3/1866; arrested 9/3/1866 (first arrested 2/9/1865; committed for trial 21/9/1865) | Sub-Inspector, Killarney | Attorney's clerk Killarney, Co. Kerry | F2682 | Tralee gaol; discharged on bail 29/4/1867 (discharged 16/9/1866) |
| Garde, Thomas Aged 30 | 13/2/1867; committed for trial | Governor, Tralee gaol | Carpenter, Killarney | F2682 | Tralee gaol; removed to Richmond bridewell; not tried, discharged on bail 24/7/1867 |

| Name | Date of Issue of Warrant/ Date of Arrest | To Whom Issued | Details | Warrant/ File No. | Where Detained and What Action Taken |
|---|---|---|---|---|---|
| Gibbons, Henry Aged 24 | 19/2/1866 | Superinten- dent Ryan, Dublin | Carpenter, 3 Cuffe's Lane, Dublin and Birkenhead; native of Tralee, Co. Kerry | | Mountjoy gaol 19/2/1866; discharged for England 27/9/1866 |
| Golden, John (aka John Goulding) Aged 23 | 22/7/1867 (already in custody; arrested in Cobh, Co. Cork 19/7/1867) | Governor, Tralee gaol | Farmer's son Cahersiveen, Co. Kerry | 7546 | Tralee gaol; tried and sentenced to five years' penal servitude at the Kerry assizes 8/8/1867; transported to Australia |
| Griffin, Thomas Aged 24 | 22/7/1867 (already in custody; arrested in Cobh, Co. Cork 19/7/1867) | Governor, Tralee gaol | Labourer and dancing master, Glenbeigh, Co. Kerry | | Tralee gaol; tried under the Whiteboy Act of 1765 at Kerry summer assizes 27/7/1867; acquitted 8/8/1867 |
| Grogan, Michael Aged 20 | 27/3/1867 (arrested in Cobh, Co. Cork) | Sub- Inspector, Kilfinane | Farmer's son, Kilteely, Co. Limerick | | Limerick gaol; tried and sentenced at the Limerick special commission to two years with hard labour 18/6/1867 |
| Harnett, Michael P. | 3/7/1866 | Sub- Inspector, Newcastle | Abbeyfeale, Co. Limerick; former sailor in the American navy | F1136 | Warrant not executed at the time |
| Harnett, Thomas Aged 25 | 9/3/1866 (already in custody; arrested 24/2/1866) | Sub- Inspector, Newcastle | 'Farmer', Newcastle West, Co. Limerick | F208 – 374 | Limerick gaol 2/4/1866; discharged on bail 30/4/1866 |
| Hartigan, Patrick | 5/4/1867 | Sub- Inspector, Limerick | Kilnaniarla, Co. Limerick | | Warrant not executed at the time; suspect sailed for America 8/4/1867 |

| Name | Date of Issue of Warrant/ Date of Arrest | To Whom Issued | Details | Warrant/ File No. | Where Detained and What Action Taken |
|---|---|---|---|---|---|
| Harvey, David (aka David Healy) Aged 22 | 28/2/1866 | Governor, Mountjoy gaol | Labourer, 6 Exchequer St, Dublin; native of Newpallas, Co. Limerick | Vol. 1 509 | Mountjoy gaol 20/2/1866; discharged 24/11/1866, 'His friends to take care of him' |
| Hassett, Michael Aged 30 | 22/2/1866 | Governor, Limerick gaol | Publican, Bridge St, and clerk in Russell's Stores, Limerick City | 3392 No. 8142 | Limerick gaol 2/4/1866; removed to Mountjoy 27/4/1866; discharged on bail 22/8/1866 |
| Hayes, Michael Aged 22 | 27/2/1867 | Governor, Limerick gaol | Baker, 28 William St, Limerick City; 'Associate of Col. Byron and Cpt Dunne' | F2470 | Limerick gaol; discharged on bail 3/5/1868 |
| Healy, Cornelius Aged 30 | 19/2/1866 | County Inspector, Tralee | Native of Kenmare, Co. Kerry; captain in the Union army | | Discharged 7/3/1866 |
| Healy, James | 16/5/1867 | Sub-Inspector, Kilfinane | Clerk, Tullyglass, Co. Limerick | | Maryborough gaol (Portlaoise); discharged 1/8/1867 |
| Healy, James | 7/3/1867 | Sub-Inspector, Kilfinane | Gunner, 13th Brigade Royal Artillery; native of Co. Limerick | | Limerick gaol; court-martialled for 'Desertion and Sedition' 3/4/1867; two years hard labour, discharged with ignominy |
| Healy, John | 15/2/1867; arrested 21/2/1867 | Sub-Inspector, Limerick | Wine merchant, Henry Street, Limerick City; returned American | F2545 | Limerick gaol 25/2/1867; discharged for America 18/6/1867 |
| Healy, John Aged 24 | 9/3/1867 (first arrested 2/9/1865); re-arrested 22/3/1867 | Sub-Inspector, Killarney | Milesman on the railway, Killarney, Co. Kerry | F2682 | Tralee gaol; discharged 16/9/1865; discharged on bail 6/5/1867 |

| Name | Date of Issue of Warrant/ Date of Arrest | To Whom Issued | Details | Warrant/ File No. | Where Detained and What Action Taken |
|---|---|---|---|---|---|
| Healy, J. J. | 21/12/1867 | Sub-Inspector, Killarney | Grocer's assistant, Henn Street, Killarney, Co. Kerry | 21757 992R | Tralee gaol; removed to Mountjoy 5/2/1868; released on bail 4/3/1868 |
| Henessey, Dennis Aged 21 | 6/3/1867 | Sub-Inspector, Kilfinane | Carpenter, Kilmallock, Co. Limerick | C. No. 7483 | Limerick gaol; tried and sentenced at the Limerick Special Commission to seven years' penal servitude 13/6/1867; transported to Australia |
| Hickey, Thomas Aged 35 | 23/2/1866 | Governor, Limerick gaol | Carpenter, Russell's Mills, Limerick City | 7899 No. 8142 | Limerick gaol; removed to Mountjoy 27/4/1866; discharged 17/8/1866 |
| Hogan, James Aged 55 | 20/5/1867 | Governor, Limerick gaol | National teacher Kilteely, Co. Limerick; 'Kilteely barracks attack' | F3779 | Limerick gaol; discharged on bail 5/3/1868 |
| Hogan, Martin Aged 29 | 28/3/1867 | Governor, Mountjoy gaol | Military prisoner; native of Limerick | 7306 | Tried by court-martial 21/8/1867; sentenced to life imprisonment, transported to Australia |
| Hogan, Patrick Aged 22 | 22/2/1866 | Governor, Limerick gaol | Shopman in Revington's, George's St, Limerick City | 3392 No. 8142 | Limerick gaol 2/4/1866; removed to Mountjoy 27/4/1866; discharged for America 27/7/1866 |

| Name | Date of Issue of Warrant/ Date of Arrest | To Whom Issued | Details | Warrant/ File No. | Where Detained and What Action Taken |
|------|------|------|------|------|------|
| Horgan, Martin Aged 24 | 28/3/1867 | Sub-Inspector, Bruff | Shoemaker and butcher, Bruff, Co. Limerick | 51619 | Limerick gaol; removed to Mountjoy 4/10/1867; discharged 2/4/1868 |
| Howard, Timothy Aged 26 | 8/3/1866 (already in custody; arrested 21/2/1866) | Governor, Limerick gaol | Dealer in cattle medicines, Rockhill, Ballingarry, Co. Limerick | F3 No. 8142 | Limerick gaol 2/4/1866; removed to Mountjoy 27/4/1866; discharged on bail 28/8/1866 |
| Joyce, Thomas Aged 22 | 9/3/1866 (arrested with 25 others, Slattery's of Cork Hill) | Superinten-dent Ryan, Dublin | Tailor, 4 Cuffe St, Dublin; native of Limerick | 4660 No. 15130 | Richmond bridewell 9/3/1866; Mountjoy gaol 13/3/1866; removed to Belfast gaol 16/8/1866; released on bail 8/10/1866 |
| Kearns, John Francis Aged 29 | 15/3/1867 | Governor, Cork gaol | Compositor; native of Limerick | | Tried and sentenced to fourteen years' penal servitude at the Cork special commission 2/8/1867 |
| Laud, George | 19/2/1866 | County Inspector, Tralee | Foreman in gunsmith's shop, Tralee, Co. Kerry | | Warrant suspended, no action taken |
| Lawler, Joseph Henry Aged 24 | 21/2/1867 (first arrested 17/2/1866) | (Super-intendent Ryan) Sub-Inspector, Limerick | Cigarmaker, 25 Ranelagh Rd, Dublin and Henry St, Limerick; returned American | No. 16727 | (Kilmainham gaol; Mountjoy gaol 8/3/1866; discharged for America 17/11/1866); Limerick gaol; re-moved to Mount-joy 30/9/1867; removed to Cork gaol 15/4/1868; discharged for America 22/4/1868 |

| Name | Date of Issue of Warrant/ Date of Arrest | To Whom Issued | Details | Warrant/ File No. | Where Detained and What Action Taken |
|---|---|---|---|---|---|
| Leahy, John Aged 24 | 11/6/1866 (already in custody); arrested 7/3/1866 | Governor, Limerick gaol | Farmer's son, Killeedy, Co. Limerick | 11331 | Limerick gaol; removed to Mountjoy 11/6/1866; discharged on bail 11/9/1866 |
| Leane, Patrick Aged 20 | 26/2/1866 | Sub-Inspector, Killarney | Farmer, Castleisland, Co. Kerry; former soldier in the American army | F101. 4921 | Tralee gaol; discharged on bail and promise to leave Ireland 19/4/1866 |
| Lee, Daniel Aged 19 | 12/6/1867 | Governor, Waterford gaol | Bootmaker, New York; native of Castleconnell, Co. Limerick; *Erin's Hope* prisoner | 11091 No. 10491 | Waterford gaol; removed to Mountjoy 14/6/1867; removed to Kilmainham 11/7/1867; removed to Sligo gaol 25/2/1868; discharged for America 6/5/1868 |
| Leslie, Francis (aka Eugene O'Shea) Aged 42 | 17/2/1866 | Superintendent Ryan, Dublin | 'Gentleman', 64 Phibsboro Road, Dublin; native of Tralee; former soldier in the American army | 3018 | Kilmainham gaol 23/2/1866; removed to Mountjoy gaol 8/3/1866; discharged for America 15/9/1866 |
| Leonard, Patrick | 7/12/1866 (arrested on suspicion 20/2/1866) | Sub-Inspector, Dunleer, Co. Louth | Lieutenant-Colonel in the American army; said to be a native of Listowel, Co. Kerry | F1667 | Absconded to America after the rising, (subsequently discharged) |

| Name | Date of Issue of Warrant/ Date of Arrest | To Whom Issued | Details | Warrant/ File No. | Where Detained and What Action Taken |
|---|---|---|---|---|---|
| Leonard, William, (aka John Hearn) Aged 21 | 17/3/1866 (already in custody as John Hearn, arrested as William Leonard 21/6/1867) | Superinten-dent Ryan, Dublin | Groom, Francis Street, Dublin; native of Listowel, Co. Kerry | C. No. 7478 | Richmond bridewell 6/3/1866; removed to Kilmainham 23/3/1866; discharged for England 25/8/1866 (Mountjoy 21/6/1867; discharged into military custody June 1867; sentenced to five years' penal servitude 27/4/1867) |
| Looney, Joseph Aged 19 | 2/9/1865 | Governor, Tralee gaol | Gardener, Killarney, Co. Kerry | | Tralee gaol; discharged 16/9/1866 |
| Luby, William | 19/2/1866 | County Inspector, Tralee | Tralee, Co. Kerry; Captain in the American army, 'Associates with Fenians' | | Warrant suspended, no action taken |
| Lundon, William Aged 28 | 20/5/1867 | Sub-Inspector, Cappamore | 'Classical teacher', now teaching in the national school Kilteely, Co. Limerick | No. 16727 | Limerick gaol 22/5/1866; removed to Mountjoy 30/8/1867; discharged on bail 28/5/1868 |
| Lyddy, Daniel (aka Daniel Ferguson) Aged 25 | 22/2/1866 | County Inspector, Limerick | Victualler and butter merchant, 72 William St, Limerick; returned American | F3166 No. 16727 | Limerick gaol; removed to Mountjoy 30/9/1867; discharged for America 11/3/1868 |
| Lyddy, Patrick | 9/3/1866 | Superinten-dent Ryan, Dublin | Dublin and 72 William St, Limerick | 3392 | Warrant suspended, no action taken |

| Name | Date of Issue of Warrant/ Date of Arrest | To Whom Issued | Details | Warrant/ File No. | Where Detained and What Action Taken |
|------|------|------|------|------|------|
| Lynch, Dennis Aged 25 | 19/2/1867 (arrested in Tarbert) | Sub-Inspector, Listowel | Cabinet turner, Tralee, Co. Kerry; former bugler in the Kerry militia | No. 16727 | Tralee gaol 20/2/1867; discharged on bail 18/3/1867 |
| Lynch, Thomas Aged 26 | 8/12/1866 | Sub-Inspector, Bantry, and Governor, Cork gaol | Draper, Bantry, Co. Cork; native of Glenflesk, Killarney, Co. Kerry | No. 12,590 | Cork gaol 11/2/1867; removed to Mountjoy 10/3/1867; discharged on bail 31/7/1867 |
| McCarthy, Daniel Aged 24 | 2/4/1866 | Superinten-dent Ryan, Dublin | Labourer, 4 Luke Street, Dublin; formerly 4 Finsbury Sq., London; native of Tralee, Co. Kerry | | Richmond bridewell; discharged for London 25/7/1866 |
| McCarthy, Florence Aged 24 | 26/2/1866 | Sub-Inspector, Killarney | Timber merchant, Killarney, Co. Kerry; former soldier in the American army | F101 | 'Decamped at the time of the arrests in Killarney September 1865'; Tralee gaol 6/3/1866; discharged on bail 23/4/1866 |
| McCoy, Patrick | 4/12/1866 | Sub-Inspector, Glin | 'Assisted his mother in the management of her two or three farms', Curraghmore, Loghill, Co. Limerick | F1835 | Detained by the Dublin Metropolitan Police; removed to Mountjoy 8/12/1866; discharged on bail 29/12/1866 |
| McDonnell, James Aged 21 | 27/2/1867 | Sub-Inspector, Limerick | Clerk in the market, Wickham St, Limerick City; 'Believed to have been involved in attack on Emly barracks' in Co. Tipperary | F2633 No. 16727 | Limerick gaol 4/3/1867; removed to Mountjoy 30/8/1867; discharged on bail 11/4/1868 |

| Name | Date of Issue of Warrant/ Date of Arrest | To Whom Issued | Details | Warrant/ File No. | Where Detained and What Action Taken |
|------|------|------|------|------|------|
| McDonnell, Thomas Aged 36 | 6/3/1866 (first arrested 25/9/1865) | Sub-Inspector, Rathkeale | Slater, Ballingarry | 3466 No. 11257 | Limerick gaol 2/4/1866; removed to Mountjoy 9/6/1866; discharged on bail 17/9/1866 |
| McElliot, James | 20/12/1866 | Sub-Inspector, Tralee | | | Cork gaol (no further report) |
| McGrath, William Aged 23 | 17/2/1866 | Superinten-dent Ryan, Dublin | Model lodging house, Marlborough St; native of Limerick; former soldier in the American army | 3018 | Kilmainham gaol 23/3/1866; discharged for America 24/8/1866 |
| McMahon, Charles Aged 49 | 28/2/1866 | Governor, Tralee gaol | Farmer and former policeman, Tralee, Co. Kerry | | Discharged 8/3/1866 |
| McMahon, Michael | 1/3/1867 (already in custody; arrested 15/2/1867) | Sub-Inspector, Limerick | Engineer, Thomondgate, Limerick City | | Limerick gaol 15/3/1867; discharged on bail 15/5/1867 |
| McMahon, Patrick | 4/12/1866 | Sub-Inspector, Glin | 'Nephew of Mrs McCoy and assisted her in farming', Curraghmore, Loghill, Co. Limerick; former soldier in the American army | 1835 | Detained by the Dublin Metropolitan Police; removed to Mountjoy 8/12/1866; discharged on bail 7/2/1867 |
| Mannix, John Aged 26 | 20/7/1867 (arrested in Tarbert March 1867) | Governor, Tralee gaol | Plasterer, Killarney, Co. Kerry | | (Warrant not executed at the time) Tralee gaol; discharged 1/4/1867 |

| Name | Date of Issue of Warrant/ Date of Arrest | To Whom Issued | Details | Warrant/ File No. | Where Detained and What Action Taken |
|------|------|------|------|------|------|
| Moloney, Thomas | 24/5/1866; arrested 29/11/1866 | Superintendent Ryan and Governor, Mountjoy gaol | Shop assistant, ships' chandlers and ironmongers; 'lately pawnbroker's clerk in Cornwallis St, Limerick'; living at 10 Abbey St, Dublin | 3391 No. 8142 | (Warrant not executed – suspect fled Limerick) Detained by the Dublin Metropolitan Police, Mountjoy gaol 3/12/1866; discharged on bail 15/5/1867 |
| Moriarty, Bartholomew Aged 18 | 2/4/1867 | Governor, Cork gaol | Stonemason, Millstreet, Co. Cork; native of Rathmore, Co. Kerry | C. No. 7469 | Cork gaol; tried and sentenced to seven years' penal servitude at Cork special commission 2/5/1867; transported to Australia |
| Moriarty, Mortimer Aged 27 | 13/2/1867 | Sub-Inspector, Killarney and Governor, Tralee gaol | Cahersiveen, Co. Kerry; former soldier in the American army | 7543 | Tralee gaol; removed to Naas gaol; tried and sentenced to ten years' penal servitude at the Kerry assizes 8/8/1867 |
| Morony, Thomas Aged 23 | 22/2/1866 | Governor, Limerick gaol | Shop assistant at Purcell's drapers, Limerick City; native of Kilteely, Co. Limerick | 3391 | Limerick gaol; discharged on bail 24/7/1866 |
| Murnan, Simon Aged 24 | 21/3/1866 | Superintendent Ryan, Dublin | Cabinetmaker, 24 Golden Lane, Dublin; native of Limerick | | Richmond bridewell; removed to Kilmainham 23/6/1866; discharged for Liverpool 31/8/1866 |

| Name | Date of Issue of Warrant/ Date of Arrest | To Whom Issued | Details | Warrant/ File No. | Where Detained and What Action Taken |
|---|---|---|---|---|---|
| Murphy, Daniel Aged 24 | 31/3/1866 | Sub-Inspector, Adare | National teacher, Mainister, Croom, Co. Limerick | 5281 | Limerick gaol 2/4/1866; discharged on bail 3/5/1866 |
| Murphy, David Aged 31 | 22/2/1866 (arrested 24/2/1868) | Superintendent Ryan and Sub-Inspector, Limerick | Attorney's clerk in Mr Fitzgerald's office, Dublin and Limerick; 'Engaged in bringing torpedoes from America' | 3392 | Warrant suspended, 'Suspect fled to London' (Limerick gaol 27/2/1868; discharged on bail 14/7/1868) |
| Murphy, John (aka Michael Murphy) Aged 22 | (12/3/1866) 25/2/1867 | Superintendent Ryan and Sub-Inspector, Limerick | Shoemaker Henry St, Limerick; native of Kilrush, Co. Clare; former clerk in the Fenian headquarters in Union Sq., New York | 4857 No. 16727 | (Warrant not executed – suspect fled to America) Limerick gaol 15/3/1867; removed to Mountjoy 30/9/1867; discharged for America 7/1/1868 |
| Murphy, Martin | 10/12/1866 | Sub-Inspector, Limerick | Foreman sawyer, Mungret Street, Limerick City | R1566 | Limerick gaol 11/12/1866; discharged on bail 18/1/1867 |
| Murphy, Michael | 15/2/1867 | Sub-Inspector, Limerick | 'No trade' | | Limerick gaol, discharged for America 7/1/1868 |
| Murray, John | 17/3/1867; re-arrested 3/3/1868 | Sub-Inspector, Limerick and Governor, Limerick gaol | Journeyman shoemaker, Thomas St, Limerick City; 'Led attack on Ardagh barracks' | | Limerick gaol 6/3/1867; discharged for America 9/4/1868 |

| Name | Date of Issue of Warrant/ Date of Arrest | To Whom Issued | Details | Warrant/ File No. | Where Detained and What Action Taken |
|---|---|---|---|---|---|
| Nagle, David Aged 23 | 2/4/1867 | Sub-Inspector, Charleville | Harnessmaker, Charleville, Co. Cork; native of Listowel, Co. Kerry | F361 | Cork gaol 2/4/1867; removed to Mountjoy 30/4/1867; discharged for America 26/11/1867 |
| Nelson, John Aged 24 | 17/2/1866 | Superintendent Ryan, Dublin | Hatter, City Mansion Hotel, Lower Bridge St, Dublin; native of Limerick; former soldier in the American army | 3018 | Kilmainham gaol; removed to Mountjoy 23/3/1866; discharged for America 25/7/1866 |
| Noonan, Joseph Aged 24 | 8/6/1867 | Governor, Tralee gaol | Builder, Cahersiveen, Co. Kerry; native of Rathcormac, Co. Cork | 7544 | Tralee gaol 15/6/1867; removed to Kilmainham gaol 5/7/1867; sentenced to seven years' penal servitude at the Kerry assizes 24/7/1867; transported to Australia |
| Noonan, Michael Aged 23 | 9/3/1867 | Sub-Inspector, Kilfinane | Cooper, Kilmallock, Co. Limerick; 'Took part in the attack on Kilmallock barracks' | Convict No. 7486 3610 | Limerick gaol; tried for treason at Limerick special commission, sentenced to five years penal servitude 15/6/1867; removed to Millbank Convict Prison 2/7/1867; transported to Australia; released 21/9/1869 |

| Name | Date of Issue of Warrant/ Date of Arrest | To Whom Issued | Details | Warrant/ File No. | Where Detained and What Action Taken |
|------|------|------|------|------|------|
| O'Brien, Bartholomew | 10/12/1866 | Sub-Inspector, Cappamore | Farmer's son, Cappamore, Co. Limerick | F1869 | Warrant not executed, 'Subject left the district' |
| O'Brien, Cornelius Aged 22 | 22/7/1867 (already in custody); arrested in Cobh 19/7/1867 | Governor, Tralee gaol | Farmer's son, Cahersiveen, Co. Kerry | | Tried and acquitted at the Kerry assizes 8/8/1867 |
| O'Brien, John | 10/12/1866 (first arrested 30/11/1866) | Sub-Inspector, Limerick | Baker, Limerick | F1862 | Limerick gaol 11/12/1866 (released on bail); discharged on bail 6/1/1867 |
| O'Brien, Patrick | 24/4/1867; arrested 24/4/1867 | Sub-Inspector, Limerick | Labourer, Kilmallock, Co. Limerick | | Limerick gaol 14/5/1867; discharged on bail 27/9/1867 |
| O'Brien, William (aka William Hogan) Aged 36 | 20/2/1866 | Governor, Mountjoy gaol | Coach trimmer, lodging at 1 Richmond Row (or Redmond's Hill), Dublin; native of Limerick | 3493 | Arrested by the Dublin Metropolitan Police; Mountjoy 23/3/1866; handed over to military escort on 10/4/1866; deserter 5th Dragoon Guards |
| O'Connell, Timothy Aged 24 | 23/4/1867 | Sub-Inspector, Tralee and Governor, Tralee gaol | Boatman, Cahersiveen, Co. Kerry | F 2543 No. 13078 | Tralee gaol 23/4/1867; removed to Mountjoy 11/10/1867; discharged for America 29/10/1867 |
| O'Connell, Thomas Aged 24 | 26/2/1866 | Governor, Limerick gaol | Abbeyfeale, Co. Limerick; former soldier in the Confederate army | F899 No. 8142 | Limerick gaol; removed to Mountjoy 27/4/1866; discharged for America 17/7/1866 |

| Name | Date of Issue of Warrant/ Date of Arrest | To Whom Issued | Details | Warrant/ File No. | Where Detained and What Action Taken |
|---|---|---|---|---|---|
| O'Connor, Henry Aged 24 | 18/2/1867 (first arrested 19/2/1866) | Superintendent Ryan, Dublin | Printer, late of Bristol, 2 Cuffe Lane, Dublin; native of Tralee, Co. Kerry | 3945 | (Discharged for England 17/9/1866) Mountjoy gaol 18/2/1867; removed to Cork gaol 15/4/1868; discharged for America 30/4/1868 |
| O'Connor, John D. | 21/12/1867 | Sub-Inspector, Killarney and Governor, Tralee gaol | Draper's clerk, High Street, Killarney, Co. Kerry | 217 57832R | Tralee gaol; removed to Mountjoy 29/1/1868; released on bail 1/5/1868 |
| O'Connor, John James Aged 25 | 26/2/1866; arrested 19/2/1867 | Sub-Inspector, Cahersiveen | Native of Valentia, Co. Kerry; 'Colonel in command of the Kerry Fenians'; former officer in the American army | F107 | Warrant not executed, suspect fled to England, 'Suspect reported in New York' |
| O'Connor, Patrick Aged 21 | 12/6/1867 | Governor, Waterford gaol | Writing clerk, native of Bruff, Co. Limerick; *Erin's Hope* prisoner | | Waterford gaol; removed to Mountjoy 14/6/1867; removed to Kilmainham 11/7/1867; discharged America 5/3/1868 |
| O'Donoghue, Maurice | 25/12/1866; arrested 18/3/1867 | (Sub-Inspector, Kilfinane) Superintendent Ryan, Dublin | Kilfinane, Co. Limerick | 4717 No. 23323 | (Warrant not executed – suspect sailed for America) Mountjoy gaol; discharged for America 21/12/1867 |

| Name | Date of Issue of Warrant/ Date of Arrest | To Whom Issued | Details | Warrant/ File No. | Where Detained and What Action Taken |
|------|------|------|------|------|------|
| O'Donovan, Edmond Aged 23 | 7/11/1867 (first arrested 26/3/1866) | Governor, Limerick gaol | Medical student (arrested Limerick station); native of Co. Clare | F4668 | Sentenced to six months' imprisonment under Arms Act; discharged from Mountjoy 25/9/1866; discharged for America 20/5/1868 |
| O'Farrell, John O'Rorke | 22/2/1866 | County Inspector, Limerick | Miller | 3392 | Warrant suspended, no action taken |
| O'Grady, Darby | 14/5/1866 | Governor, Limerick gaol | Newcastle West | 9521 | Papers sent to the attorney-general 16/5/1866, no further report |
| O'Grady, John | 10/12/1866 | Superinten- dent Ryan, Dublin | Sailor, 105 Marlborough St, Dublin; native of Limerick; former gunner in the American artillery | | Arrested by the Dublin Metropolitan Police; Mountjoy gaol 10/12/1866; discharged for America 6/7/1867 |
| O'Keeffe, Edward Aged 30 | 5/1/1867 | Superinten- dent Ryan, Dublin | Shoemaker, Essex St, Dublin and Liverpool; native of Duress, Croom, Co. Limerick | | Mountjoy gaol 5/1//1867; discharged for Liverpool 1/4/1868 |
| O'Kelly, John Aged 20 | 12/3/1866 (first arrested 21/9/1865) | Governor, Tralee gaol | 'No trade', Tralee, Co. Kerry | | Tralee gaol 2/4/1866; discharged on bail 19/4/1866 |
| O'Leary, Jeremiah Aged 26 | 31/3/1866 | Sub- Inspector, Adare | National teacher, Croom, Co. Limerick | 5281 | Limerick gaol 2/4/1866; discharged on bail 18/4/1866 |
| O'Neill, John | 22/2/1866 | County Inspector, Limerick | House painter, Limerick City | 3392 | Warrant suspended, no action taken |

| Name | Date of Issue of Warrant/ Date of Arrest | To Whom Issued | Details | Warrant/ File No. | Where Detained and What Action Taken |
|---|---|---|---|---|---|
| O'Reilly, James Aged 22 | 1/3/1867; arrested 22/2/1867 | Sub-Inspector, Tralee | Draper's assistant, Cahersiveen; native of Waterville | C. No. 7544 | (Warrant not executed, subject already in custody) Tralee gaol 4/3/1867; Richmond bridewell 16/3/1867; removed to Naas gaol 10/7/1867; sentenced to seven years' penal servitude at the Kerry summer assizes 24/7/1867; transported to Australia |
| O'Rourke, James | 14/5/1866 | Governor, Limerick gaol | Bruff, Co. Limerick | 9521 | Papers sent to the attorney-general 16/5/1866, no further report |
| O'Rourke, Phillip Aged 20 | 14/3/1867 | Sub-Inspector, Killarney | Labourer, Muckross, Co. Kerry; returned American | F2979 | Tralee gaol 22/3/1867; discharged for America 18/6/1867 |
| O'Shea, John Aged 38 | 2/7/1866 | Sub-Inspector, Tralee | Shipwright, Tralee, Co. Kerry; American citizen | F1139 | Tralee gaol; discharged on bail 11/8/1866 |
| O'Shea, John Aged 40 | 22/7/1866 | Governor, Tralee gaol | Farmer, Cahersiveen | | Tralee gaol; Richmond bridewell 16/3/1867; discharged 13/6/1867 |

| Name | Date of Issue of Warrant/ Date of Arrest | To Whom Issued | Details | Warrant/ File No. | Where Detained and What Action Taken |
|------|------|------|------|------|------|
| O'Sullivan, William Aged 58 | 9/3/1867 | Sub-Inspector, Kilfinane | Hotel-keeper, Kilmallock | No. 16014 C. No. 7485 | Limerick gaol 5/3/1867; sentenced to five years' penal servitude at the Limerick special commission 17/6/1867; removed to Mountjoy 12/9/1867; discharged on condition that he does not visit Co. Limerick 23/3/1868 |
| Pegum, John | 22/2/1866 | County Inspector, Limerick | Carpenter, Connolly's Range, Limerick | 3392 | Warrant suspended, no action taken |
| Pender, John | 10/12/1866 | Sub-Inspector, Limerick | Pawnbroker's clerk, Limerick | F1957 | Limerick gaol, discharged on bail 8/2/1867 |
| Power, Edward | 3/12/1866 | Superintendent Ryan, Dublin | Apothecary, 3 Upper Temple St, Dublin; native of Tralee, Co. Kerry | 21763 7389 | Arrested by the Dublin Metropolitan Police; Mountjoy gaol 4/12/1866; removed to Kilmainham 1/2/1867; sentenced to fifteen years' penal servitude at the Dublin special commission 14/2/1867 |
| Power, James Aged 21 | 23/2/1866 | Governor, Limerick gaol | Ironmonger's clerk, Mulgrave St, Limerick City; living at Denmark St, Limerick City | F899 No. 8142 | Limerick gaol 20/2/1866; removed to Mountjoy 27/4/1866; discharged on bail 7/7/1866 |

| Name | Date of Issue of Warrant/ Date of Arrest | To Whom Issued | Details | Warrant/ File No. | Where Detained and What Action Taken |
|---|---|---|---|---|---|
| Power, John | 22/2/1866 | Sub-Inspector, Limerick | Shopman, O'Connor & Morgans, Playhouse Lane, Limerick | 3391 | Warrant suspended, no action taken |
| Quaid, William Aged 27 | 26/2/1866 | Superintendent Ryan, Dublin | Clerk, 32 Harold's Cross, Dublin; native of Rathkeale; returned American | | Kilmainham gaol 23/3/1866; discharged on bail 18/10/1866 |
| Quane, David Aged 29 | 27/2/1866 | Sub-Inspector, Kilfinane | Instructor in agriculture, Ballylanders, Co. Limerick | F156 No. 8794 | Limerick gaol 2/4/1866; remanded to Mountjoy 12/5/1866; discharged on bail 16/7/1866 |
| Reardon, Michael Aged 25 | 9/3/1867 | Sub-Inspector, Kilfinane | Labourer, Kilmallock | | Limerick gaol; sentenced to two years' hard labour at the Limerick special commission 19/6/1867 |
| Reardon, Patrick Aged 20 | 6/3/1867 | Sub-Inspector, Kilfinane | Car driver, Kilmallock, Co. Limerick | C. No. 7474 | Limerick gaol; sentenced to seven years' penal servitude at the Limerick special commission 11/6/1867; transported to Australia |
| Ryan, Jeremiah | 22/2/1866 | Sub-Inspector, Limerick | Post office assistant, Limerick | 3392 | Warrant suspended, no action taken |
| Ryan, Jeremiah (aka Jerry Ryan) Aged 21 | 4/5/1866 | County Inspector, Limerick | Cabinetmaker, Limerick City | F970 | Limerick gaol; discharged for America 29/5/1866 |

| Name | Date of Issue of Warrant/ Date of Arrest | To Whom Issued | Details | Warrant/ File No. | Where Detained and What Action Taken |
|------|------|------|------|------|------|
| Shaw, Jeremiah Aged 23 | 12/3/1866 (first arrested 25/9/1865) | Sub-Inspector, Killarney and Governor, Tralee gaol | Shopman, Killarney | 5053 | Tralee gaol 12/4/1866 (never tried); discharged on condition of leaving Ireland 19/5/1866 |
| Sheahan, Daniel Jeremiah | 1/3/1867 | County Inspector, Tralee | Shop assistant, Killarney | | Tralee gaol 27/6/1867; removed to Mountjoy 3/10/1867; removed to Naas gaol; discharged for America 5/2/1868 |
| Sheahan, John Aged 29 | 24/2/1866; re-arrested 7/3/1867 | Sub-Inspector, Rathkeale | Stone-cutter and publican, Rathkeale; former militia man | F3 – 3846 No. 11257 | Limerick gaol 27/2/1866; removed to Mountjoy 9/6/1866; discharged on bail 13/8/1866; sentenced to seven years' penal servitude at Limerick special commission |
| Sheahan, John | – | Sub-Inspector, Cahersiveen | Cahersiveen | 7842 | Tralee gaol Sentenced to seven years' penal servitude at Tralee summer assizes 24/7/1867 Transported to Australia |
| Sheahan, John (aka John Shiel) Aged 25 | 19/2/1866 | Superinten-dent Ryan, Dublin | Tailor, 2 Cuffe Lane, Dublin; native of Limerick | 3945 | Arrested by the Dublin Metropolitan Police; Mountjoy gaol 19/2/1866; discharged for England 10/11/1866 |

| Name | Date of Issue of Warrant/ Date of Arrest | To Whom Issued | Details | Warrant/ File No. | Where Detained and What Action Taken |
|---|---|---|---|---|---|
| Sheahan, John | 13/3/1867 | Governor, Limerick gaol | Labourer, Bulgaden, Co. Limerick; Private in the West Cork militia | | Sentenced to seven years' penal servitude at the Limerick special commission June 1867; transported to Australia |
| Sheahan, Martin | 21/2/1866 (first arrested 20/9/1865) | Governor, Limerick gaol | Tailor employed by Cannock & Tait's, Limerick | F899 | Limerick gaol 20/2/1866; discharged 25/4/1866 |
| Southwell, Thomas Aged 27 | 5/4/1866 | Sub-Inspector, Rathkeale | Shoemaker, Rathkeale | F674 No. 11257 | Limerick gaol 11/4/1866; removed to Mount-joy 9/6/1866; discharged for America 22/5/1867 |
| Stack, William Moore | 5/12/1866 | Superinten-dent Ryan, Dublin | Law clerk, 12 Portland Place, Dublin; native of Knockanure, Co. Kerry | 32015 7390 | Arrested by the Dublin Metropolitan Police; Mountjoy gaol 10/12/1866; removed to Kilmainham 1/2/1867; sentenced to ten years' penal servitude at the Dublin special commission February 1867 |
| Stinson, James Weytea Aged 30 | 1/3/1866 | Sub-Inspector, Limerick | Printer and compositor; Sergeant in Co. Limerick militia | 4056 No. 8142 | Limerick gaol 2/4/1866; remanded to Mountjoy 27/4/1866; discharged on bail 14/5/1866 |
| Sullivan, Batt | 21/12/1867 | Sub-Inspector, Killarney and Governor, Tralee gaol | Grocer's assistant, New Street, Killarney | | Tralee gaol 24/12/1867; removed to Mountjoy 29/1//1868; discharged on bail 1/5/1868 |

| Name | Date of Issue of Warrant/ Date of Arrest | To Whom Issued | Details | Warrant/ File No. | Where Detained and What Action Taken |
|---|---|---|---|---|---|
| Sullivan, John | 19/2/1866 | County Inspector, Tralee | Claims to have been a soldier in the American army | | Warrant suspended, no action taken |
| Sullivan, Thomas | 19/2/1866 | County Inspector, Tralee | Draper's assistant, The Mall, Tralee, Co. Kerry | | Warrant suspended, no action taken |
| Synan, Daniel Aged 21 | – | Superintendent Ryan, Dublin | Medical student, 1 Synge St, Dublin; native of George's St, Limerick City; 'Arrested at Tallaght' | 1566 R | Kilmainham gaol; Dublin special commission April 1867 |
| Thornhill, Henry Aged 24 | 31/3/1866 | Sub-Inspector, Adare | Croom, Co. Limerick; former soldier in the papal brigade; had been in America | 5281 | Limerick gaol 2/4/1866; discharged on bail 14/4/1866 |
| Vaughan, Daniel Aged 35 | 23/2/1866 | Governor, Limerick gaol | Carpenter, Thomondgate, Limerick; former soldier in the American army | F899 | Limerick gaol 20/2/1866; discharged on bail 4/5/1866 |
| Wall, William Aged 22 | 17/3/1866 (already in custody; arrested 20/2/1866) | Sub-Inspector, Kilfinane | Teacher in the workhouse school, Kilmallock | F480 F296 No. 794 | Limerick gaol 24/2/1866; remanded to Mountjoy 12/5/1866; discharged for America 18/8/1866 |
| Wallace, John Aged 24 | 16/3/1866; arrested 18/6/1866 | Sub-Inspector, Kilfinane | Farmer's son, Kilfinane | F495 | Limerick gaol 18/6/1866; discharged on bail 21/8/1866 |

| Name | Date of Issue of Warrant/ Date of Arrest | To Whom Issued | Details | Warrant/ File No. | Where Detained and What Action Taken |
|---|---|---|---|---|---|
| Walsh, Patrick | 9/3/1867 | Sub-Inspector, Kilfinane | Former clerk in O'Sullivan's Hotel, Kilmallock | 3377 C. No. 7472 | Sentenced to fifteen years' penal servitude at the Limerick special commission 11/6/1867 |
| Walsh, Stephen B. Aged 26 | 23/2/1866 | Sub-Inspector, Kilfinane | Shopkeeper's son, Kilmallock | No. 8794 | Limerick gaol 27/2/1866; removed to Mountjoy 3/5/1866; discharged on bail 4/6/1866 |
| Wheelan, James Aged 55 | 26/3/1866 | Sub-Inspector, Newcastle West | Slater and plasterer | No. 11257 | Limerick gaol 26/3/1866; removed to Mountjoy 9/6/1866; discharged 11/7/1866 |
| Whelston, Thomas Aged 30 | 19/2/1866 | Superinten-dent Ryan, Dublin | Cabinetmaker, 3 Mecklenburg St, Dublin; native of Tralee | No. 3945 | Belfast gaol; removed to Mountjoy gaol 17/2/1866; discharged for Glasgow 14/9/1866 |

# APPENDIX 2

## FENIAN ARRESTS BY COUNTIES OF RESIDENCE

| | | | | | |
|---|---|---|---|---|---|
| Antrim | 37 | Galway | 32 | Monaghan | 3 |
| Armagh | 4 | Kerry | 17 | Queen's County (Offaly) | 10 |
| Carlow | 10 | Kildare | 12 | Roscommon | 20 |
| Cavan | 4 | Kilkenny | 24 | Sligo | 13 |
| Clare | 28 | King's County (Laois) | 4 | Tipperary | 58 |
| Cork | 144 | Leitrim | 9 | Tyrone | 9 |
| Donegal | 4 | Limerick | 65 | Waterford | 31 |
| Down | 4 | Longford | 3 | Westmeath | 20 |
| Dublin | 346 | Louth | 5 | Wexford | 3 |
| Fermanagh | 2 | Mayo | 45 | Wicklow | 8 |

# APPENDIX 3

## GAOLS IN WHICH FENIAN PRISONERS WERE LODGED

| | | | | | |
|---|---|---|---|---|---|
| Armagh | 6 | Galway | 31 | Nenagh | 22 |
| Belfast | 35 | Kilkenny | 22 | Omagh | 10 |
| Carlow | 10 | Kilmainham (Dublin) | 129 | Richmond (Dublin) | 95 |
| Carrick-on-Shannon | 9 | Lifford | 5 | Roscommon | 27 |
| Castlebar | 40 | Limerick | 66 | Sligo | 15 |
| Cavan | 2 | Londonderry | 1 | Tralee | 18 |
| Clonmel | 55 | Longford | 4 | Trim | 6 |
| Cork | 162 | Maryborough (Portlaoise) | 8 | Tullamore | 7 |
| Drogheda | 3 | Monaghan | 3 | Waterford | 49 |
| Dundalk | 4 | Mountjoy (Dublin) | 179 | Wexford | 3 |
| Ennis | 19 | Mullingar | 12 | Wicklow | 10 |
| Enniskillen | 2 | Naas | 8 | | |

# APPENDIX 4

## FENIAN SUSPECTS AND THOSE COMMITTED FOR TRIAL IN LIMERICK AND KERRY

| Name | Address and Occupation | Date of Information or Date and Place of Committal | Date of Release | Remarks from police reports |
|---|---|---|---|---|
| Ahern, Thomas Aged 22 | Horse trainer, Kilmallock, Co. Limerick | Limerick gaol 25/3/1867 | | Sentenced to twelve months for 'Whiteboyism' at the special commission July 1867 |
| Ahern, William | Mason, Limerick City | 27/5/1869 | | 'Reputed Fenian absconded to America' |
| Ambrose, Robert Aged 15 | Farmer's son, Dunganville, Newcastle West, Co. Limerick | Limerick gaol 21/10/1867 | Discharged on bail 4/11/1867 | 'Suspected of being concerned in attack on Ardagh barracks', 'Surrendered to Mr Moriarty RM' |
| Ambrose, Thomas | Farmer's son, Dunganville, Newcastle West, Co. Limerick | Limerick gaol 4/3/1867 | Discharged 22/3/1867 | 'Suspected of being concerned in attack on Ardagh barracks' |
| Baily, Patrick | Ship's carpenter, Francis St, Limerick | Limerick gaol 22/2/1867 | | |
| Barrett, Patrick | Late 64th London Volunteers, Mungret St, Limerick City | | | 'Arrested while drunk. In possession of letter from David Murphy, Fenian centre' |
| Barrett, Patrick Aged 28 | Nailer, Bruree, Co. Limerick | Limerick gaol 6/3/1867; arraigned before Limerick special commission | | 'Took part in the attack on Kilmallock barracks', sentenced to twelve months for 'Whiteboyism' at the special commission July 1867 |
| Beary, Michael | Farmer, Cappamore, Co. Limerick | Limerick gaol 15/3/1867 | Discharged 4/4/1867 | 'Looked upon as a Fenian centre' |

| | | | | |
|---|---|---|---|---|
| Begly, Thomas Aged 19 | Shoemaker, Ballyagran, Co. Limerick | Limerick gaol 4/4/1867 | | 'Took part in the attack on Kilmallock barracks', sentenced to twelve months for 'Whiteboyism' at the special commission July 1867 |
| Benson, George | Shop assistant, Limerick City | Limerick gaol 7/3/1867 | Discharged 3/4/1867 | |
| Bereton, James | Limerick | Arraigned before the Limerick special commission | Discharged | |
| Birmingham, Richard | Farmer's son, Kilfinane | 25/11/1866 | | 'Engaged in making ball cartridge' |
| Bourke, Ned | Rahard, Oola, Co. Limerick | 25/11/1866 | | 'Meetings in house and pikemaking' |
| Bourke, John | Clerk in Limerick City, Caherconlish, Co. Limerick | 30/11/1866 | | '"B" in the movement – active' |
| Bourke, John | Labourer, Boher, Co. Limerick | Limerick gaol 7/3/1867 | Discharged on bail 20/6/1867 | Bailed at the special commission |
| Bourke, Patrick | Athlunkard St, Limerick City | 30/11/1866 | | 'Keeping company with Fenians' |
| Bradshaw, Benjamin | Shoemaker, Limerick City | 25/11/1866 | | 'House of resort for Fenian agents' |
| Bradshaw, Thomas | Carpenter, Cappamore, Co. Limerick | 4/12/1866 | | 'Associates with Fenians' |
| Brazill, Patrick | Manager at O'Callaghan's Tannery; clerk at Todd Burns, Dublin 1871, Sexton St, Limerick City | February 1866 6/10/1871 | | 'Active in acquiring arms 1866', 'Fenian organiser 1869', 'Fenian head centre in Limerick September 1871' |
| Brennan, Patrick | Cooper, Cahersiveen, Co. Kerry | Cahersiveen Bridewell 16/2/1867 | Discharged on bail 23/2/1867 | 'Suspected of taking part in the attack on Kells coastguard station' |
| Bridgeman, Michael (aka Thomas Bridgeman) | Foynes(?), Co. Limerick | Limerick gaol 15/3/1867 | Discharged 2/5/1867 | 'Suspected of taking part in the attack on Ardagh barracks' |

| | | | | |
|---|---|---|---|---|
| Buckley, John | Limerick | | Discharged on bail July 1867 | 'Illegal drilling', bailed at the special commission |
| Burke, John | Small farmer's son, Cappamore, Co. Limerick | 4/11/1866 | | 'Associates with known Fenians' |
| Burke, John | Cullen, Co. Limerick | 1/12/1869 | | 'Fenian captain' 'Very active' |
| Cahill, Edward Aged 26 | Kilteely, Co. Limerick | Arraigned before Limerick special commission | Discharged | 'Suspected of taking part in the attack on Kilteely barracks' |
| Cahill, Richard Aged 21 | Kilteely, Co. Limerick | Arraigned before Limerick special commission | | 'Took part in the attack on Kilteely barracks', sentenced to twelve months for 'Whiteboyism' at the special commission July 1867 |
| Cantillon, Robert Aged 23 | Labourer, Kilmallock, Co. Limerick | Limerick gaol 6/3/1867 | | 'Took part in the attack on Kilmallock barracks', sentenced to twelve months for 'Whiteboyism' at the special commission July 1867 |
| Carroll, John Aged 20 | Tailor, Cappamore, Co. Limerick | (Arraigned before Limerick special commission June 1867) 1/12/1869 | | 'Took part in the attack on Kilteely barracks. Attempted to leave the county at the time of the rising', sentenced to two years for 'Whiteboyism' at the special commission July 1867, 'Captain in Oola, December 1869' |
| Carty, Patrick | Cappamore, Co. Limerick | 7/12/1869 | | 'Fenian suspect' |
| Casey, Daniel | Small farmer's son, Cappamore, Co. Limerick | Arrested 2/4/1867 | Discharged 9/4/1867 | 'Consorts with known Fenians' |

| | | | | |
|---|---|---|---|---|
| Casey, Patrick | Kilnagoneeny, Oola, Co. Limerick | 4/11/1869 | | '"B" or colonel in the Fenians. Bought revolvers and distributed them' |
| Casey, Patrick | Small farmer's son, Cappamore, Co. Limerick | Arrested 2/4/1867 | Discharged 9/4/1867 | 'Consorts with known Fenians', (Centre for Oola 1871) |
| Casey, William | Small farmer's son, Cappamore, Co. Limerick | 4/12/1866 | | 'Consorts with known Fenians' |
| Cashel, John | Labourer, Kilmallock, Co. Limerick | Detained on remand 12/12/1867 | | |
| Clancy, John | Labourer, Limerick | Limerick gaol 11/3/1867 | Discharged 23/3/1867 | |
| Cleary, John Aged 19 | Farmer's son, Bulgaden, Co. Limerick | Limerick gaol 13/3/1867 | Discharged on bail 10/4/1867 | 'Suspected of being concerned in attack on Kilmallock barracks', bailed at the special commission |
| Clifford, John | Labourer, Limerick | Cork City gaol 14/3/1867 | Discharged | |
| Coffey, James | Postmaster, Beaufort, Co. Kerry | | | 'Fenian suspect' |
| Coffey, Jeremiah | Shoemaker, Killarney, Co. Kerry | 21/2/1866 | | 'On bail on the charge of Fenianism' |
| Collins, John | Tailor, Limerick | July 1868 | | 'Former sailor in the American navy' |
| Collins, Patrick Aged 17 | Labourer, Ardagh, Co. Limerick | Limerick gaol 15/4/1867 | Discharged on bail 8/7/1867 | 'Suspected of being concerned in attack on Ardagh barracks', bailed at the special commission |
| Comerford, Isaac | Limerick | August 1869 | | 'Arrested for assault. Active in swearing in Fenians' |
| Condon, John | Labourer, Newcastle West, Co. Limerick | Limerick gaol 13/4/1867 | Discharged on bail 15/6/1867 | |
| Condon, Richard | Former soldier in the British army, Newcastle West, Co. Limerick | 28/11/1868 | | 'Frequents company of Fenians' |

| | | | | |
|---|---|---|---|---|
| Connell, Daniel | Painter, Tralee, Co. Kerry | 18/2/1866 | | 'Constant attender at the Fenian rooms. Reads the new Irish People newspaper' |
| Connell, James | Kilteely, Co. Limerick | 6/6/1867 | Discharged on bail 18/8/1867 | 'Suspected of taking part in the attack on Kilteely barracks' |
| Connell, Michael Aged 21 | Farmer's son, Kilscannell, Ardagh, Co. Limerick | Limerick gaol 27/4/1867 | Discharged on bail 6/7/1867 | 'Suspected of being concerned in attack on Ardagh barracks', bailed at the special commission |
| Connell, Michael | Pensioner of 106th Regiment, native of Limerick | Tullamore gaol 11/4/1867 | Discharged | |
| Connell, Michael | Labourer, Pallaskenry, Co. Limerick | Limerick gaol 15/2/1867 | Discharged on bail 22/3/1867 | Bailed at the special commission |
| Connell, Richard | Ardagh, Co. Limerick | Limerick gaol 9/4/1867 | Discharged | 'Suspected of taking part in the attack on Ardagh barracks' |
| Connery, Patrick | Cooper, Bruff, Co. Limerick | 25/11/1866 | | 'Reckless' 'Associates with Fenians' |
| Connor, James | Tarbert, Co. Kerry | 11/12/1866 | | 'Said to have been sworn in by Garett McMahon' |
| Connor, Michael (aka Michael Daly) | Shop porter, Newcastle West | 25/11/1866 | | 'Out on bail – attending Fenian meetings' |
| Connors, Daniel | Native of Limerick | Ennis gaol July 1867 | Discharged on bail | 'Illegal drilling' |
| Connors, Dennis Aged 19 | Cattle dealer, Kilmallock, Co. Limerick | Limerick gaol 6/3/1867 | | 'Took part in the attack on Kilmallock barracks', sentenced to twelve months for 'Whiteboyism' at the special commission July 1867 |
| Connors, John | Farmer's son, Kilscannell, Coolacappa, Co. Limerick | Limerick gaol 15/3/1867 | Discharged 22/3/1867 | 'Suspected of being concerned in attack on Ardagh barracks' |

| | | | | |
|---|---|---|---|---|
| Connors, Joseph Aged 27 | Farmer's son Kilscannell, Coolacappa, Co. Limerick | Limerick gaol 15/2/1867 | Discharged on bail 20/7/1867 | 'Suspected of being concerned in attack on Ardagh barracks', bailed at the special commission |
| Connors, Michael | Weaver, Bruff, Co. Limerick | 25/11/1866 | | Soldier in the militia, 'Drilling secretly' |
| Cooke, Patrick | Doon, Co. Limerick | November 1869 | | 'Leader in the commemoration of those hanged in Manchester' |
| Conway, John Aged 22 | Labourer, Rathreagh, Cahermoyle, Co. Limerick | Limerick gaol 30/4/1867 | Discharged on bail 8/7/1867 | 'Suspected of being concerned in attack on Ardagh barracks', bailed at the special commission |
| Corbett, Patrick | 'No occupation', Cappamore, Co. Limerick | 4/12/1866 | | Recruiting and making bullets |
| Cosgrave, Michael | Draper's assistant, Kilcolman, Co. Limerick | Limerick gaol 9/3/1867 | Discharged 22/3/1867 | |
| Costelloe, Nicholas | Labourer, Doon, Co. Limerick | Limerick gaol 20/4/1867 | Discharged 1/5/1867 | |
| Cotter, James | Ardagh, Co. Limerick | Limerick gaol 20/4/1867 | Discharged | 'Suspected of being concerned in attack on Ardagh barracks' |
| Cremin, Cornelius Aged 27 | Ardagh, Co. Limerick | Limerick gaol 18/3/1867 | Discharged on bail 6/7/1867 | 'Fenian centre – suspected of being concerned in attack on Ardagh barracks' Bailed at the special commission |
| Cronin, Jeremiah | Former soldier in the American army, Killarney, Co. Kerry | 1/2/1866 | | 'Drill instructor' |
| Cronin, John | Former soldier in the American army, Killarney, Co. Kerry | 1/2/1866 | | 'Drill instructor' |

| | | | | |
|---|---|---|---|---|
| Cronin, Michael | Shoemaker, Killarney, Co. Kerry | 21/2/1866 | | 'On bail on the charge of Fenianism' |
| Crowley, James | Farmer, Kilfinane, Co. Limerick | November 1869 | | Returned American, 'Supposed Fenian centre' |
| Crowley, Patrick | Storekeeper, Bruree, Co. Limerick | Limerick gaol 18/3/1867 | Discharged on bail 19/6/1867 | Bailed at the special commission |
| Crowley, Patrick | Kilmallock, Co. Limerick | Arraigned before Limerick special commission | Discharged on bail | 'Suspected of taking part in the attack on Kilmallock barracks', bailed at the special commission |
| Curley, Daniel Aged 18 | Labourer, Bruree, Co. Limerick | Limerick gaol 18/3/1867 | Discharged on bail 19/6/1867 | 'Suspected of taking part in the attack on Kilmallock barracks' Bailed at the special commission |
| Cusack, Michael | Ironmonger and dealer in firearms, Limerick | August 1871 | | 'Conduct suspicious' |
| Cussin, Thomas | Shoemaker, native of Limerick | Dundalk gaol 28/9/1867 | Discharged 16/10/1867 | |
| Daly, Cornelius | Bookkeeper William St, Limerick City | Limerick gaol 22/2/1867 | | '"B" in the city' |
| Daly, Michael | Painter, Boherboy, Limerick City | Arraigned before Limerick special commission | Discharged | 'Associates with known Fenian agents' |
| Daly, Michael | Shop porter, Newcastle West, Co. Limerick | 28/11/1866 | | 'On bail but attends Fenian meetings' |
| Daly, Michael | Labourer, Bruree, Co. Limerick | Limerick gaol 15/3/1867 | Discharged on bail 19/6/1867 | Bailed at the special commission |
| Daly, Patrick | Labourer and militia man, Ardagh, Co. Limerick | Limerick gaol 9/3/1867 | | 'Suspected of being concerned in attack on Ardagh barracks' |
| Danagher, William Aged 28 | Labourer, Ardagh, Co. Limerick | Limerick gaol 23/3/1867 | Discharged on bail 6/7/1867 | 'Suspected of being concerned in attack on Ardagh barracks', bailed at the special commission |

| | | | | |
|---|---|---|---|---|
| Darcy, Michael | Tailor, Bruff, Co. Limerick | 25/11/1866 | | 'Keeps open house for Fenians' |
| Dee, John | Cappamore, Co. Limerick | 4/12/1866 | | 'Endeavoured to swear in Fenians' |
| Dee, Maurice | Small farmer's son, Cappamore, Co. Limerick | 4/12/1866 | | 'Confessed and repented, but still engaged in Fenianism' |
| Deginn, William | Servant, Annacotty, Co. Limerick | Limerick gaol 11/3/1867 | Discharged 25/5/1867 | |
| Dinison, Thomas | Shoemaker, Cappamore, Co. Limerick | 4/12/1866 | | 'Centre, engaged in recruiting and very active' |
| Dixon, John Thomas | Shoemaker, Nicker, Co. Limerick | Limerick gaol 9/3/1867 | Sent to Ballybough depot 6/7/1867 | (Deserter) |
| Donnellan, Timothy | Master weaver, Limerick City | 30/11/1866 | | 'Actively engaged – seen marching men in city' |
| Donoghue, Dennis | Weaver, Adare, Co. Limerick | 2/12/1866 | | 'Very much suspected' |
| Donoghue, Nicholas | 'No occupation', Limerick City | 30/11/1866 | | 'Continually in the company of Fenians' |
| Donovan, Matthew | Cork cutter, Limerick City | 30/11/1866 | | 'Active agent' |
| Donovan, Matthew | Small farmer's son, Cappamore, Co. Limerick | 4/12/1866 | | 'Associates with Fenians' |
| Dowran, James (aka James Donovan) | Tralee, Co. Kerry | Arraigned 21/7/1867 | | Arraigned for treason felony at the Kerry summer assizes 25/7/1867 |
| Dugann, William Aged 19 | Labourer, Ardagh, Co. Limerick | Limerick gaol 15/3/1867 | Discharged 20/7/1867 | 'Suspected of being concerned in attack on Ardagh barracks' |
| Dunne, Dennis | Listowel, Co. Kerry | 16/2/1866 | | 'Fenian suspect' |
| Dunne, Patrick | Carpenter, Newcastle West, Co. Limerick | Limerick gaol 9/3/1867 | Discharged 22/3/1867 | 'Strongly suspected Fenian' |

| | | | | |
|---|---|---|---|---|
| Dwyer, John | Blacksmith, Newcastle West, Co. Limerick | Limerick gaol 9/3/1867 | Discharged 29/3/1867 | 'Returned from America where he fled' |
| Dwyer, Patrick | Kilmallock, Co. Limerick | Arraigned before Limerick special commission | | 'Took part in the attack on Kilmallock barracks', sentenced to twelve months for 'Whiteboyism' at the special commission July 1867 |
| Egan, Patrick | Baker, Cappamore, Co. Limerick | 4/12/1866 | Bound to the peace 5/12/1866 | 'Using treasonable language and singing seditious songs' |
| Ellard, Benjamin | Nailer, Cappamore, Co. Limerick | 4/2/1866 | | 'Suspected of recruiting and of making bullets' |
| Falvey, Patrick | Labourer, Cahersiveen, Co. Kerry | Cahersiveen bridewell 16/2/1867 | Discharged on bail 23/2/1867 | 'Suspected of taking part in the attack on Kells coastguard station' |
| Felton, John | Nailer, Newcastle West, Co. Limerick | 21/11/1866 | | 'Strongly suspected Fenian' |
| Finerty, William | Gardener, Ardagh | 2/12/1866 | | 'Movements not as suspicious as last winter' |
| FitzGerald, James | Tarbert, Co. Kerry | 16/2/1866 | | 'Fenian suspect' |
| FitzGerald, John | 'No occupation', Limerick City | 30/11/1866 | | Returned American 'supposed Fenian messenger – Brother(?) of David Murphy, centre for Limerick' |
| FitzGerald, Michael | Baker, Newcastle West, Co. Limerick | 28/11/1866 | | 'Reputed Fenian – left home in February, has just returned' |
| FitzGerald, Patrick | Newcastle West, Co. Limerick | Committed for trial 4/12/1867 | | 'Seditious expressions' |
| FitzGerald, Thomas | Clerk in the market, Limerick City | 30/11/1866 | | 'Noted Fenian' |
| Fleming, John | Harnessmaker, Tralee, Co. Kerry | 1/2/1866 | | 'Constant attender at the Fenian rooms' |

| | | | | |
|---|---|---|---|---|
| Fleming, Michael | Labourer, Cahernane, Killarney, Co. Kerry | 21/2/1866 | | 'On bail on charge of Fenianism' |
| Flynn, Peter | Shoemaker, Kenmare, Co. Kerry | 26/11/1866 | | 'House strongly suspected as a place of Fenian meetings' |
| Foley, Michael | Nailer, Cahersiveen, Co. Kerry | 16/3/1867, committed for trial Richmond bridewell | | |
| Foley, Michael Aged 25 | Labourer, Ardpatrick, Co. Limerick | Limerick gaol 11/3/1867 | | 'Took part in the attack on Kilmallock barracks', charged with 'Whiteboyism', sentenced to 12 months at the Limerick special commission June 1867 |
| Foley, Patrick | Tinsmith, Tralee, Co. Kerry | 18/2/1866 | | 'Suspect since 1848 – centre for Tralee' |
| Foley, Richard | Painter and glazier, Killarney, Co. Kerry | 21/2/1866 | | 'Associates with known Fenians' |
| Foran, John | 'No occupation', Newcastle West, Co. Limerick | 28/11/1866 | | Returned American |
| Frawley, John | Mason, Bruff, Co. Limerick | 25/11/1866 | | 'Reckless – declares himself a Fenian' |
| Garvey, Michael | Shoemaker, Tralee, Co. Kerry | Tralee gaol 9/3/1867 | Discharged 29/3/1867 | |
| Gavan, Michael | House painter, Limerick City | 1866 | | 'Associates with Fenians' |
| Geary, John | Newcastle West, Co. Limerick | 28/11/1866 | | Returned American 'Fenian agent' |
| Geary, Patrick Aged 21 | Kilmallock, Co. Limerick | Arraigned before Limerick special commission | Discharged | 'Suspected of being concerned in attack on Kilmallock barracks' |
| Griffin, Patrick Aged 23 | Cahersiveen, Co. Kerry | Arraigned for trial at the Kerry summer assizes | Discharged | 'Suspected of taking part in the Kerry rising' |

| | | | | |
|---|---|---|---|---|
| Grimes, Dennis | Son of Patrick Grimes | 19/2/1867 | | 'Prominent Fenian in the city' |
| Grimes, Patrick | Tobacconist, Limerick City | 20/11/1866 | | 'Reputed Fenians frequent his house' |
| Hammersly, Thomas | Limerick | Arraigned before Limerick special commission | | |
| Hanrahan, John | Limerick City | May 1869 | | 'Reputed Fenian – gone to America' |
| Hanrahan, Matthew | Shoemaker, Limerick City | 30/11/1866 | | 'Active member' |
| Hawthorne, Christopher Aged 26 | Tailor, Newcastle West, Co. Limerick | Limerick gaol 28/3/1867 | Discharged on bail 20/6/1867 | 'Suspected of being concerned in attack on Kilmallock barracks', bailed by the special commission |
| Hayes, Dominic | Kilmallock, Co. Limerick | November 1869 | | Returned American, 'Absconded after attack on barracks' |
| Hayes, Garrett | Stonecutter, Limerick | 'On remand' Galway gaol 27/3/1867 | Discharged on bail 10/4/1867 | |
| Hayes, James | Carpenter, Adare, Co. Limerick | 2/12/1866 | | 'Movements suspicious' |
| Hayes, Jeremiah | Car driver, Killarney, Co. Kerry | | | Returned American, 'Supposed drill instructor' |
| Hayes, Jeremiah | Tralee, Co. Kerry | 14/2/1866 | | 'Drilling at night' |
| Healy, Michael | Clerk in Mr Leahy's office Killarney, Co. Kerry | 21/2/1866 | | 'Associates with known Fenians' |
| Hennessy, James | Labourer, Glenville, Broadford, Co. Limerick | Limerick gaol 22/3/1867 | Discharged on bail 8/7/1867 | 'Suspected of being concerned in attack on Ardagh barracks', bailed at the special commission |
| Hickey, John | Ballyloughane, Kilteely, Co. Limerick | Sub-Inspector, Newcastle West 7/1/1867 | | Returned American |

| Hickey, John | Labourer, Abington, Co. Limerick | Limerick gaol 7/3/1867 | Discharged on bail 20/6/1867 | Bailed by the special commission |
|---|---|---|---|---|
| Hickey, Thomas | Blacksmith, Boherboy, Limerick City | Limerick gaol 22/2/1867 | | |
| Hoare, Patrick | Adare, Co. Limerick | 28/10/1867 | | 'One of those who assembled at Crecora Cross on 27 October 1867' |
| Hogan, John | Kilteely, Co. Limerick | Arrested 14/2/1869 | Discharged April 1869 | 'Took part on attack on the barracks 7 March 1867' |
| Hogan, John (W?) | Draper's assistant, Limerick City | 1866 | | 'Very active' |
| Holmes, Daniel | Labourer, Kilmallock, Co. Limerick | Maryborough gaol (Portlaoise) 16/5/1867 | Discharged 8/7/1867 | |
| Holmes, Henry | Labourer, Kilmallock, Co. Limerick | Maryborough gaol (Portlaoise) 16/5/1867 | Discharged 8/7/1867 | |
| Horan, Dennis | Tralee, Co. Kerry | 16/2/1866 | | 'Drilling at night' |
| Horan, Dennis | Tralee, Co. Kerry | 18/2/1866 | | 'Drilling at night' |
| Horgan, Thomas | Shoemaker, Kilteely, Co. Limerick | Limerick gaol 18/3/1867 | Discharged 29/3/1867 | |
| Hurley, John | Pawnbroker's clerk, Limerick City | 30/11/1866 | | 'Active agent' |
| Irvine, William | 'No occupation', Limerick City | 30/11/1866 | | 'Well-known associate of reputed Fenians' |
| Johnston, George | Tralee, Co. Kerry | 16/2/1866 | | 'Seen sharpening a sword and going through exercises with a gun' |
| Jones, James | Farmer's son, Ballyrowden, Co. Limerick | Limerick gaol 24/5/1867 | Discharged 29/5/1867 | |
| Jordan, James | Sawyer, Pennywell, Limerick City | Limerick gaol 12/3/1867 | Discharged 23/3/1867 | |

| | | | | |
|---|---|---|---|---|
| Joyce, James | Labourer, Effin, Co. Limerick | Maryborough gaol, (Portlaoise) 16/5/1867 | Discharged 1/7/1867 | |
| Keane, Joseph | Militia man, Newcastle West, Co. Limerick | 28/11/1866 | | 'Associates with reputed Fenians' |
| Keavin, James | Labourer, Ardagh, Co. Limerick | Limerick gaol 9/3/1867 | Discharged 22/3/1867 | 'Suspected of being concerned in attack on Ardagh barracks' |
| Keilty, James | Slater and plasterer, Cahersiveen, Co. Kerry | | | 'Engaged in 1867 rising' |
| Kelly, John | Tralee, Co. Kerry | 16/2/1866 | | 'Drilling at night' |
| Kenealy, John | Newcastle West, Co. Limerick | Limerick gaol 4/12/1869 | | 'Seditious expressions' |
| Kennedy, John | Adare, Co. Limerick | 28/10/1867 | | 'One of those who assembled at Crecora Cross on 27 October 1867' |
| Kennedy, Joseph Aged 31 | Farmer, Glin, Co. Limerick | Limerick gaol 5/4/1867 | Discharged on bail 8/7/1867 | 'Suspected of being concerned in attack on Ardagh barracks', bailed by the special commission |
| Kennedy, Patrick Aged 17 | Small farmer, Bruree, Co. Limerick | Limerick gaol 26/3/1867 | Discharged on bail 19/6/1867 | 'Suspected of being concerned in attack on Kilmallock barracks', bailed by the special commission |
| Kennedy, Thomas | Large farmer's son, Cappamore, Co. Limerick | 4/12/1866 | | 'Consorts with noted Fenians' |
| Kenny, John | Labourer, Effin, Co. Limerick | Limerick gaol 27/3/1867 | Discharged on bail 4/7/1867 | |
| Keough, Thomas | Labourer, Kilteely, Co. Limerick | Limerick gaol 2/4/1867, re-arrested 19/7/1867 | Discharged on bail 6/5/1867, discharged on bail 23/7/1867 | Bailed by the special commission |
| Kerby, Jeremiah | Large farmer's son, Cappamore, Co. Limerick | 4/12/1866 | | 'Consorts with known Fenians' |

| | | | | |
|---|---|---|---|---|
| Kerins, Roger | Labourer Ardagh, Co. Limerick | Limerick gaol 9/3/1867 | Discharged 22/3/1867 | 'Suspected of being concerned in attack on Ardagh barracks' |
| King, Charles | Blacksmith, Newcastle West, Co. Limerick | 28/11/1866 | | 'Suspected Fenian' |
| Kinnavan, John | Grocer's assistant, Limerick City | 1866 | | 'Companion of Colonel Byron, American officer' |
| Kirby, Michael | Newcastle West, Co. Limerick | Limerick gaol 4/12/1869 | | 'Shouted for the Irish Republic – bail refused' |
| Kirby, Patrick | Painter, Newcastle West, Co. Limerick | 28/11/1866 | | 'Served in the American army – suspected Fenian' |
| Lacy, Patrick | Blacksmith, Newcastle West, Co. Limerick | 28/11/1866 | | 'Attended Fenian meeting at Ashford' |
| Laffan, Thomas Aged 23 | Ardagh, Co. Limerick | 20/7/1867 | Discharged | 'Suspected of taking part in the attack on Kilmallock barracks' |
| Leahy, James | Harnessmaker, Adare, Co. Limerick | 2/12/1866 | | 'Movements suspicious' |
| Leahy, James Aged 22 | Small farmer, Cappamore, Co. Limerick | Limerick gaol 13/3/1867 | Discharged on bail 19/6/1867 | 'Took part in the attack on Kilmallock barracks', bailed at the special commission |
| Leonard, Patrick | Labourer, Cappamore, Co. Limerick | 4/12/1866 | | 'In company of noted Fenians' |
| Leary, John | Farm servant, Newcastle West, Co. Limerick | 28/11/1866 | | 'Attended Fenian meeting at Ashford' |
| Liston, Michael Aged 19 | Farmer's son, Coolacappa, Co. Limerick | Limerick gaol 27/4/1867 | Discharged on bail 6/7/1867 | 'Suspected of taking part in the attack on Ardagh barracks', bailed at the special commission |
| Lodge, Michael | Mechanic, Limerick City | 8/12/1866 | | 'Active member, has receipt for liquid fire' |
| Lynch, Thomas | 'No occupation', former soldier in the British army, Newcastle West, Co. Limerick | 28/11/1866 | | 'Suspected Fenian' |

| | | | | |
|---|---|---|---|---|
| McCarthy, Daniel | Law clerk Newcastle West, Co. Limerick | 28/11/1866 | | 'Suspected greatly of Fenianism' |
| McCarthy, John Aged 20 | – | Arraigned before the Limerick special commission | | 'Took part in the attack on Kilmallock barracks', sentenced to twelve months for 'Whiteboyism' at the Limerick special commission June 1867 |
| McCarthy, Michael | Tarbert, Co. Kerry | 16/2/1866 | | 'Fenian suspect' |
| McCarthy, Owen | Farmer's son, Kilfinane, Co. Limerick | 26/11/1866 | | 'Making cartridges' |
| McCarthy, William | Son of hotel-keeper, Kenmare, Co. Kerry | 26/11/1866 | | 'Accompanies known Fenians' |
| McGrath, Dennis | Baker, Limerick City; native of Thurles, Co. Tipperary | Limerick gaol 2/3/1867 | Discharged on bail 20/3/1867 | |
| McGrath, John | Labourer Kilmallock, Co. Limerick | Limerick gaol 9/3/1867 | Discharged on bail 19/6/1867 | Bailed by the special commission |
| McGrath, Joseph | Carpenter Cappamore, Co. Limerick | 4/12/1866 | | 'Fenian in appearance as well as in principles' |
| McGrath, Patrick | Labourer, Kilmallock, Co. Limerick | Limerick gaol 6/3/1867 | | Sentenced to twelve months for 'Whiteboyism' at the Limerick special commission June 1867 |
| McGuire, John Aged 15 | Kilmallock, Co. Limerick | Arraigned before Limerick special commission | Discharged | 'Suspected of taking part in the attack on Kilmallock barracks' |
| McGuire, Patrick Aged 60 | Kilmallock, Co. Limerick | Arraigned before Limerick special commission | Discharged | 'Suspected of taking part in the attack on Kilmallock barracks' |
| McKenna, Maurice | Tralee, Co. Kerry | 16/2/1866 | | 'Drilling at night' |
| McMahon, Charles | Tralee, Co. Kerry | 16/2/1866 | | 'Drilling at night' |

| | | | | |
|---|---|---|---|---|
| McMahon, Edward | Farmer, Newcastle West | 28/11/1866 | | 'Reputed Fenian – fled the district July 1866, just returned' |
| McMahon, John | Millwright, Limerick City | Ennis gaol 1866 | Discharged on bail 1867 | 'Illegal drilling' |
| McMahon, Michael | Limerick City | 30/11/1866 | | 'Actively engaged in Fenianism' |
| McMahon, Patrick | Labourer, Glin, Co. Limerick | 25/11/1866 | | 'Using treasonable language' |
| McNamara, John | 'No occupation', Cappamore, Co. Limerick | 4/12/1866 | | 'Endeavouring to recruit and making bullets' |
| McNamara, Michael | Tailor, Doon, Co. Limerick | Limerick gaol 28/3/1867 | Discharged on bail 20/6/1867 | Bailed by the special commission |
| McNamara, Michael | Blacksmith, Boher, Co. Limerick | Limerick gaol 15/3/1867 | | |
| McNamara, Patrick | 'No occupation', Cappamore, Co. Limerick | 4/12/1866 | | 'Endeavouring to recruit and making bullets' |
| McNamara, Patrick Aged 21 | Tailor, Doon, Co. Limerick | Limerick gaol 28/3/1867 | | 'Suspected of taking part in the attack on Kilteely barracks', sentenced to nine months for 'Whiteboyism' at the Limerick special commission June 1867 |
| Magner, John Aged 22 | Farmer's son, Cahermoyle or Coolacappa, Co. Limerick | Limerick gaol 15/3/1867 | Discharged on bail 8/7/1867 | 'Suspected of being concerned in attack on Ardagh barracks', bailed at the special commission |
| Mahoney, John, (aka James Mahoney) Aged 18 | Labourer, Ardagh, Co. Limerick | Limerick gaol 15/3/1867 | Discharged on bail 8/7/1867 | 'Suspected of being concerned in attack on Ardagh barracks', bailed at the special commission |
| Managhan, Daniel (aka William Managhan) | Attorney's clerk, Windmill Road, Limerick City | Limerick gaol 22/2/1866 | | 'Very active' |
| Mannix, George | Attorney's clerk, Military Road, Limerick City | Limerick gaol 22/2/1866 | | 'Very active' |

| | | | | |
|---|---|---|---|---|
| Mannix, Timothy | Labourer, Cahersiveen, Co. Kerry | Cahersiveen bridewell 16/2/1867 | Discharged on bail 23/2/1867 | 'Suspected of taking part in the attack on Kells coastguard station' |
| Mannix, William | Limerick City | May 1869 | | 'Reputed Fenian – gone to America' |
| Marshall, William (aka John Rourke) | Limerick | Waterford gaol 2/11/1867 | Discharged 8/11/1867 | Returned from England |
| Massey, George Aged 40 | Labourer, Ardagh, Co. Limerick | Limerick gaol 15/3/1867 | Discharged on bail 20/7/1867 | 'Suspected of being concerned in attack on Ardagh barracks', pleaded guilty to 'Whiteboyism' |
| Maybury, George | Boatbuilder, Kenmare, Co. Kerry | 26/11/1866 | | 'Arrested as member of the Phoenix Society' |
| Meany, Patrick | Bruff, Co. Limerick | 25/11/1866 | | 'Very active commander and attender at Fenian meetings' |
| Meehan, Thomas Aged 22 | Feathermonger, Knockaderry, Co. Limerick | Limerick gaol 30/3/1867 | | 'Took part in the attack on Kilmallock barracks', sentenced to twelve months for 'Whiteboyism' at the Limerick special commission June 1867 |
| Moloney, Michael | Plasterer, Limerick City | 30/11/1866 | | 'Deeply concerned in the conspiracy' |
| Moloney, James Aged 18 | Baker, Newcastle West, Co. Limerick | Limerick gaol 23/3/1867 | Discharged on bail 21/7/1867 | 'Suspected of taking part in the attack on Ardagh barracks', bailed at the special commission |
| Moloney, John | Painter, Adare, Co. Limerick | 2/12/1866 | | 'Movements suspected' |
| Moloney, J. W. | Limerick | Ennis gaol | Discharged on bail | 'Illegal drilling' |
| Moore, James Aged 18 | Kilcolman, Co. Limerick | Limerick gaol 15/3/1867 | Discharged on bail 6/7/1867 | 'Suspected of taking part in the attack on Ardagh barracks', bailed at the special commission |
| Moore, John | Bruff, Co. Limerick | 25/11/1866 | | 'Very active – enrols members' |

| Moroney, James | Ardagh, Co. Limerick | Limerick gaol 15/3/1867 | Discharged | 'Suspected of taking part in the attack on Ardagh barracks' |
|---|---|---|---|---|
| Moroney, Michael Aged 21 | Small farmer's son, Bruree, Co. Limerick | Limerick gaol 16/4/1867 | Discharged on bail 19/6/1867 | 'Suspected of taking part in the attack on Kilmallock barracks', bailed at the special commission |
| Morrissy, Cornelius | Clerk, Limerick City | 30/11/1866 | | 'Prominent Fenian' |
| Mulcair, Jeremiah | Shoemaker, Limerick City | January 1868 | | 'Fenian suspect' |
| Mullins, Daniel | Publican; former soldier in the papal brigade Limerick City | 8/12/1866 | | 'Active member' |
| Mulqueen, John | Butcher, Limerick City | 8/12/1866 | | 'Very active member – house a place of meeting for Fenian Brotherhood' |
| Murphy, Cornelius | Butcher, Kenmare, Co. Kerry | 26/11/1867 | | 'Apparent leader until the suspension of Habeas Corpus' |
| Murphy, James | Leather cutter, William St, Limerick City | 8/12/1866 | | 'Boasts of being an employee at the Fenian headquarters in New York' |
| Murphy, Martin | Foreman sawyer, Limerick City | 30/11/1866 | | 'Active in organising the conspiracy' |
| Murphy, Patrick Aged 40 | Weaver, Ardagh, Co. Limerick | Limerick gaol 15/3/1867 | Discharged on bail 6/7/1867 | 'Suspected of taking part in the attack on Ardagh barracks', bailed at the special commission |
| Murray, James (aka John Murray) | Shoemaker; former captain in the American army Limerick City | 8/12/1866 Arraigned before Limerick special commission | Discharged on bail | 'Active man', 'Suspected of leading the attack on Ardagh barracks', bailed at the special commission |
| Nash, William Aged 18 | Land surveyor, Ardagh, Co. Limerick | Limerick gaol 15/4/1867 | Discharged on bail 8/7/1867 | 'Suspected of being concerned in attack on Ardagh barracks', bailed at the special commission |
| Naughton, Thomas | Labourer, Tarbert, Co. Kerry | Limerick gaol 9/3/1867 | | |

| | | | | |
|---|---|---|---|---|
| Naughton, William Aged 21 | Labourer, Reens, Rathkeale, Co. Limerick | Limerick gaol 15/3/1867 | Discharged on bail 8/7/1867 | 'Suspected of being concerned in attack on Ardagh barracks', bailed at the special commission |
| Neilan, Edward | Tailor, Herbertstown, Co. Limerick | Limerick gaol 18/3/1867 | Discharged on bail 13/5/1867 | |
| Nelligan, Patrick | Mason, Tralee, Co. Kerry | March 1869 | Discharged on bail | 'Attempting to seduce a soldier' |
| Neville, Michael | Labourer, Reens, Rathkeale, Co. Limerick | Limerick gaol 15/3/1867 | Discharged on bail 2/4/1867 | 'Suspected of taking part in the attack on Ardagh barracks' |
| Neville, Patrick | Newcastle West, Co. Limerick | Limerick gaol 4/12/1869 | | 'Using seditious expressions' |
| Newe, Thomas | Shop assistant, Kilmallock, Co. Limerick | 27/12/1867 | | 'Fenian suspect' |
| Noonan, John | Clerk, Limerick City | 30/11/1866 | | 'Prominent organiser' |
| O'Brien, Cornelius | Farmer's son, Foilmore, Cahersiveen, Co. Kerry | Tralee gaol 22/7/1867 | Discharged 12/8/1867 | |
| O'Brien, Daniel | Publican, Limerick City | 30/11/1866 | | 'House of resort by known Fenians' |
| O'Brien, John Aged 50 | Labourer, Glin, Co. Limerick | Limerick gaol 5/4/1867 | Discharged on bail 8/7/1867 | 'Suspected of being concerned in attack on Ardagh barracks', bailed at the special commission |
| O'Brien, John | Baker, Mary St, Limerick City | 30/11/1866 | | 'Active organiser – arrested for tearing down proclamation' |
| O'Brien, John | Son of well-off farmer, Boleragh, Cahersiveen, Co. Kerry | Cahersiveen bridewell 16/2/1867 | Discharged on bail 23/2/1867 | 'Suspected of taking part in the attack on Kells coastguard station' |
| O'Brien, Michael | Doon, Co. Limerick | November 1869 | | 'Leader in the demonstration to commemorate those hanged at Manchester' |
| O'Brien, Richard | Labourer, Cappamore, Co. Limerick | 4/12/1866 | | 'Endeavoured to administer the Fenian oath' |

| O'Brien, Roger | Son of well-off farmer, Boleragh, Cahersiveen, Co. Kerry | Cahersiveen bridewell 16/2/1867 | Discharged on bail 23/2/1867 | 'Suspected of taking part in the attack on Kells coastguard station' |
|---|---|---|---|---|
| O'Connor, David | Weaver, Bruff, Co. Limerick | Limerick gaol 1/4/1867 | Discharged on bail 9/4/1867 | |
| O'Connor, Michael | Tarbert, Co. Kerry | 16/2/1866 | | 'Fenian suspect' |
| O'Connor, Nicholas | Car owner, Limerick City | 30/11/1866 | | 'Copy of the Fenian oath found on him' |
| O'Connor, William | Car owner, Limerick City | 30/11/1866 | | 'Continually in Fenian company – arrested for shouting for Fenianism' |
| O'Donnell, Daniel | Baker, Newcastle West, Co. Limerick | 28/11/1866 | | 'Reputed Fenian – fled on the suspension of Habeas Corpus – just returned' |
| O'Donnell, John | Harnessmaker, Limerick | 1866 | | 'Very active' |
| O'Donnell, Patrick | Small farmer's son, Cappamore, Co. Limerick | 4/12/1866 | | 'Associates with Fenians' |
| O'Donnell, Thomas Aged 19 | Kilmallock, Co. Limerick | Limerick gaol 9/3/1867 | | 'Took part in the attack on Kilmallock barracks', sentenced to twelve months for 'Whiteboyism' at the Limerick special commission June 1867 |
| O'Donnell, William | Clerk, Limerick City | 30/11/1866 | | 'Boasts of being a Fenian' |
| O'Grady, Darby | Shopkeeper, Newcastle West | 28/11/1866 | | 'Attended treasonable meeting while out on bail' |
| O'Neill, John | Tailor, Ballybunion, Co. Kerry | Limerick gaol 18/3/1867 | Discharged 21/5/1867 | |
| O'Neill, John W. | Ahane, Brosna, Co. Kerry | Cork gaol 1866 | | 'Well-known Fenian – arrested on suspicion' |
| Osborne, John | Labourer, Bruff, Co. Limerick | Limerick gaol 6/3/1867 | Discharged 23/3/1867 | |

| | | | | |
|---|---|---|---|---|
| O'Shaughnassy, John | Comfortable farmer, Ballincally, Ardagh, Co. Limerick | July 1868 | Discharged on bail 25/7/1868 | 'Led attack on Ardagh barracks – returned from America' |
| O'Shea, Dennis | Publican, Kenmare, Co. Kerry | 26/11/1866 | | 'Leader and organiser in the locality – Phoenix man in 1858' |
| O'Sullivan, Cornelius | 'No occupation', father master of the workhouse in Kenmare, Co. Kerry | 1866 | . | 'Consorts with Fenians – was a Phoenix suspect in 1858' |
| O'Sullivan, Daniel | Military pensioner, Kenmare, Co. Kerry | 1866 | | 'Strongly suspected' |
| O'Sullivan, William (Jnr) Aged 18 | 'No occupation', son of the hotel-keeper in Kilmallock, Co. Limerick | Arraigned before Limerick special commission | | 'Took part in the attack on Kilmallock barracks', sentenced to five years' penal servitude at the Limerick special commission |
| Peterson, Edward | Stoker on Liverpool steamer, Castleconnell, Co. Limerick | Waterford gaol 14/12/1866 | | 'Says he could give information on James Stephens' |
| Pigott, Patrick Aged 22 | Labourer, Kilmallock, Co. Limerick | Limerick gaol 6/3/1867, re-arrested 7/3/1869 | Bound over March 1869 | 'Took part in the attack on Kilmallock barracks', sentenced to twelve months for 'Whiteboyism' at the Limerick special commission June 1867 'Marching and singing seditious songs' |
| Purtill, Edward | Castleconnell, Co. Limerick | 11/12/1866 | | 'Returned from Liverpool – a stranger with no money' |
| Quane, David | Farmer, Kilfinane, Co. Limerick | 25/11/1866 | | 'Fenian suspect' |
| Quinlivan, Daniel Aged 20 | Blacksmith, Ashgrove, Co. Limerick | Limerick gaol 15/3/1866 | Discharged on bail 8/7/1867 | 'Suspected of being concerned in attack on Ardagh barracks', bailed at the special commission |

| | | | | |
|---|---|---|---|---|
| Quinn, John Aged 18 | Farmer's son, Ardagh, Co. Limerick | Limerick gaol 14/4/1866 | Discharged on bail 20/7/1867 | 'Suspected of being concerned in attack on Ardagh barracks', bailed at the special commission |
| Quinn, Michael | Leather cutter, Limerick City | 30/11/1866 | | 'Actively furthering acts of conspiracy' |
| Quirke, John | Son of comfortable farmer, Foilduv, Cahersiveen, Co. Kerry | Cahersiveen bridewell 16/2/1867 | Discharged on bail 23/2/1867 | 'Suspected of taking part in the attack on Kells coastguard station' |
| Quirke, Maurice | Mason, Mountcollins, Co. Limerick | 1869 | | 'Suspect that arms are buried in his house' |
| Quirke, Timothy | Son of comfortable farmer, Foilduv, Cahersiveen, Co. Kerry | | | |
| Real, Michael | Slater, Bruff, Co. Limerick | 25/11/1866 | | 'Reckless – associate of Fenians' |
| Reagan, Michael | Farmer, Adare, Co. Limerick | 2/12/1866 | | 'Movements suspicious' |
| Reardon, Owen | Naval pensioner, Limerick City | July 1868 | | 'Fenian suspect' |
| Reddan, David | Adare, Co. Limerick | 28/10/1867 | | 'One of those who assembled at Crecora Cross 27/10/1867' |
| Regan, Patrick Aged 19 | Labourer, Bruree, Co. Limerick | Limerick gaol 18/3/1867 | Discharged on bail 19/6/1867 | 'Suspected of taking part in the attack on Kilmallock barracks', bailed at the special commission |
| Reidy, John Aged 18 | Labourer, Ardagh, Co. Limerick | Limerick gaol 15/3/1867 | Discharged on bail 9/7/1867 | 'Suspected of being concerned in attack on Ardagh barracks', bailed at the special commission |
| Rice, John | Sergeant in the City Artillery, Limerick | 1866 | | 'Associate of Colonel Byron, Fenian organiser' |
| Riggs, Peter | Limerick | Limerick gaol | Discharged 20/4/1867 | |

| | | | | |
|---|---|---|---|---|
| Riordan, Edward | Horse trainer, Kilmallock | 1869 | | 'Fenian suspect' |
| Riordan, James | Kerry | Tralee gaol 4/1/1868 | | |
| Riordan, John | Labourer, Cappamore, Co. Limerick | 4/12/1866 | | 'Consorts with Fenians' |
| Riordan, Michael | Labourer, Native of Co. Limerick | Dundalk gaol 10/3/1867 | Discharged 4/4/1867 | |
| Riordan, Patrick Aged 20 | Blacksmith, Ballingarry, Co. Limerick | Limerick gaol 9/3/1867 | | 'Took part in the attack on Kilmallock barracks', sentenced to twelve months for 'Whiteboyism' at the Limerick special commission June 1867 |
| Riordan, Robert Aged 34 | Limerick | Arraigned before the Limerick special commission | | 'Took part in the attack on Kilmallock barracks', sentenced to twelve months for 'Whiteboyism' at the Limerick special commission June 1867 |
| Roche, John | Adare, Co. Limerick | 28/10/1867 | | 'One of those who assembled at Crecora Cross 27 October 1867' |
| Roche, Redmond | Listowel, Co. Kerry | 1866 | | 'Correspondent of Dr Power, Fenian centre' |
| Roche, William | Tobacco spinner, St Mary's, Limerick | Limerick gaol 5/3/1867 | Discharged 23/3/1867 | |
| Rose, William | Fisherman, Castleconnell, Co. Limerick | 24/11/1866 | Bound to the peace | 'Using seditious language' |
| Ryan, George | Carpenter, Doon, Co. Limerick | Limerick gaol 13/3/1867 | Discharged 20/3/1867 | |
| Ryan, John Aged 18 | Domestic servant, Nicker, Co. Limerick | Limerick gaol 12/3/1867 | | 'Took part in the attack on Kilteely barracks', sentenced to six months for 'Whiteboyism' at Limerick summer assizes 1867 |

| | | | | |
|---|---|---|---|---|
| Ryan, John | Draper's assistant, Limerick City | 1866 | | 'Very active' |
| Ryan, Michael | Shoemaker, Bruff, Co. Limerick | 25/11/1866 | | 'Very active Fenian' |
| Ryan, Patrick | Limerick | Arraigned before Limerick special commission | Discharged | |
| Ryan, Patrick | Doon, Co. Limerick | November 1869 | | 'Leader in commemoration of Fenians hung in Manchester' |
| Ryan, William | Servant boy, Cappamore, Co. Limerick | 4/12/1866 | | 'Consorts with Fenians' |
| Ryan, William Aged 32 | Slater Cappamore, Co. Limerick | Limerick gaol 12/3/1867 | Discharged on bail 26/6/1867 | 'Suspected of taking part in the attack on Kilteely barracks', bailed by the special commission |
| Scanlan, Edward | 'Idle', Adare, Co. Limerick | 2/2/1866 | | 'Grounds for suspecting him' |
| Shea, Patrick | Labourer Ardagh, Co. Limerick | Limerick gaol 9/3/1867 | Discharged 22/3/1867 | |
| Sheahan, James Aged 18 | Labourer, Ardagh, Co. Limerick | Limerick gaol 5/4/1867 | Discharged on bail 8/7/1867 | 'Suspected of taking part in the attack on Ardagh barracks', bailed by the special commission |
| Sheehan, Martin (aka Martin Sheehy) | Tailor, Mary St, Limerick City | Limerick gaol 22/2/1867 | | 'Fenian suspect' |
| Sheehy, Mrs | Limerick | March 1869 | | 'A Fenian medium' |
| St Laurence, Thomas | Commercial traveller, Limerick City | 30/11/1866 | | 'Friend of Colonel Byron and associated with reputed Fenians' |
| St Laurence, William | Hatter, Limerick City | 30/11/1867 | | 'Continually in Fenian company' |

| | | | | |
|---|---|---|---|---|
| Stokes, William | Publican, Newcastle West, Co. Limerick | 28/11/1866 | | 'Deprived of licence for use of treasonable language' |
| Taylor, Charles | Tralee, Co. Kerry | 16/2/1866 | | 'Constant attender at Fenian rooms – discharged from employment for his Fenian principles' |
| Thompson, James | Hardware clerk, Cahersiveen, Co. Kerry | Cahersiveen Bridewell 16/2/1867 | Discharged 23/2/1867 | 'Suspected of taking part in the attack on Kells coastguard station' |
| Thornhill, Henry | 'Idle' – lives with father, Adare, Co. Limerick | 2/12/1866 | | 'Movements suspicious' |
| Timmons, Patrick | Clerk, Newcastle West, Co. Limerick | 30/11/1866 | | 'Actively engaged in Fenianism' |
| Toomey, John | Adare, Co. Limerick | March 1869 | Bound to the peace | 'Marching and singing seditious songs' |
| Toomey, Thomas | Draper; former soldier in the American army Newcastle West, Co. Limerick | 28/11/1866 | | 'Fenian suspect' |
| Toomey, Timothy | Mason, 'No fixed residence' | Tralee gaol 17/8/1867 | Discharged 24/8/1867 | |
| Turner, Thomas Aged 23 | Farmer's son, Kilmallock, Co. Limerick | Limerick gaol 14/4/1867 | Discharged on bail 19/6/1867 | 'Took part in the attack on Kilmallock barracks', bailed at the special commission |
| Turner, William Aged 19 | Farmer's son, Kilmallock, Co. Limerick | Limerick gaol 6/3/1867 | | 'Took part in the attack on Kilmallock barracks', sentenced to twelve months for 'Whiteboyism' at the Limerick special commission June 1867 |
| Upton, John | Printer, Limerick City | 30/11/1866 | | 'Active agent' |
| Upton, William | Ardagh, Co. Limerick | October 1869 | | 'Fled to America after attack on Ardagh barracks – has just returned' |

| | | | | |
|---|---|---|---|---|
| Vaughan, Daniel | Carpenter, Limerick | 1866 | | 'Very active' |
| Wallace, William | Labourer, Adare, Co. Limerick | 2/12/1866 | | 'Movements very suspicious' |
| Wallace, William | Groom, Ardpatrick, Co. Limerick | Limerick gaol 12/3/1867 | Discharged 18/3/1867 | |
| Walsh, Edward | Printer, Limerick City | 8/11/1866 | | 'Acting head centre' |
| Walsh, Jack | Carpenter's apprentice, Tankardstown, Co. Limerick | Limerick gaol 30/4/1867 | Discharged on bail 20/6/1867 | Bailed by the special commission |
| Walsh, John | Painter, Kilfinane, Co. Limerick | 25/11/1866 | | 'Seen with reputed Fenians and is one!' |
| Walsh, Michael | Labourer, Kilfinane, Co. Limerick | Limerick gaol 23/3/1867 | Discharged on bail 30/5/1867 | |
| Walsh, Michael (aka Michael Massey) Aged 20 | Labourer, Kilfinane, Co. Limerick | Limerick gaol 23/3/1867 | Discharged on bail 19/6/1867 | Bailed by the special commission |
| Walsh, Patrick | Labourer, Bruree, Co. Limerick | Limerick gaol 26/3/1867 | Discharged on bail 8/7/1867 | |
| Walsh, Patrick (aka Patrick Ward) Aged 25 | Small farmer's son, Ardagh, Co. Limerick | Limerick gaol 15/3/1867 | | 'Took part in the attack on Kilmallock barracks', sentenced to twelve months for 'Whiteboyism' at the Limerick special commission June 1867 |
| Walsh, Peter | Millman, Bruree, Co. Limerick | Maryborough gaol, (Portlaoise) 16/3/1867 | Discharged 6/7/1867 | |
| Walsh, Robert | Shoemaker, Tarbert, Co. Kerry | 11/12/1866 | | 'Sworn in by Garret Mahoney' |

| | | | | |
|---|---|---|---|---|
| Walsh, William | Limerick | Arraigned before Limerick special commission June 1867 | Discharged | |
| Ward, Patrick Aged 17 | Limerick | Arraigned before Limerick special commission June 1867 | Discharged | 'Suspected of taking part in the attack on Ardagh barracks' |
| Wheelan, Timothy | Farmer's son, Kilteely, Co. Limerick | Limerick gaol 27/4/1867, re-arrested 18/7/1867 | Discharged on bail 8/5/1867, discharged on bail 23/7/1867 | |
| Woods, Thomas | Small farmer, Bruff, Co. Limerick | 25/11/1866 | Discharged on bail | 'Using seditious language' |

# Bibliography

## Manuscript Sources

### *NATIONAL ARCHIVES*
Chief secretary's office registered (CSOR) papers 1863–9
Fenian briefs (boxes 1–4)
Fenian papers R and F series
Fenian police reports (boxes 1–4)
Habeas Corpus Suspension Act – arrests
Habeas Corpus Suspension Act – papers
List of Fenian suspects

### *NATIONAL LIBRARY*
Anderson papers
Crean papers
Green papers
Larcom papers
Luby papers
Mayo (Naas) papers
Sean Ó Luing papers
T. F. O'Sullivan papers

### *NATIONAL ARCHIVES OF THE UNITED KINGDOM*
Admiralty papers
Colonial Office papers: CO537, CO906
Foreign Office papers: FO5, FO383
Home Office papers: HO12, HO44, HO45, HO46, HO122, HO144
London Metropolitan Police papers: MEPO1, MEPO3
War Office papers: WO33, WO35, WO139

### *BRITISH LIBRARY*
Papers of Lord Monck
Papers of Sir Hugh Rose (Lord Strathnairn)

### *ISLINGTON AND HOLBORN LIBRARIES*
Clerkenwell explosion details

### *KERRY COUNTY LIBRARY – LOCAL HISTORY SECTION*
Files on Fenian rising in Kerry

### *NATIONAL UNIVERSITY OF IRELAND – DUBLIN*
Irish Folklore Commission Archive

## NEWSPAPERS

An Gael

Clonmel Commercial

Cork Constitution

Cork Herald

Daily Express

Dublin Evening Mail

Evening Telegraph

Freeman's Journal

Illustrated Police News

Illustrated Times

Kerry Evening Post

The Kerryman

Limerick Chronicle

London Evening News

New York Irish American

New York Times

The Irish People

The Illustrated London News

The Irish Times

The Nation

The Times (London)

Toronto Globe

Tralee Chronicle

Waterford News

# Printed Sources

## BOOKS

Anderson, R., *Sidelights on the Home Rule Movement* (John Murray, London, 1906)

Anon., *Correspondence relating to the Fenian Invasion and the Rebellion in the Southern States* (Government publication, Ottawa, 1869)

—— *James Stephens: Chief Organiser Irish Republic* (privately published, New York, 1866)

—— *Report of the Special Commission in Cork and Limerick* (Alex Thom, Dublin, 1867)

—— *Report of the Special Commission in Dublin* (Alex Thom, Dublin, 1866)

—— *The Irish Library – The Fenian Movement* (John Ousley, London, 1908)

—— *Un Irlandais à la Presse Française Dite Liberale* (publisher not given, Paris, 1865)

Berkeley, G. F., *The Irish Battalion in the Papal Army* (Talbot Press, Dublin, 1929)

Bourke, M., *John O'Leary* (Anvil Books, Tralee, 1967)

Chamney, W. G., *'The Fenian Conspiracy': Report of the Trial of Thomas F. Burke and others for high treason and treason felony &c.* (Alex Thom, Dublin, 1869)

Cole, J. A., *Prince of Spies* (Faber & Faber, London, 1984)

Comerford, R. V., *The Fenians in Context* (Wolfhound Press, Dublin, 1985)

D'Arcy, W., *The Fenian Movement in the United States* (Catholic University Press, Washington, 1947)

Deniffe, J., *Personal Recollections* (Irish University Press, Shannon 1969)

Devoy, J., *Devoy's Post Bag* (C. J. Fallon, Dublin, vol. 1: 1948, vol. 2: 1953)

—— *Recollections of an Irish Rebel* (Irish University Press, Shannon, 1969)

—— *Scrapbook of Newspaper Cuttings* (vol. 1, Dublin, n.d.)

Doheny, M., *The Felon's Track* (M. H. Gill & Son, Dublin, 1914)

Dooley, T., *The Greatest of the Fenians: John Devoy and Ireland* (Wolfhound Press, Dublin, 2003)

Frezza, Di S. F., *Dei Camerieri &c.* (Befani, Rome, 1894)

Glynn, A., *High Upon the Gallows Tree* (Anvil Books, Tralee, 1967)

Harmon, M., *Fenians and Fenianism: centenary essays* (Scepter, Dublin, 1968)

Kee, R., *The Green Flag* (Weidenfeld & Nicolson, London, 1972)

Kelleher, M., *Ireland's Trained and Marshalled Manhood: Gender Perspectives in Nineteenth-Century Ireland* (Irish Academic Press, Dublin, 1997)

Kenny, M., *The Fenians – Photographs &c. in the National Library* (National Library of Ireland, Dublin, 1994)

—— *William Francis Roantree* (Coicéim, Dublin, 1996)

Laubenstein, W., *The Emerald Whaler* (Mayflower, London, 1960)

Le Caron, H., *Twenty-Five Years in the British Secret Service* (Heinemann, London, 1892)

Marx, K., *The Fenians* (British & Irish Communist Party, London, reprint 1967)

Moody, T. W. (ed.), *The Fenian Movement* (Mercier Press, Cork, 1968)

Morgan, J., *'Whistle Up the Marching Tune': The Life of General Sweeny* (Nova University, Fort Lauderdale, 1994)

Neidhardt, W. S., *Fenianism in North America* (State University Press, Pennsylvania, 1963)

Newsinger, J., *Fenianism in Mid-Victorian Britain* (Pluto Press, London, 1994)

Ó Broin, L., *Fenian Fever: an Anglo-American dilemma* (New York University Press, New York, 1971)

O'Higgins, B., *The Wolfe Tone Annual* (self-published, Dublin 1938)

—— *The Wolfe Tone Annual* (self-published, Dublin 1954)

—— *The Wolfe Tone Annual* (self-published, Dublin 1957)

O'Kelly, S., *The Bold Fenian Men* (Irish News Service, Dublin, 1967)

O'Leary, J., *Recollections* (Irish University Press, Shannon, 1968)

Ó Luing, S., *Fremantle Mission* (Anvil Books, Tralee, 1965)

—— *John Devoy* (Cló Morainn, Dublin, 1961)

—— *Ó Donnabháin Rossa* I & II (Sairséal & Dill, Dublin, 1969)

O'Mullane, S., *The Erin's Hope* (Catholic Truth Society, Dublin, 1924)

Phelan, J., *The Ardent Exile* (Macmillan, Toronto, 1951)

Power, J. O'C., *Irish Political Prisoners* (White & Fawcett, London, 1874)

Protestant Mission Union, *Fenianism and Its Cause and Cure* (no publisher given, Dublin, n.d.)

Quinlivan, P. and Rose, P., *The Fenians in England* (John Calder, London, 1982)

Rafferty, O., *The Church, The State and The Fenian Threat* (Macmillan, New York, 1999)

Ramón, M., *A Provisional Dictator* (University Collage Dublin Press, Dublin, 2007)

Rose, P., *The Manchester Martyrs* (Lawrence & Wishart, London, 1970)

Rutherford, W., *'67 Retrospection, A Concise History of the Fenian Rising* (O'Loughlin, Shields & Boland, Dublin, 1903)

—— *The Secret History of the Fenian Conspiracy* (Kegan Paul, London, 1877)

Ryan, D., *The Fenian Chief* (M. H. Gill & Son, Dublin, 1967)

—— *The Phoenix Flame* (Barker, London, 1937)

Ryan, M. F., *Fenian Memories* (M. H. Gill & Son, Dublin, 1945)

Sarbaugh, T. J., *Post Civil War Fever and Adjustment: fenianism in the Californian context 1858-72* (Northeastern University, Boston, 1992)

Savage, J., *Fenian Heroes and Martyrs* (P. Donohue, Boston, 1868)

Sheehan, Canon P. , *Literary Life* (Phoenix, Dublin, n.d.)

—— 'Moonlight and Memory', *Literary Life* (Phoenix, Dublin, n.d.)

—— *The Graves of Kilmorna* (Clonmore & Reynolds, Dublin, 1915)

Slattery, T. P., *'They Got To Find Mee Guilty Yet'* (Doubleday Press, Toronto, 1972)

Stephens, P., *The Voyage of the Catalpa: a perilous journey and six Irish rebels escape to freedom* (Weidenfeld & Nicolson, London, 2003)

Sullivan, A. M., *Story Of Ireland* (M. H. Gill & Son, Dublin, 1910)

—— *Speeches from the Dock* (Excelsior, New York, 1881)

Sullivan, T. D., *A Memoir of A. M. Sullivan* (self-published, Dublin, 1885)

Takagami, S. I., *The Dublin Fenians* (ICES, Hosei University, Tokyo, 1993)

Williams, T. D., *Secret Societies in Ireland* (Gill & Macmillan, Dublin, 1973)

## PERIODICALS

*All the Year Round*

*Catholic Bulletin*

*Clogher Record* (1957, 1967)

*Dublin University Magazine* ( July 1866)

*Eire–Ireland Fall* (1979)

*Evangelical Mission*

*Irish Ecclesiastical Record* (February 1968)

*Irish Historical Studies* (1968)

*Irish Sword* (Summer 1967; Winter 1968; Winter 1986; Summer 1992; Summer 2007)

*Irishman*

*Journals of the Cork Historical and Archaeological Society*

*Journals of the Kerry Historical and Archaeological Society* (Series 1, nos 1–6: 1968–73)

*New York Phoenix*

*North Munster Antiquarian Journal* (1967, vol. X, no. 2)

*Saturday Review*

*Seanchas Ardmhacha* ( Journal of the Armagh Diocesan Historical Society, 1967; 1999)

*The Spectator*

# INDEX

## L

## M